IN MEMORIAM

AN AUTHORITATIVE TEXT

BACKGROUNDS AND SOURCES

CRITICISM

≫ A NORTON CRITICAL EDITION ≪

ALFRED, LORD TENNYSON

IN MEMORIAM

AN AUTHORITATIVE TEXT
BACKGROUNDS AND SOURCES
CRITICISM

≫≪

Selected and Edited by

ROBERT H. ROSS

BOWLING GREEN STATE UNIVERSITY

W · W · NORTON & COMPANY

New York · London

"The Three Faces of *In Memoriam*" by Robert H. Ross. Published in this volume for the first time by permission of Robert H. Ross.

"The Challenge of Geology," "Further Reassurances," and "Chronology" from *In Memoriam: The Way of a Soul* by Eleanor B. Mattes, © 1951 by Eleanor B. Mattes. Reprinted by permission of Exposition Press, Inc.

"In Memoriam" from *More Nineteenth-Century Studies: A Group of Honest Doubters* by Basil Willey, Columbia University Press, New York and Chatto and Windus, London, 1956. Reprinted by permission of the publisher.

"In Memoriam" from *Selected Essays* by T. S. Eliot, Faber and Faber, London, 1936, and from *Selected Essays*, New Edition, by T. S. Eliot, copyright, 1932, 1936, 1950, by Harcourt Brace Jovanovich, Inc.; copyright, 1960, 1964, by T. S. Eliot. Reprinted by permission of the publisher.

"Faith, Doubt, and Mystical Experience in *In Memoriam*" by Carlisle Moore in *Victorian Studies* 7 (1963). Reprinted by permission of *Victorian Studies*.

"The Structure of *In Memoriam*" from *A COMMENTARY ON TENNYSON'S* "In Memoriam" by A. C. Bradley. Reprinted by permission of St. Martin's Press, Inc., and Macmillan, London and Basingstoke.

"Some Deficiencies of *In Memoriam*" from *Tennyson Sixty Years After* by Paull F. Baum. Reprinted by permission of University of North Carolina Press.

"The Two Kingdoms in *In Memoriam*" by John D. Rosenberg, from the *Journal of English and Germanic Philology*, 58 (1959). Reprinted by permission of University of Illinois Press.

"*In Memoriam*: The Way of the Poet" by E. D. H. Johnson in *Victorian Studies* 2 (1958). Reprinted by permission of *Victorian Studies*.

"*In Memoriam*: The Way of the Soul" from *Tennyson: The Growth of a Poet* by Jerome Hamilton Buckley, Harvard University Press, Cambridge, Mass., Copyright, 1960, by the President and Fellows of Harvard College. Reprinted by permission of the publisher.

"Theme and Symbol in *In Memoriam*" from *Theme and Symbol in Tennyson's Poems to 1850* by Clyde de L. Ryals, University of Pennsylvania Press, Philadelphia, 1964. Reprinted by permission of the publisher.

"*In Memoriam* and Modern Poetry" from *The Language of Tennyson's* "In Memoriam" by Alan Sinfield, Basil and Blackwell, Oxford, 1971. Reprinted by permission of the publisher.

Copyright © 1973 by W. W. Norton & Company, Inc.

FIRST EDITION

Library of Congress Cataloging in Publication Data

Tennyson, Alfred Tennyson, Baron, 1809–1892.
   In memoriam.

   (A Norton critical edition)
   Bibliography: p.
   I. Ross, Robert H., ed.   II. Title.
   PR5562.A1 1973   821'.8   72–13041
   ISBN 0-393-04365-7
   ISBN 0-393-09379-4 {pbk}

PRINTED IN THE UNITED STATES OF AMERICA

Contents

Preface

The standard text of *In Memoriam* is found in the Eversley Edition
of Tennyson's *Works*. Comprising nine volumes published in
1907–8, the Eversley Edition was edited and annotated by the
poet's son Hallam, Lord Tennyson, and includes annotations by
Tennyson himself. Several major manuscripts of *In Memoriam* are
available to scholars in the *Tennyson Notebook* of 1833, the J. M.
Heath *Commonplace Book*, the Harvard Library notebooks, the
Huntington Library collection, and the manuscript in the Usher
Gallery at the Tennyson Centre in Lincoln. The most significant
manuscript of the poem, however, which is owned by the Library of
Trinity College, Cambridge, still remains under partial interdict.
Only recently has the Trinity Library permitted scholars to examine
the manuscript in detail. Professor Christopher Ricks, the first
modern editor of Tennyson to have access to the Trinity notebooks,
made such use of them as he could in compiling his recent edition
of Tennyson's *Works* (Longman/Norton Annotated English Poets,
1969). The Library's interdict against copying or quoting from
them in perpetuity, however—which was imposed by Hallam Tenny-
son, following his father's wishes, many years ago—severely limits
their present usefulness, and so the Eversley remains the most relia-
ble text of *In Memoriam*.

With the exception of changing the section headings from
Roman to Arabic numerals, I have allowed the Eversley text to
stand. Contrary to some recent editorial practice, I have not, for
instance, modernized Tennyson's spelling (e.g., "though" for
"tho' "), nor have I supplied the *e* for the poet's apostrophe in such
words as *heav'n*. I have tried to retain as nearly as possible the
visual and aural qualities of the nineteenth-century text.

My notes, however, are aimed at the twentieth-century reader.
For the most part they attempt to identify some of Tennyson's allu-
sions or to supply biographical or historical information for the gen-
eral modern reader. Occasionally I also supply short explications of
some of the more obscure passages, but my intention is more to sug-
gest than to prescribe. A few of my notes function essentially as
cross-references. Lacking any but the loosest formal structure—the
three Christmases (Sections 28, 78, 104) afford the keystones for
what little there is—*In Memoriam* is nevertheless a skillfully unified
poem. Its unity inheres, however, not in its architectonics but in a
series of remarkably rich internal patterns of recurrent themes,

images, metaphors, and symbols which roll from lyric to lyric throughout the poem. It is of some importance, then, occasionally to commend such patterns to the reader's particular attention and to refer him to similar or contrasting passages in other sections of *In Memoriam* or, infrequently, in other Tennyson poems.

Some of the most interesting glosses on *In Memoriam* have been provided either by Tennyson himself or by his son—and editor— Hallam in the appendix to the Eversley Edition of the poem. Some of my notes are verbatim quotations from that source. I do not intend thereby to suggest that the annotations of either the poet or his son should necessarily be taken as the authoritative last word on certain passages of the poem; the reader must give such interpretations what weight he will in the light of his own knowledge and reading skills. My intention is only to make them readily available. Those notes from the Eversley in which Tennyson is speaking directly as annotator have been enclosed in quotation marks and followed by "—Tennyson." Those in which Hallam Tennyson is speaking as editor have been enclosed in quotation marks and followed by "—Hallam Tennyson." It is to be understood that the source of all such notes, unless otherwise indicated, is the Eversley Edition, and no further attribution is therefore given. Most of the critical essays in this volume carry with them their authors' original footnotes. In the rare instance where an additional note of my own seems required, it is followed by [*Editor*].

Selecting critical essays for a book such as this is a notably chancy undertaking. In the case of *In Memoriam* one's choice is made the more difficult by both the immense quantity of available criticism and the unusually high quality of the scholarly attention which the poem has attracted, particularly during the past two to three decades when important new assessments of all the major Victorian poets, including Tennyson, have burgeoned as never before. Any scholar familiar with the field could immediately suggest the names of distinguished modern critics—Hough, Rutland, Pitt, Shannon, Svaglic, Carr, to name but a few—whose contributions to *In Memoriam* scholarship might profitably have been included in these pages. But choose one must, and within prescribed limits of space. My choices, therefore, imply no claim to inclusiveness: the pieces I have selected comprise only a part of the best that has been said and thought on *In Memoriam*. An extensive critical bibliography, however, may help guide the interested reader to additional major critical assessments of the poem.

The purposes of the general reader seemed best served by arranging the critical essays under two general headings, "Backgrounds and Sources" and "Criticism." Though the distinction implied by such a division is necessarily imprecise, the essays in "Backgrounds and

Sources" deal by and large with the subject of the poet in his poem. Their authors approach *In Memoriam* from the viewpoint of, broadly speaking, biographers and intellectual or literary historians. Thus they examine such matters as the origins of the poem, the events surrounding its composition and publication, its contemporary reception and influence, the chronology of its parts, and the biographical knowledge about Tennyson required for an informed reading of his poem. In this section too will be found Tennyson's own comments on *In Memoriam* as well as a modern scholarly examination of three important intellectual sources of the poem: the works of the pre-Darwinian scientists, Lyell, Herschel, and Chambers. My small essay "The Three Faces of *In Memoriam*" summarizes briefly the traditional critical approaches to the poem. In placing it at the beginning of this section, I hope that it may serve to alert the reader at the outset to the various subjects and critical assumptions he will encounter in all the rest of the subsequent essays.

Unlike those in "Backgrounds and Sources," the essays in the "Criticism" section are not only analytical but also, to one degree or another, judgmental. Beyond that, however, no single subject binds them together. The first three critics in this section tend to view *In Memoriam* in what may be called its public context: they analyze the uniquely Victorian matrix of the poem and examine its relationship to the intellectual currents of the mid-nineteenth century (Willey), or they deal with the perennial question of religious faith and doubt in *In Memoriam* (Eliot and Moore). Beginning with A. C. Bradley's well known essay, however, the critics become increasingly concerned with the private, even the belletristic, qualities of *In Memoriam*; they tend to assume that the poem is to be judged as poem, as a wrought verbal object, that is, susceptible to being analyzed and judged according to its own internal principles. Thus three critics examine, among other things, the structure of *In Memoriam* (Bradley, Baum, and Rosenberg)—and in the process come to some strikingly divergent conclusions. Another conceives of the poem as primarily embodying Tennyson's struggle toward the formulation of a satisfactory aesthetic creed (Johnson). Yet others analyze several unifying patterns of imagery inherent in the poem (Buckley), study the intricate relationships among the poem's themes and symbols (Ryals), and examine the significance of the language and tone of *In Memoriam* (Sinfield).

Most of my work in annotating and assembling materials for this volume was done during several long sojourns in New Hampshire, where I relied heavily on the excellent Victorian collection of the Dartmouth College Library. I am deeply indebted to the members of the staff, and especially to the College Librarian, Mr. Edward Connery Lathem, for their interest and assistance and for providing x · *Preface*

me with the kinds of facilities and services which help transform scholarly labor into the genuine pleasure it ought always ideally to be. I am also grateful to Dr. Corinne Taylor for her help and to Washington State University for the financial grant-in-aid which made her services available to me. A knowledgeable Victorian scholar, Mrs. Taylor performed many of the bibliographical chores initially required to get this book under way.

ROBERT H. ROSS

The Text of
In Memoriam

In Memoriam A.H.H.

[PROLOGUE]

Strong Son of God, immortal Love,[1]
  Whom we, that have not seen thy face,
  By faith, and faith alone, embrace,
Believing where we cannot prove;

Thine are those orbs of light and shade;[2]   5
  Thou madest Life in man and brute;
  Thou madest Death; and lo, thy foot
Is on the skull which thou hast made.

Thou wilt not leave us in the dust:
  Thou madest man, he knows not why,   10
  He thinks he was not made to die;
And thou hast made him: thou art just.

Thou seemest human and divine,
  The highest, holiest manhood, thou.
  Our wills are ours, we know not how;   15
Our wills are ours, to make them thine.

Our little systems have their day;[3]
  They have their day and cease to be:
  They are but broken lights of thee,
And thou, O Lord, art more than they.   20

We have but faith: we cannot know;
  For knowledge is of things we see;
  And yet we trust it comes from thee,
A beam in darkness: let it grow.

Let knowledge grow from more to more,   25
  But more of reverence in us dwell;
  That mind and soul, according well,
May make one music as before,[4]

1. "This might be taken in a St. John sense"—Tennyson. "In him was life, and the life was the light of men. The light shines in the darkness, and the darkness has not overcome it" (John i.4–5).
2. The moon and the planets, half lighted by the sun, half in shade.
3. I.e., our humanly conceived theological, metaphysical, and scientific systems, or modes of perceiving reality.

4. "Before": in past ages of faith, before modern science had created the gulf between intellectual "knowledge" on the one hand and instinctive "reverence" on the other (lines 25–26). The same theme recurs frequently among the Victorian poets. Cf. Matthew Arnold, *Dover Beach, Stanzas from the Grande Chartreuse.*

But vaster. We are fools and slight;
　　We mock thee when we do not fear:⁣   30
　　But help thy foolish ones to bear;
Help thy vain worlds to bear thy light.⁵

Forgive what seem'd my sin in me;
　　What seem'd my worth since I began;
　　For merit lives from man to man,   35
And not from man, O Lord, to thee.

Forgive my grief for one removed,
　　Thy creature, whom I found so fair.
　　I trust he lives in thee, and there
I find him worthier to be loved.   40

Forgive these wild and wandering cries,
　　Confusions of a wasted youth;
　　Forgive them where they fail in truth,
And in thy wisdom make me wise.

                         1849⁶

1

I held it truth, with him who sings
　　To one clear harp in divers tones,
　　That men may rise on stepping stones
Of their dead selves to higher things.¹

But who shall so forecast the years   5
　　And find in loss a gain to match?
　　Or reach a hand thro' time to catch
The far-off interest of tears?²

Let Love clasp Grief lest both be drown'd,
　　Let darkness keep her raven gloss: 10
　　Ah, sweeter to be drunk with loss,
To dance with death, to beat the ground,

---

5. The light of modern scientific knowledge.
6. Arthur Henry Hallam died suddenly on September 15, 1833, in Vienna, while touring the Continent with his father. He was twenty-two years old. News of his death reached Tennyson on October 1, and before the year was out the poet had begun composing the series of lyric poems which, many years later, he would assemble and publish as *In Memoriam*. These "elegies," as Tennyson called them, were composed sporadically over a period of perhaps twelve years. "The sections were written at many different places," Tennyson explained, "and as the phases of our intercourse came to my memory and suggested them. I did not write them with any view of weaving them into a whole, or for publication, until I found that I had written so many" (*Memoir*, I, 304). Having decided tentatively upon publication in 1849, Tennyson assembled and arranged the Elegies into a single long poem and composed his Prologue. In early 1850 he circulated among his friends a few copies of a privately printed early version of the poem called, significantly, *Fragments of an Elegy*. At his wife's suggestion the title was changed to *In Memoriam*, and the poem was published anonymously on June 1, 1850.
1. Lines 1–4: The allusion is to Goethe, according to Tennyson, but the specific reference is obscure.
2. "The good that grows for us out of grief"—Tennyson.

Than that the victor Hours should scorn
   The long result of love, and boast,
   'Behold the man that loved and lost,[3]   15
But all he was is overworn.'

3. Cf. Section 27, lines 13–16.

2

Old yew, which graspest at the stones
   That name the under-lying dead,
   Thy fibres net the dreamless head,
Thy roots are wrapt about the bones.

The seasons bring the flower again,   5
   And bring the firstling to the flock;
   And in the dusk of thee, the clock
Beats out the little lives of men.[1]

O not for thee the glow, the bloom,
   Who changest not in any gale,   10
   Nor branding summer suns avail
To touch thy thousand years of gloom:[2]

And gazing on thee, sullen tree,
   Sick for thy stubborn hardihood,
   I seem to fail from out my blood   15
And grow incorporate into thee.

1. Lines 1–8: The yew is pictured as growing in the churchyard, the clock as striking the hours from the church-tower. 2. Lines 9–12: The dark-green foliage of the English yew, an unusually long-lived tree, does not change color with the seasons.

3

O Sorrow, cruel fellowship,
   O Priestess in the vaults of Death,
   O sweet and bitter in a breath,
What whispers from thy lying lip?

'The stars,' she whispers, 'blindly run;   5
   A web is wov'n across the sky;
   From out waste places comes a cry,
And murmurs from the dying sun:[1]

'And all the phantom, Nature, stands—
   With all the music in her tone,   10
   A hollow echo of my own,—[2]
A hollow form with empty hands.'

1. An allusion to the then recently advanced nebular hypothesis, which conceived the sun as a dying star eventually to become an inert, burnt-out cinder. Cf. Sections 89, lines 47–48; and 118, lines 7–9. 2. Sorrow, personified, is speaking; phantom Nature's song merely echoes Sorrow's own despair.

And shall I take a thing so blind,[3]
   Embrace her as my natural good;
   Or crush her, like a vice of blood,
Upon the threshold of the mind?   15

3. Section 3 embodies the speaker's "first realization of blind sorrow,"—Tennyson. Also implicit in Sorrow's message is the doctrine of scientific determinism, which holds that the cosmos is a purposeless agglomeration of matter; that Nature, contrary to the Romantic view, is neither sentient nor benign (line 12); and that life is controlled by mechanical laws of necessity which preclude both free will in man and cosmic control by God. A crucial metaphysical and moral question in Victorian England, determinism, with its manifold implications for "the way of the soul," as the poet subtitled *In Memoriam*, also becomes a central issue throughout the poem.

4

To Sleep I give my powers away;
   My will is bondsman to the dark;
   I sit within a helmless bark,
And with my heart I muse and say:

O heart, how fares it with thee now,   5
   That thou should'st fail from thy desire,
   Who scarcely darest to inquire,
'What is it makes me beat so low?'

Something it is which thou hast lost,
   Some pleasure from thine early years.   10
   Break, thou deep vase of chillling tears,
That grief hath shaken into frost!

Such clouds of nameless trouble cross
   All night below the darken'd eyes;
   With morning wakes the will, and cries,   15
'Thou shalt not be the fool of loss.'

5[1]

I sometimes hold it half a sin
   To put in words the grief I feel;
   For words, like Nature, half reveal
And half conceal the Soul within.

But, for the unquiet heart and brain,   5
   A use in measured language lies;
   The sad mechanic exercise,
Like dull narcotics, numbing pain.

In words, like weeds,[2] I'll wrap me o'er,
   Like coarsest clothes against the cold: 10
   But that large grief which these enfold
Is given in outline and no more.

1. This is the first of several sections on the theme of the adequacy—more properly, inadequacy—of poetry as a vehicle for conveying deeply felt human experience. Cf. Sections 8, 16, 20, 21, 23.
2. I.e., widow's weeds, garments worn as symbols of mourning.

6

One writes, that 'Other friends remain,'
    That 'Loss is common to the race'—
    And common is the commonplace,
And vacant chaff well meant for grain.

That loss is common would not make   5
    My own less bitter, rather more:
    Too common! Never morning wore
To evening, but some heart did break.

O father, wheresoe'er thou be,
    Who pledgest now thy gallant son;   10
    A shot, ere half thy draught be done,
Hath still'd the life that beat from thee.

O mother, praying God will save
    Thy sailor,—while thy head is bow'd,
    His heavy-shotted hammock-shroud   15
Drops in his vast and wandering grave.

Ye know no more than I who wrought
    At that last hour to please him well;
    Who mused on all I had to tell,
And something written, something thought;[1]   20

Expecting still his advent home;
    And ever met him on his way
    With wishes, thinking, 'here to-day,'
Or 'here to-morrow will he come.'

O somewhere, meek, unconscious dove,   25
    That sittest ranging[2] golden hair;
    And glad to find thyself so fair,
Poor child, that waitest for thy love!

For now her father's chimney glows
    In expectation of a guest;   30
    And thinking 'this will please him best,'
She takes a riband or a rose;

For he will see them on to-night;
    And with the thought her colour burns;
    And, having left the glass, she turns   35
Once more to set a ringlet right;

And, even when she turn'd, the curse
    Had fallen, and her future Lord
    Was drown'd in passing thro' the ford,
Or kill'd in falling from his horse.   40

1. According to his son, Tennyson was   Hallam's death.
writing a letter to Hallam at the hour of   2. Arranging.

O what to her shall be the end?
    And what to me remains of good?
    To her, perpetual maidenhood,[3]
And unto me no second friend.

3. To the girl described in lines 25–40.

7

Dark house, by which once more I stand
    Here in the long unlovely street,[1]
    Doors, where my heart was used to beat
So quickly, waiting for a hand,

A hand that can be clasp'd no more—   5
    Behold me, for I cannot sleep,
    And like a guilty thing I creep
At earliest morning to the door.

He is not here; but far away
    The noise of life begins again,   10
    And ghastly thro' the drizzling rain
On the bald street breaks the blank day.

1. Hallam had lived in the house at 67 Wimpole Street, London. Cf. the speaker's second visit to Hallam's house in a changed mood, Section 119.

8

A happy lover who has come
    To look on her that loves him well,
    Who 'lights and rings the gateway bell,
And learns her gone and far from home;

He saddens, all the magic light   5
    Dies off at once from bower and hall,
    And all the place is dark, and all
The chambers emptied of delight:

So find I every pleasant spot
    In which we two were wont to meet,   10
    The field, the chamber and the street,
For all is dark where thou art not.

Yet as that other, wandering there
    In those deserted walks, may find
    A flower beat with rain and wind,   15
Which once she fostered up with care

So seems it in my deep regret,
    O my forsaken heart, with thee
    And this poor flower of poesy
Which little cared for fades not yet.   20

But since it pleased a vanish'd eye,
    I go to plant it on his tomb,
    That if it can it there may bloom,
Or dying, there at least may die.

9[1]

Fair ship, that from the Italian shore[2]
    Sailest the placid ocean-plains
    With my lost Arthur's loved remains,
Spread thy full wings, and waft him o'er.

So draw him home to those that mourn   5
    In vain; a favourable speed
    Ruffle thy mirror'd mast, and lead
Thro' prosperous floods his holy urn.

All night no ruder air perplex
    Thy sliding keel, till Phosphor,[3] bright   10
    As our pure love, thro' early light
Shall glimmer on the dewy decks.

Sphere all your lights around, above;
    Sleep, gentle heavens, before the prow;
    Sleep, gentle winds, as he sleeps now,   15
My friend, the brother of my love;

My Arthur, whom I shall not see
    Till all my widow'd race be run;
    Dear as the mother to the son,
More than my brothers are to me.   20

1. This poem, composed perhaps as early as two months after Hallam's death, was one of the first written of the elegies which now make up *In Memoriam*. Tennyson considered Sections 9–20 to be something of a unit because of their common subjects: Hallam's death, the return of the body to England, and the burial at Clevedon.
2. The ship returning Hallam's body sailed for England from Trieste.
3. The morning star. Cf. the Phosphor-Hesper linking in Section 121.

10

I hear the noise about thy keel;
    I hear the bell struck in the night:
    I see the cabin-window bright;
I see the sailor at the wheel.

Thou bring'st the sailor to his wife,   5
    And travell'd men from foreign lands;
    And letters unto trembling hands;
And, thy dark freight, a vanish'd life.

So bring him: we have idle dreams:
    This look of quiet flatters thus   10

Our home-bred fancies: O to us,
The fools of habit, sweeter seems

To rest beneath the clover sod,
That takes the sunshine and the rains,
Or where the kneeling hamlet drains   15
The chalice of the grapes of God;[1]

Than if with thee the roaring wells
Should gulf him fathom-deep in brine;
And hands so often clasp'd in mine,
Should toss with tangle and with shells.   20

1. Lines 12–16: Either the churchyard (lines 13–14) or the chancel (lines 15–16), being hallowed ground, would be preferable to the sea burial imagined in the following lines.

11

Calm is the morn without a sound,
Calm as to suit a calmer grief,
And only thro' the faded leaf
The chestnut pattering to the ground:

Calm and deep peace on this high wold,   5
And on these dews that drench the furze,
And all the silvery gossamers
That twinkle into green and gold:[1]

Calm and still light on yon great plain
That sweeps with all its autumn bowers,   10
And crowded farms and lessening towers,
To mingle with the bounding main:

Calm and deep peace in this wide air,
These leaves that redden to the fall;
And in my heart, if calm at all,   15
If any calm, a calm despair:

Calm on the seas, and silver sleep,
And waves that sway themselves in rest,
And dead calm in that noble breast
Which heaves but with the heaving deep.   20

1. Lines 7–8: The dew-laden strands of cobweb ("gossamers") show green and gold as they reflect the morning sunlight.

12

Lo, as a dove when up she springs
To bear thro' Heaven a tale of woe,
Some dolorous message knit below
The wild pulsation of her wings;[1]

1. Like many other images, that of the dove recurs later in the poem, where the effect is very different from the despair suggested in this stanza. Cf. Section 103.

Like her I go; I cannot stay;   5
    I leave this mortal ark behind,
    A weight of nerves without a mind,
And leave the cliffs, and haste away

O'er ocean-mirrors rounded large,
    And reach the glow of southern skies,   10
    And see the sails at distance rise,
And linger weeping on the marge,

And saying; 'Comes he thus, my friend?
    Is this the end of all my care?'
    And circle moaning in the air: 15
'Is this the end? Is this the end?'

And forward dart again, and play
    About the prow, and back return
    To where the body sits, and learn
That I have been an hour away.   20

13

Tears of the widower, when he sees
    A late-lost form that sleep reveals,
    And moves his doubtful arms, and feels
Her place is empty, fall like these;

Which weep a loss for ever new,   5
    A void where heart on heart reposed;
    And, where warm hands have prest and
        closed,
Silence, till I be silent too.

Which weep the comrade of my choice,
    An awful thought, a life removed,   10
    The human-hearted man I loved,
A Spirit, not a breathing voice.

Come Time, and teach me, many years,[1]
    I do not suffer in a dream;
    For now so strange do these things seem, 15
Mine eyes have leisure for their tears;

My fancies time to rise on wing,
    And glance about the approaching sails,
    As tho' they brought but merchants' bales,
And not the burthen that they bring.   20

1. "Time" and "many years" are in apposition.

14

If one should bring me this report,
    That thou[1] hadst touch'd the land to-day,

1. "Thou": the ship.

And I went down unto the quay,
And found thee lying in the port;

And standing, muffled round with woe,   5
Should see thy passengers in rank
Come stepping lightly down the plank,
And beckoning unto those they know;

And if along with these should come
The man I held as half-divine;[2]   10
Should strike a sudden hand in mine,
And ask a thousand things of home;

And I should tell him all my pain,
And how my life had droop'd of late,
And he should sorrow o'er my state   15
And marvel what possess'd my brain;

And I perceived no touch of change,
No hint of death in all his frame,
But found him all in all the same,
I should not feel it to be strange.   20

2. "My father said, [Hallam] was as
near perfection as mortal man could be"
—Hallam Tennyson. In this line, as an
occasional reader has observed, Tenny-
son unintentionally comes close to blas-
phemy.

15
To-night the winds begin to rise
And roar from yonder dropping day:
The last red leaf is whirl'd away,
The rooks are blown about the skies;

The forest crack'd, the waters curl'd,   5
The cattle huddled on the lea;
And wildly dash'd on tower and tree
The sunbeam strikes along the world:

And but for fancies, which aver
That all thy motions gently pass   10
Athwart a plane of molten glass,
I scarce could brook the strain and stir

That makes the barren branches loud;
And but for fear it is not so,
The wild unrest that lives in woe[1]   15
Would dote and pore on yonder cloud

1. Cf. the "wild unrest" of this section
with the "calm despair" of Section 11
(line 16). Both moods are alluded to
again in stanza 1 of Section 16.

That rises upward always higher,
    And onward drags a labouring breast,
    And topples round the dreary west,
A looming bastion fringed with fire.   20

16[1]

What words are these have fall'n from me?
    Can calm despair and wild unrest
    Be tenants of a single breast,
Or sorrow such a changeling be?

Or doth she only seem to take   5
    The touch of change in calm or storm;
    But knows no more of transient form
In her deep self, than some dead lake

That holds the shadow of a lark
    Hung in the shadow of a heaven?   10
    Or has the shock, so harshly given,
Confused me like the unhappy bark

That strikes by night a craggy shelf,
    And staggers blindly ere she sink?
    And stunn'd me from my power to think   15
And all my knowledge of myself;

And made me that delirious man
    Whose fancy fuses old and new,
    And flashes into false and true,
And mingles all without a plan?   20

1. In this section, the I "questions himself about these alternations of 'calm despair' and 'wild unrest.' Do these changes only pass over the surface of the mind while in the depth still abides his unchanging sorrow? or has his reason been stunned by his grief?"—Hallam Tennyson.

17[1]

Thou comest, much wept for: such a breeze
    Compell'd thy canvas, and my prayer
    Was as the whisper of an air
To breathe thee over lonely seas.

For I in spirit saw thee move   5
    Thro' circles of the bounding sky,
    Week after week: the days go by:
Come quick, thou bringest all I love.

Henceforth, wherever thou may'st roam,
    My blessing, like a line of light,   10
    Is on the waters day and night,
And like a beacon guards thee home.

1. This and Section 18 were among the first written poems of *In Memoriam*.

So may whatever tempest mars
  Mid-ocean, spare thee, sacred bark;   15
  And balmy drops in summer dark
Slide from the bosom of the stars.

So kind an office hath been done,
  Such precious relics brought by thee;
  The dust of him I shall not see
Till all my widow'd race be run.[2]   20

2. Cf. the image of the grieving widower, Section 13, lines 1–8.

18

'Tis well; 'tis something; we may stand
  Where he in English earth is laid,[1]
  And from his ashes may be made
The violet of his native land.

'Tis little; but it looks in truth   5
  As if the quiet bones were blest
  Among familiar names to rest
And in the places of his youth.

Come then, pure hands, and bear the head[2]
  That sleeps or wears the mask of sleep, 10
  And come, whatever loves to weep,
And hear the ritual of the dead.

Ah yet, ev'n yet, if this might be,
  I, falling on his faithful heart,
  Would breathing thro' his lips impart 15
The life that almost dies in me;

That dies not, but endures with pain,
  And slowly forms the firmer mind,
  Treasuring the look it cannot find,
The words that are not heard again.   20

1. Hallam was buried in St. Andrew's Church at Clevedon on January 3, 1834. Tennyson did not actually visit Clevedon until many years later.
2. Tenants on the Clevedon estate bore Hallam's body to its grave.

19[1]

The Danube to the Severn gave[2]
  The darken'd heart that beat no more;
  They laid him by the pleasant shore,
And in the hearing of the wave.

1. This poem was written at Tintern Abbey, which is on the Wye near Clevedon. Cf. "Tears, Idle Tears" from *The Princess*, which was composed at the same place.
2. Vienna, where Hallam died, is on the Danube, and Clevedon, where he was buried, is on the Severn.

There twice a day the Severn fills;   5
　　The salt sea-water passes by,
　　And hushes half the babbling Wye,
And makes a silence in the hills.³

The Wye is hush'd nor moved along,
　　And hush'd my deepest grief of all,   10
　　When fill'd with tears that cannot fall,
I brim with sorrow drowning song.

The tide flows down, the wave again
　　Is vocal in its wooded walls;
　　My deeper anguish also falls,   15
And I can speak a little then.

3. Lines 5–8: "Taken from my own ob-   The Wye, which joins the Severn just
servation—the rapids of the Wye are   above Clevedon, is backed up by the tides
stilled by the incoming sea"—Tennyson.   for about half its course.

20

The lesser griefs that may be said,
　　That breathe a thousand tender vows,
　　Are but as servants in a house
Where lies the master newly dead;

Who speak their feeling as it is,   5
　　And weep the fulness from the mind:
　　'It will be hard,' they say, 'to find
Another service such as this.'

My lighter moods are like to these,
　　That out of words a comfort win;   10
　　But there are other griefs within,
And tears that at their fountain freeze;

For by the hearth the children sit
　　Cold in that atmosphere of Death,
　　And scarce endure to draw the breath,   15
Or like to noiseless phantoms flit:

But open converse is there none,
　　So much the vital spirits sink
　　To see the vacant chair, and think,
'How good! how kind! and he is gone.'   20

21

I sing to him that rests below,
　　And, since the grasses round me wave,

I take the grasses of the grave,
And make them pipes whereon to blow.[1]

The traveller hears me now and then,   5
And sometimes harshly will he speak:
'This fellow would make weakness weak,
And melt the waxen hearts of men.'[2]

Another answers, 'Let him be,
He loves to make parade of pain   10
That with his piping he may gain
The praise that comes to constancy.'

A third is wroth: 'Is this an hour
For private sorrow's barren song,
When more and more the people throng   15
The chairs and thrones of civil power?[3]

'A time to sicken and to swoon,
When Science reaches forth her arms[4]
To feel from world to world, and charms
Her secret from the latest moon?'[5]   20

Behold, ye speak an idle thing:
Ye never knew the sacred dust:
I do but sing because I must,
And pipe but as the linnets sing:

And one is glad; her note is gay,   25
For now her little ones have ranged;
And one is sad; her note is changed,
Because her brood is stol'n away.

1. Lines 1–4: One of the poet's infrequent uses of the pastoral convention customarily adopted by elegists. Most of the great English elegies adhere more rigorously to the classical pastoral tradition than In Memoriam (e.g., Milton's Lycidas, Shelley's Adonais, Arnold's Thyrsis), a difference which is in part explained by the long time span over which the lyrics constituting In Memoriam were composed and the fact that Tennyson's initial conception of them was as independent, more or less self-contained poems (see note 6 to the Prologue). In this stanza Tennyson also assumes that Hallam was buried in the churchyard, whereas the body was actually entombed inside the church at Clevedon.
2. In stanzas 2–5 the poet considers the charges which may be brought against him and his poem by the average reader of his "mother age": excessive sentimentality (lines 7–8), love of praise (lines 9–12), and selfish, self-imposed isolation from the stirring events of his time (lines 13–20). Cf. Section 5.
3. Lines 15–16: Perhaps a reference to Chartism, a populist political movement, which, in 1838, presented to Parliament The People's Charter demanding legislation to remedy the economic plight and increase the political power of the English laborer.
4. Telescopes.
5. Lines 17–20: Generally, an allusion to the important astronomical discoveries of the age. Specifically, perhaps, a reference to the discovery of the planet Neptune; since the discovery occurred in 1846, the allusion suggests a relatively late date of composition for this section. One commentator claims that it was written "by 1845"; others suggest 1846—one even 1847—as a more likely date.

22

The path by which we twain did go,
   Which led by tracts that pleased us well,
   Thro' four sweet years arose and fell,
From flower to flower, from snow to snow:

And we with singing cheer'd the way,   5
   And, crown'd with all the season lent,
   From April on to April went,
And glad at heart from May to May:

But where the path we walk'd began
   To slant the fifth autumnal slope,[1]   10
   As we descended following Hope,
There sat the Shadow fear'd of man;

Who broke our fair companionship,
   And spread his mantle dark and cold,
   And wrapt thee formless in the fold,   15
And dull'd the murmur on thy lip,

And bore thee where I could not see
   Nor follow, tho' I walk in haste,
   And think, that somewhere in the waste
The Shadow sits and waits for me.   20

1. Lines 1–10: Tennyson first met Hallam in 1828. Their friendship lasted through four full years (line 3), and Hallam died in September 1833, on "the autumnal slope" of the fifth year (line 10).

23

Now, sometimes in my sorrow shut
   Or breaking into song by fits,[1]
   Alone, alone, to where he sits,
The Shadow cloak'd from head to foot,

Who keeps the keys of all the creeds,   5
   I wander, often falling lame,
   And looking back to whence I came,
Or on to where the pathway leads;

And crying, How changed from where it ran
   Thro' lands where not a leaf was dumb;   10
   But all the lavish hills would hum
The murmur of a happy Pan:[2]

When each by turns was guide to each,
   And Fancy light from Fancy caught,

1. See note 6 to the Prologue.
2. Pan, the Greek god of forests, pastures, flocks, and shepherds, represents unrestrained nature.

And Thought leapt out to wed with Thought   15
Ere Thought could wed itself with Speech;

And all we met was fair and good,
    And all was good that Time could bring,
    And all the secret of the Spring
Moved in the chambers of the blood;   20

And many an old philosophy
    On Argive heights divinely sang,
    And round us all the thicket rang
To many a flute of Arcady.³

3. Lines 21–24: *Argive*—Greek. *Arcady* —Arcadia, a rural region of Greece, conventionally the locus for pastoral poetry. The stanza as a whole is a rather inflated way of saying that Tennyson and Hallam read much Greek philosophy and poetry together.

24

And was the day of my delight
    As pure and perfect as I say?
    The very source and fount of Day
Is dash'd with wandering isles of night.¹

If all was good and fair we met,   5
    This earth had been the Paradise
    It never look'd to human eyes
Since our first Sun arose and set.

And is it that the haze of grief
    Makes former gladness loom so great?   10
    The lowness of the present state,
That sets the past in this relief?

Or that the past will always win
    A glory from its being far;
    And orb into the perfect star   15
We saw not, when we moved therein?²

1. Sun spots.
2. Cf. *Locksley Hall Sixty Years After*, lines 189–92.

25

I know that this was Life,—the track
    Whereon with equal feet we fared;
    And then, as now, the day prepared '
The daily burden for the back.

But this it was that made me move   5
    As light as carrier-birds in air;
    I loved the weight I had to bear,
Because it needed help of Love:

Nor could I weary, heart or limb,
  When mighty Love would cleave in twain   10
  The lading¹ of a single pain,
And part it, giving half to him.

26

Still onward winds the dreary way;
  I with it; for I long to prove
  No lapse of moons can canker Love,
Whatever fickle tongues may say.

And if that eye which watches guilt¹   5
  And goodness, and hath power to see
  Within the green the moulder'd tree,
And towers fall'n as soon as built—

Oh, if indeed that eye foresee
  Or see (in Him is no before)   10
  In more of life true life no more
And Love the indifference to be,²

Then might I find, ere yet the morn
  Breaks hither over Indian seas,
  That Shadow waiting with the keys,   15
To shroud me from my proper scorn.³

1. The heavy burden.
1. "The Eternal Now. I AM"—Tennyson. Thus, the eye of God.
2. I.e., that love will become indifference in the future. Some commentators suggest the insertion of "in" between "And" and "Love."
3. "Proper scorn": self-scorn.

27¹

I envy not in any moods
  The captive void of noble rage,
  The linnet born within the cage,
That never knew the summer woods:

I envy not the beast that takes   5
  His license² in the field of time,
  Unfetter'd by the sense of crime,
To whom a conscience never wakes;

Nor, what may count itself as blest,
  The heart that never plighted troth   10
  But stagnates in the weeds of sloth;
Nor any want-begotten rest.³

1. For those analysts who argue that *In Memoriam* is structurally divided into four parts (e.g., Bradley), this section is the concluding lyric of Part I. The affirmation of the final stanza suggests, they point out, that the speaker has been able at least to discern some meaning in his sorrow.
2. Lines 5–6: He who lives without self-restraint.
3. Undeserved rest, not earned by emotional commitment, struggle, or sorrow.

I hold it true, whate'er befall;
I feel it, when I sorrow most;
'Tis better to have loved and lost   15
Than never to have loved at all.[4]

4. Lines 15–16: Cf. Section 1, lines 13–16; Section 85, lines 1–4.

28[1]

The time draws near the birth of Christ:
The moon is hid; the night is still;
The Christmas bells from hill to hill
Answer each other in the mist.

Four voices of four hamlets round,[2]   5
From far and near, on mead and moor,
Swell out and fail, as if a door
Were shut between me and the sound:

Each voice four changes on the wind,[3]
That now dilate, and now decrease,   10
Peace and goodwill, goodwill and peace,
Peace and goodwill, to all mankind.

This year I slept and woke with pain,
I almost wish'd no more to wake,
And that my hold on life would break   15
Before I heard those bells again:

But they my troubled spirit rule,
For they controll'd me when a boy;
They bring me sorrow touch'd with joy,
The merry merry bells of Yule.[4]   20

1. If, as many commentators hold, the structural divisions of the poem are marked by the three Christmases, then Part II begins with this section, which describes the first Christmas after Hallam's death (1833) and extends through Section 77. Being Christmas lyrics, Sections 28, 29, and 30 have a natural unity of their own.
2. The four villages around the poet's home at Somersby in Lincolnshire.
3. Sets of bells are pealed in varying sequences, or changes.
4. The church bells at Somersby were customarily rung on Christmas Eve.

29

With such compelling cause to grieve
As daily vexes household peace,
And chains regret to his decease,
How dare we keep our Christmas-eve;

Which brings no more a welcome guest   5
To enrich the threshold of the night
With shower'd largess of delight
In dance and song and game and jest?

Yet go, and while the holly boughs
 Entwine the cold baptismal font,   10
 Make one wreath more for Use and Wont,
That guard the portals of the house;[1]

Old sisters of a day gone by,[2]
 Gray nurses, loving nothing new;
 Why should they miss their yearly due 15
Before their time? They too will die.

1. Lines 9–12: The speaker bids the members of his family go decorate the church for Christmas as was their custom, though because of his private grief he will not himself take part in the public ritual this year.
2. The "sisters" are the "Use and Wont" of line 11.

30

With trembling fingers did we weave
 The holly round the Christmas hearth;
 A rainy cloud possess'd the earth,
And sadly fell our Christmas-eve.[1]

At our old pastimes in the hall   5
 We gambol'd, making vain pretence
 Of gladness, with an awful sense
Of one mute Shadow watching all.[2]

We paused: the winds were in the beech:
 We heard them sweep the winter land; 10
 And in a circle hand-in-hand
Sat silent, looking each at each.

Then echo-like our voices rang;
 We sung, tho' every eye was dim,
 A merry song we sang with him   15
Last year: impetuously we sang:

We ceased: a gentler feeling crept
 Upon us: surely rest is meet:
 'They rest,' we said, 'their sleep is sweet,'
And silence follow'd, and we wept.   20

Our voices took a higher range;
 Once more we sang: 'They do not die
 Nor lose their mortal sympathy,
Nor change to us, although they change;

'Rapt from the fickle and the frail   25
 With gather'd power, yet the same,

1. Compare the adverb in this line with that applied to the second Christmas Eve (Section 78, line 4) and to the third (Section 105, line 4).
2. I.e., the shadow of Hallam.

Pierces the keen seraphic flame
From orb to orb, from veil to veil.'

Rise, happy morn, rise, holy morn,
    Draw forth the cheerful day from night: 30
    O Father, touch the east, and light
The light that shone when Hope was born.

31

When Lazarus left his charnel-cave,
    And home to Mary's house return'd,[1]
    Was this demanded—if he yearn'd
To hear her weeping by his grave?

'Where wert thou, brother, those four days?'   5
    There lives no record of reply,
    Which telling what it is to die
Had surely added praise to praise.

From every house the neighbours met,
    The streets were fill'd with joyful sound,   10
    A solemn gladness even crown'd
The purple brows of Olivet.[2]

Behold a man raised up by Christ!
    The rest remaineth unreveal'd;
    He told it not; or something seal'd   15
The lips of that Evangelist.[3]

1. Lines 1–2: Lazarus, brother of Mary and Martha, had died and had been buried in a cave for five days when Christ miraculously raised him from the dead. See John xi.32–44. Cf. Browning's very different treatment of the same miracle in *An Epistle Containing the Strange Medical Experiences of Karshish.*
2. A hill near Jerusalem.
3. St. John, whose gospel recounts the miracle.

32

Her eyes are homes of silent prayer,
    Nor other thought her mind admits
    But, he was dead, and there he sits,
And he that brought him back is there.

Then one deep love doth supersede   5
    All other, when her ardent gaze
    Roves from the living brother's face,
And rests upon the Life indeed.

All subtle thought, all curious fears,
    Borne down by gladness so complete,   10
    She bows, she bathes the Saviour's feet
With costly spikenard and with tears.[1]

1. Lines 11–12: When Christ visited Lazarus's house after the miracle, in perfect love Mary anointed His feet and wiped them with her hair. See John xii.

Thrice blest whose lives are faithful prayers,
    Whose loves in higher love endure;
    What souls possess themselves so pure,   15
Or is there blessedness like theirs?

33[1]

O thou that after toil and storm
    Mayst seem to have reach'd a purer air,
    Whose faith has centre everywhere,
Nor cares to fix itself to form,

Leave thou thy sister when she prays,   5
    Her early Heaven, her happy views;
    Nor thou with shadow'd hint confuse
A life that leads melodious days.

Her faith thro' form is pure as thine,
    Her hands are quicker unto good: 10
    Oh, sacred be the flesh and blood
To which she links a truth divine!

See thou, that countest reason ripe
    In holding by the law within,[2]
    Thou fail not in a world of sin,   15
And ev'n for want of such a type.

1. With echoes of the Lazarus story still in mind, in this poem Tennyson imagines another brother and sister of his own Victorian age. The sister's faith, like Mary's, is intuitive, uncritical, even naive. The brother's is more intellectual and thoughtful because it has had to survive the assaults of modern rationalistic doubt and skepticism. The poet warns the brother against a too-prideful scoffing at his sister's simple faith. This section should be compared to Section 96, where, under somewhat similar circumstances, a different judgment on Tennyson's part is implied.

2. I.e., in holding an intellectual faith based on rationality and logic, not on mere intuitive apprehension.

34[1]

My own dim life should teach me this,
    That life shall live for evermore,
    Else earth is darkness at the core,
And dust and ashes all that is;

This round of green, this orb of flame,[2]   5
    Fantastic beauty; such as lurks
    In some wild Poet, when he works
Without a conscience or an aim.

1. In this poem and those following, one arrives at an unequivocal statement of the central dilemma forced upon Tennyson by the fact of Hallam's death: if there is no personal immortality, then life for the speaker is devoid of any ultimate purpose or significance, and he would wish only to die. The question he must face, then—and the one with which he wrestles throughout much of the rest of the poem—is as simple as it is basic. In light of the various kinds of evidence both pro and con, can one achieve—and defend—a firm belief in the immortality of the soul?

2. The earth and sun.

What then were God to such as I?
   'Twere hardly worth my while to choose   10
   Of things all mortal, or to use
A little patience ere I die;

'Twere best at once to sink to peace,
   Like birds the charming serpent draws,
   To drop head-foremost in the jaws   15
Of vacant darkness and to cease.

35

Yet if some voice that man could trust
   Should murmur from the narrow house,[1]
   'The cheeks drop in; the body bows;
Man dies: nor is there hope in dust:'

Might I not say? 'Yet even here,   5
   But for one hour, O Love, I strive
   To keep so sweet a thing alive:'
But I should turn mine ears and hear

The moanings of the homeless sea,
   The sound of streams that swift or slow   10
   Draw down Aeonian hills, and sow
The dust of continents to be;[2]

And Love would answer with a sigh,
   'The sound of that forgetful shore[3]
   Will change my sweetness more and more,   15
Half-dead to know that I shall die.'

O me, what profits it to put
   An idle case? If Death were seen
   At first as Death, Love had not been,
Or been in narrowest working shut,   20

Mere fellowship of sluggish moods,
   Or in his coarsest Satyr-shape
   Had bruised the herb and crush'd the grape,
And bask'd and batten'd in the woods.

1. I.e., the grave.
2. Lines 9–12: The image of erosion and sedimentation was derived from Tennyson's reading of Lyell's *Principles of Geology* (1830–33). *Aeonian* (line 11):

"The everlasting hills. The vastness of the Ages to come may seem to militate against that Love"—Tennyson.
3. The shore of the river Lethe, for the ancients the boundary of the underworld.

36

Tho' truths in manhood darkly join,
   Deep-seated in our mystic frame,
   We yield all blessing to the name
Of Him that made them current coin;

For Wisdom dealt with mortal powers,   5
  Where truth in closest words shall fail,
  When truth embodied in a tale
Shall enter in at lowly doors.[1]

And so the Word had breath,[2] and wrought
  With human hands the creed of creeds   10
  In loveliness of perfect deeds,
More strong than all poetic thought;

Which he may read that binds the sheaf,
  Or builds the house, or digs the grave,
  And those wild eyes that watch the wave[3]   15
In roarings round the coral reef.

1. Lines 5–8: "For divine Wisdom had to deal with the limited powers of humanity, to which truth logically argued out would be ineffectual, whereas truth coming in the story of the Gospel can influence the poorest"—Tennyson.
2. "In the beginning was the Word, and the Word was with God, and the Word was God. He was in the beginning with God; all things were made through him, and without him was not anything made that was made. ... And the Word became flesh and dwelt among us, full of grace and truth" (John i.1–3, 14).
3. "By this is intended the Pacific Islanders, 'wild' having a sense of 'barbarian' in it"—Tennyson. Cf. *Locksley Hall*, lines 157–80.

37

Urania[1] speaks with darken'd brow:
  'Thou pratest here where thou art least;
  This faith has many a purer priest,
And many an abler voice than thou.

'Go down beside thy native rill,   5
  On thy Parnassus[2] set thy feet,
  And hear thy laurel whisper sweet
About the ledges of the hill.'

And my Melpomene[3] replies,
  A touch of shame upon her cheek: 10
  'I am not worthy ev'n to speak
Of thy prevailing mysteries;

'For I am but an earthly Muse,
  And owning but a little art
  To lull with song an aching heart,   15
And render human love his dues;

'But brooding on the dear one dead,
  And all he said of things divine,

1. In Greek mythology the Muse of astronomy. Perhaps following the suggestion implied by her name (which, translated, means "the heavenly one"), Milton transformed her into the Muse of the loftiest poetry, that inspired by heaven. See *Paradise Lost* VII.1–20.
2. A Greek mountain sacred to the Muses.
3. The Muse of elegiac poetry (such as *In Memoriam*), hence "earthly" (line 13). The resolution of the conflict between the two Muses occurs in Section 103.

20

(And dear to me as sacred wine
To dying lips is all he said),

'I murmur'd, as I came along,
Of comfort clasp'd in truth reveal'd;
And loiter'd in the master's field,[4]
And darken'd sanctities with song.'

4. "The province of Christianity"—Tennyson.

38

With weary steps I loiter on,
    Tho' always under alter'd skies
    The purple from the distance dies,
My prospect and horizon gone.

No joy the blowing season[1] gives,   5
    The herald melodies of spring,
    But in the songs I love to sing
A doubtful gleam of solace lives.

If any care for what is here
    Survive in spirits render'd free,   10
    Then are these songs I sing of thee
Not all ungrateful to thine ear.

1. "The blossoming season"—Tennyson.   sequent spring song.
Cf. the tone of Section 83, another, sub-

39[1]

Old warder of these buried bones,
    And answering now my random stroke
    With fruitful cloud and living smoke,[2]
Dark yew, that graspest at the stones

And dippest toward the dreamless head,   5
    To thee too comes the golden hour
    When flower is feeling after flower;
But Sorrow—fixt upon the dead,

And darkening the dark graves of men,—
    What whisper'd from her lying lips?   10
    Thy gloom is kindled at the tips,
And passes into gloom again.

1. Written in April 1868 and added to   2. "The yew, when flowering, in a wind
In Memoriam in 1870, this poem echoes   or if struck sends up its pollen like
the imagery and themes of Sections 2   smoke"—Tennyson.
and 3.

40

Could we forget the widow'd hour
    And look on Spirits breathed away,
    As on a maiden in the day
When first she wears her orange-flower!

When crown'd with blessing she doth rise   5
　　To take her latest leave of home,
　　And hopes and light regrets that come
Make April of her tender eyes;

And doubtful joys the father move,
　　And tears are on the mother's face,   10
　　As parting with a long embrace
She enters other realms of love;

Her office there to rear, to teach,
　　Becoming as is meet and fit
　　A link among the days, to knit   15
The generations each with each;

And, doubtless, unto thee[1] is given
　　A life that bears immortal fruit
　　In those great offices that suit
The full-grown energies of heaven.   20

Ay me, the difference I discern!
　　How often shall her old fireside
　　Be cheer'd with tidings of the bride,
How often she herself return,

And tell them all they would have told,[2]   25
　　And bring her babe, and make her boast,
　　Till even those that miss'd her most
Shall count new things as dear as old:

But thou and I have shaken hands,
　　Till growing winters lay me low;   30
　　My paths are in the fields I know.
And thine in undiscover'd lands.

1. Hallam.
2. I.e., all they "would desire to be told"—Hallam Tennyson.

41
Thy spirit ere our fatal loss
　　Did ever rise from high to higher;
　　As mounts the heavenward altar-fire,
As flies the lighter thro' the gross.

But thou art turn'd to something strange,   5
　　And I have lost the links that bound
　　Thy changes; here upon the ground,
No more partaker of thy change.

Deep folly! yet that this could be—
　　That I could wing my will with might   10

To leap the grades of life and light,
And flash at once, my friend, to thee.

For tho' my nature rarely yields
    To that vague fear implied in death;
    Nor shudders at the gulfs beneath,   15
The howlings from forgotten fields;[1]

Yet oft when sundown skirts the moor
    An inner trouble I behold,
    A spectral doubt which makes me cold,
That I shall be thy mate no more,   20

Tho' following with an upward mind
    The wonders that have come to thee,
    Thro' all the secular to-be,
But evermore a life behind.

1. Lines 13–16: "The eternal miseries of the Inferno"—Tennyson. Hallam Tennyson refers the reader specifically to the Trimmers in Dante's *Inferno*, those spirits who, never having made a commitment either to good or to evil while alive, are denied entrance either to heaven or to hell after death. They "lived without blame, and without praise. They are mixed with that caitiff choir of the angels, who were not rebellious, nor were faithful to God; but were for themselves. Heaven chased them forth to keep its beauty from impair; and deep Hell receives them not, for the wicked would have some glory over them" (*Inferno* III.35–42).

42

I vex my heart with fancies dim:
    He still outstript me in the race;
    It was but unity of place
That made me dream I rank'd with him.

And so may Place retain us still,   5
    And he the much-beloved again,
    A lord of large experience, train
To riper growth the mind and will:

And what delights can equal those
    That stir the spirit's inner deeps,   10
    When one that loves but knows not, reaps
A truth from one that loves and knows?

43

If Sleep and Death be truly one,
    And every spirit's folded bloom
    Thro' all its intervital gloom[1]
In some long trance should slumber on;

Unconscious of the sliding hour,   5
    Bare of the body, might it last,

1. "In the passage between this life and the next"—Tennyson.

And silent traces of the past
Be all the colour of the flower:

So then were nothing lost to man;
    So that still garden of the souls   10
    In many a figured leaf enrolls
The total world since life began;

And love will last as pure and whole
    As when he loved me here in Time,
    And at the spiritual prime[2]   15
Rewaken with the dawning soul.

2. "Dawn of the spiritual life hereafter"—Tennyson.

44[1]

How fares it with the happy dead?[2]
    For here the man is more and more;
    But he forgets the days before
God shut the doorways of his head.[3]

The days have vanish'd, tone and tint,   5
    And yet perhaps the hoarding sense
    Gives out at times (he knows not whence)
A little flash, a mystic hint;

And in the long harmonious years
    (If Death so taste Lethean springs),[4]   10
    May some dim touch of earthly things
Surprise thee ranging with thy peers.

If such a dreamy touch should fall,
    O turn thee round, resolve the doubt;
    My guardian angel will speak out   15
In that high place, and tell thee all.

1. For several possible readings of this section, one of the most obscure in the poem, see Bradley's *Commentary*, pp. 125–135. (See Bibliography at the end of this volume.)
2. Cf. the echo of Section 4, line 5.
3. "Closing of the skull after babyhood. The dead after this life may have no remembrance of life, like the living babe who forgets the time before the sutures of the skull are closed, yet the living babe grows in knowledge, and though the remembrance of his earliest days has vanished, yet with his increasing knowledge there comes a dreamy vision of what has been; it may be so with the dead; if so, resolve my doubts, etc."—Tennyson.
4. In classical myth drinking the waters of the river Lethe induced forgetfulness of all that had gone before.

45

The baby new to earth and sky,
    What time his tender palm is prest
    Against the circle of the breast,
Has never thought that 'this is I:'

But as he grows he gathers much,   5
   And learns the use of 'I,' and 'me,'
   And finds 'I am not what I see,
And other than the things I touch.'

So rounds he to a separate mind
   From whence clear memory may begin,   10
   As thro' the frame that binds him in
His isolation grows defined.

This use may lie in blood and breath,
   Which else were fruitless of their due,
   Had man to learn himself anew   15
Beyond the second birth of Death.[1]

1. The purpose of life, the speaker argues, is to establish an individual consciousness, or identity (line 9). Surely, then, the dead must retain some memory of their earthly life; otherwise, man would have to learn himself anew after death, thus rendering the purpose of living merely a waste of "blood and breath" (lines 13–16).

46

We ranging down this lower track,
   The path we came by, thorn and flower,
   Is shadow'd by the growing hour,
Lest life should fail in looking back.

So be it: there no shade can last   5
   In that deep dawn behind the tomb,
   But clear from marge to marge shall bloom
The eternal landscape of the past;

A lifelong tract of time reveal'd;
   The fruitful hours of still increase;   10
   Days order'd in a wealthy peace,
And those five years its richest field.[1]

O Love, thy province were not large,
   A bounded field, nor stretching far;
   Look also, Love, a brooding star,   15
A rosy warmth from marge to marge.[2]

1. Lines 5–12: After death the speaker will comprehend all time past, which will lead him to see that the five years' friendship with Hallam was the "richest field" in the landscape of his life.
2. "Memory fails here, but memory in the next life . . . will see Love shine forth as if the Lord of the whole life (not merely of those five years of friendship),—the wider landscape aglow with the sunrise of 'that deep dawn behind the tomb' "—Hallam Tennyson.

47[1]

That each, who seems a separate whole,
   Should move his rounds, and fusing all

1. "The individuality lasts after death, and we are not utterly absorbed into the Godhead. If we are to be finally merged into the Universal Soul, Love asks to have at least one more parting before we lose ourselves"—Tennyson. Thus the speaker resists the notion of the total destruction of personality after death.

The skirts of self again, should fall
Remerging in the general Soul,

Is faith as vague as all unsweet: 5
   Eternal form shall still divide
   The eternal soul from all beside;
And I shall know him when we meet:

And we shall sit at endless feast,
   Enjoying each the other's good: 10
   What vaster dream can hit the mood
Of Love on earth? He seeks at least

Upon the last and sharpest height,
   Before the spirits fade away,
   Some landing-place, to clasp and say,   15
'Farewell! We lose ourselves in light.'

48
If these brief lays, of Sorrow born,
   Were taken to be such as closed
   Grave doubts and answers here proposed,
Then these were such as men might scorn:

Her care is not to part[1] and prove;   5
   She takes, when harsher moods remit,
   What slender shade of doubt may flit,
And makes it vassal unto love:

And hence, indeed, she sports with words,
   But better serves a wholesome law,   10
   And holds it sin and shame to draw
The deepest measure from the chords:

Nor dare she trust a larger lay,
   But rather loosens from the lip
   Short swallow-flights of song, that dip   15
Their wings in tears, and skim away.

1. To analyze.

49
From art, from nature, from the schools,[1]
   Let random influences glance,
   Like light in many a shiver'd lance
That breaks about the dappled pools:

The lightest wave of thought shall lisp,   5
   The fancy's tenderest eddy wreathe,
   The slightest air of song shall breathe
To make the sullen surface crisp.

1. I.e., theological and philosophical systems.

And look thy look, and go thy way,[2]
   But blame not thou the winds that make   10
   The seeming-wanton ripple break,
The tender-pencil'd shadow play.

Beneath all fancied hopes and fears
   Ay me, the sorrow deepens down,
   Whose muffled motions blindly drown   15
The bases of my life in tears.

2. The poet addresses an observer, such as the traveler in Section 21.

50[1]

Be near me when my light is low,[2]
   When the blood creeps, and the nerves prick
   And tingle; and the heart is sick,
And all the wheels of Being slow.

Be near me when the sensuous frame   5
   Is rack'd with pangs that conquer trust;
   And Time, a maniac scattering dust,
And Life, a Fury slinging flame.

Be near me when my faith is dry,
   And men the flies of latter spring,   10
   That lay their eggs, and sting and sing
And weave their petty cells and die.

Be near me when I fade away,
   To point the term of human strife,
   And on the low dark verge of life   15
The twilight of eternal day.

1. Tennyson suggested that Sections 50–58 formed a group. In them the speaker's doubts about immortality, springing primarily from his readings in geology, seem almost to overcome what frail trust he has so far been able to muster.
2. The poet addresses the spirit of Hallam.

51

Do we indeed desire the dead
   Should still be near us at our side?
   Is there no baseness we would hide
No inner vileness that we dread?

Shall he for whose applause I strove,   5
   I had such reverence for his blame,
   See with clear eye some hidden shame
And I be lessen'd in his love?

I wrong the grave with fears untrue:
   Shall love be blamed for want of faith?   10
   There must be wisdom with great Death:
The dead shall look me thro' and thro'.

Be near us when we climb or fall:
    Ye watch, like God, the rolling hours
    With larger other eyes than ours,   15
To make allowance for us all.

52[1]

I cannot love thee as I ought,
    For love reflects the thing beloved;
    My words are only words, and moved
Upon the topmost froth of thought.

'Yet blame not thou thy plaintive song,'   5
    The Spirit of true love replied;
    'Thou canst not move me from thy side,
Nor human frailty do me wrong.

'What keeps a spirit wholly true
    To that ideal which he bears?   10
    What record? not the sinless years
That breathed beneath the Syrian blue:[2]

'So fret not, like an idle girl,
    That life is dash'd with flecks of sin.
    Abide: thy wealth is gather'd in,   15
When Time hath sunder'd shell from pearl.'

1. The argument in this difficult section rests on the speaker's distinction between perfect, infinite love, which exists in the realm of the ideal, and the imperfect, finite love of our real, human world. Perfect love like Christ's, the speaker complains, cannot be sustained by imperfect human beings, because human love requires the physical presence of the loved one. Nevertheless, in spite of human imperfection and death, which physically sunders the beloved from the lover, the *spirit* of love endures; personified, it counsels the speaker to "abide" in the sure faith that the ideal of love survives all "human frailty" and finitude. 2. Lines 11–12: The years of Christ's life recorded in the Gospels.

53

How many a father have I seen,
    A sober man, among his boys,
    Whose youth was full of foolish noise,
Who wears his manhood hale and green:

And dare we to this fancy give,   5
    That had the wild oat not been sown,
    That soil, left barren, scarce had grown
The grain by which a man may live?

Or, if we held the doctrine sound
    For life outliving heats of youth,   10
    Yet who would preach it as a truth
To those that eddy round and round?

Hold thou the good: define it well:
  For fear divine Philosophy
  Should push beyond her mark, and be   15
Procuress to the Lords of Hell.[1]

1. Lines 5–16: "There is a passionate heat of nature in a rake sometimes. The nature that yields emotionally may turn out straighter than a prig's. Yet we must not be making excuses, but we must set before us a rule of good for young as for old"—Tennyson.

54[1]

Oh yet we trust that somehow good
  Will be the final goal of ill,
  To pangs of nature, sins of will,
Defects of doubt, and taints of blood;

That nothing walks with aimless feet;   5
  That not one life shall be destroy'd,
  Or cast as rubbish to the void,
When God hath made the pile complete,

That not a worm is cloven in vain;
  That not a moth with vain desire   10
  Is shrivell'd in a fruitless fire,
Or but subserves another's gain.

Behold, we know not anything;
  I can but trust that good shall fall
  At last—far off—at last, to all,[2]   15
And every winter change to spring.

So runs my dream: but what am I?
  An infant crying in the night:
  An infant crying for the light:
And with no language but a cry.   20

1. In Sections 54–56 the speaker's faith all but gives way in the face of the rational evidence against immortality implied, he believes, by the geological discoveries of his age. When he reconsiders the same kind of evidence later in the poem, however, his faith and trust have come to have more secure bases, and the implications that he subsequently draws from contemporary scientific thinking are quite different from those drawn here. Cf. especially Sections 118, 120.
2. Cf. the Epilogue, lines 141–44.

55

The wish, that of the living whole
  No life may fail beyond the grave,
  Derives it not from what we have
The likest God within the soul?[1]

Are God and Nature then at strife,[2]   5
  That Nature lends such evil dreams?

1. "The inner consciousness—the divine in man"—Tennyson.
2. I.e., does the evidence of nature not seem to deny the existence of immortality and to contradict the concept that love is the ultimate law of creation?

So careful of the type[3] she seems,
So careless of the single life;

That I, considering everywhere
Her secret meaning in her deeds,   10
And finding that of fifty seeds[4]
She often brings but one to bear,[5]

I falter where I firmly trod,
And falling with my weight of cares
Upon the great world's altar-stairs   15
That slope thro' darkness up to God,

I stretch lame hands of faith, and grope,
And gather dust and chaff, and call
To what I feel is Lord of all,
And faintly trust the larger hope.[6]   20

3. Species.
4. " 'Fifty' should be 'myriad' "—Tennyson.
5. Lines 7–12: Tennyson here suggests the principle of natural selection long before Darwin made it a Victorian commonplace. Primarily because it implied that nature was indifferent to man, natural selection subsequently became, for many thoughtful Victorians, one of the most unsettling concepts in Darwin's theory of evolution as set forth in *The Origin of Species* (1859). Tennyson, according to his son, "was occasionally much troubled with the intellectual problem of the apparent profusion and waste of life and by the vast amount of sin and suffering throughout the world, for these semed to militate against the idea of the Omnipotent and All-loving Father" (*Memoir*, I, 313).
6. "My father means by 'the larger hope' that the whole human race would, through perhaps ages of suffering, be at length purified and saved . . ."—Hallam Tennyson.

56[1]

'So careful of the type?' but no.
From scarped cliff and quarried stone
She cries, 'A thousand types are gone:
I care for nothing, all shall go.[2]

'Thou makest thine appeal to me: 5
I bring to life, I bring to death:
The spirit does but mean the breath:[3]
I know no more.' And he, shall he,

Man, her last work, who seem'd so fair,
Such splendid purpose in his eyes,   10
Who roll'd the psalm to wintry skies,
Who built him fanes of fruitless prayer,

Who trusted God was love indeed
And love Creation's final law—

1. This section, which derives largely from Tennyson's reading of Lyell's *Principles of Geology* (1830–33), marks the depth of the speaker's despair. It may be contrasted to the Prologue, wherein the poet's faith reaches its triumphant height, and to Section 118.
2. Lines 1–4. From the evidence of fossils found in quarried stone and cliffs cut away so that rock strata are exposed ("scarped"), we know that not only individuals but entire species have become extinct.
3. In Latin *spiritus* means "breath."

Tho' Nature, red in tooth and claw   15
With ravine, shriek'd against his creed—

Who loved, who suffer'd countless ills,
    Who battled for the True, the Just.
    Be blown about the desert dust,
Or seal'd within the iron hills?   20

No more? A monster then, a dream,
    A discord. Dragons of the prime,[4]
    That tare each other in their slime,
Were mellow music match'd with him.[5]

O life as futile, then, as frail![6]   25
    O for thy voice to soothe and bless![7]
    What hope of answer, or redress?
Behind the veil, behind the veil.

4. "The geologic monsters of early ages" —Tennyson. Particularly dinosaurs.
5. Lines 21–23: If the ultimate law of life is not love but ravine (lines 13–16), then the prehistoric monsters "red in tooth and claw" were at least more in harmony with the natural order than man, for they were incapable of deluding themselves with cruel hopes and dreams of immortality.
6. I.e., if man is no more than another species doomed to extinction (lines 19–20), then life is pointless.
7. The voice of Hallam.

57

Peace; come away: the song of woe
    Is after all an earthly song:
    Peace; come away: we do him wrong
To sing so wildly: let us go.

Come; let us go: your cheeks are pale;[1]   5
    But half my life I leave behind:
    Methinks my friend is richly shrined;
But I shall pass; my work will fail.

Yet in these ears, till hearing dies,
    One set slow bell will seem to toll   10
    The passing of the sweetest soul
That ever look'd with human eyes.

I hear it now, and o'er and o'er,
    Eternal greetings to the dead;
    And 'Ave, Ave, Ave,'[2] said,   15
'Adieu, adieu' for evermore.

1. Lines 1–5: Some commentators believe that these lines are addressed to Tennyson's sister Emily, who was Hallam's fiancée; others that they are addressed more generally to the poet's fellow mourners.
2. Latin: "hail!"

58[1]

In those sad words I took farewell:
 Like echoes in sepulchral halls,
 As drop by drop the water falls
In vaults and catacombs, they fell;

And, falling, idly broke the peace   5
 Of hearts that beat from day to day,
 Half-conscious of their dying clay,
And those cold crypts where they shall cease.

The high Muse[2] answer'd: 'Wherefore grieve
 Thy brethren with a fruitless tear?   10
 Abide a little longer here,
And thou shalt take a nobler leave.'

1. In Sections 57 and 58 perhaps something of a turning point in the poem has been reached. That the speaker is beginning to recover significantly from the bleak despair of the immediately preceding sections is suggested by Tennyson's own comparison of Section 58 to his

Ulysses: "*Ulysses* was written soon after Arthur Hallam's death, and gave my feelings about the need for going forward and braving the struggle of life perhaps more simply than anything in *In Memoriam*"—Tennyson.
2. Urania. Cf. Section 37.

59[1]

O Sorrow, wilt thou live with me
 No casual mistress, but a wife,
 My bosom-friend and half of life;
As I confess it needs must be;

O Sorrow, wilt thou rule my blood,   5
 Be sometimes lovely like a bride,
 And put thy harsher moods aside,
If thou wilt have me wise and good.

My centered passion cannot move,
 Nor will it lessen from to-day;   10
 But I'll have leave at times to play
As with the creature of my love;

And set thee forth, for thou art mine,
 With so much hope for years to come,
 That, howsoe'er I know thee, some   15
Could hardly tell what name were thine.

1. This poem, which was inserted in the fourth edition of *In Memoriam* in 1851, was designed to parallel Section 3. Sorrow is addressed in each poem. In Section 3, Sorrow declares the universe to be pointless and futile and thus strikes the prevailing tone for roughly the first

half of the poem. Here, however, Sorrow is addressed more hopefully (in a marriage metaphor), which suggests the proper tone for the speaker's spiritual recovery in the second half of *In Memoriam.*

60[1]

He past; a soul of nobler tone:
  My spirit loved and loves him yet,
  Like some poor girl whose heart is set
On one whose rank exceeds her own.

He mixing with his proper sphere,   5
  She finds the baseness of her lot,
  Half jealous of she knows not what,
And envying all that meet him there.

The little village looks forlorn;
  She sighs amid her narrow days,   10
  Moving about the household ways,
In that dark house where she was born.

The foolish neighbours come and go,
  And tease her till the day draws by:
  At night she weeps, 'How vain am I!   15
How should he love a thing so low?'

1. Most analysts of the structure of *In Memoriam* group Sections 60–65 together because of their common theme.

61

If, in thy second state sublime,[1]
  Thy ransom'd reason change replies[2]
  With all the circle of the wise,[3]
The perfect flower of human time;

And if thou cast thine eyes below,   5
  How dimly character'd and slight,
  How dwarf'd a growth of cold and night,
How blanch'd with darkness must I grow!

Yet turn thee to the doubtful shore,[4]
  Where thy first form was made a man;   10
  I loved thee, Spirit, and love, nor can
The soul of Shakespeare love thee more.[5]

1. I.e., in your afterlife.
2. "Ransom'd": regained by Christ's sacrifice of His life. "Change": exchange.
3. I.e., with wise men who have now, perhaps, been sainted.
4. I.e., to the now dimly discernible life of man on earth. Here, as in the two stanzas above, Dantean imagery is suggested.
5. Shakespeare also enshrined his love for a friend in poetry (i.e., in the Sonnets).

62

Tho' if an eye that's downward cast
  Could make thee somewhat blench or fail,
  Then be my love an idle tale,
And fading legend of the past;[1]

1. Lines 1–4: In view of the allusion to Shakespeare in the stanza above, cf. the echo of Sonnet 116, lines 13–14.

And thou, as one that once declined,   5
    When he was little more than boy,
    On some unworthy heart with joy,
But lives to wed an equal mind;

And breathes a novel world, the while
    His other passion wholly dies,   10
    Or in the light of deeper eyes
Is matter for a flying smile.

63

Yet pity for a horse o'er-driven,
    And love in which my hound has part,
    Can hang no weight upon my heart
In its assumptions up to heaven;

And I am so much more than these,   5
    As thou, perchance, art more than I,
    And yet I spare them sympathy,
And I would set their pains at ease.

So mayst thou watch me where I weep,
    As, unto vaster motions bound,   10
    The circuits of thine orbit round
A higher height, a deeper deep.[1]

1. Lines 9–12: Metaphorically the speaker's orbit is that of the earth around the sun; Hallam's is the larger orbit of a far larger planet.

64[1]

Dost thou look back on what hath been,
    As some divinely gifted man,
    Whose life in low estate began
And on a simple village green;

Who breaks his birth's invidious bar,   5
    And grasps the skirts of happy chance,
    And breasts the blows of circumstance,
And grapples with his evil star;

Who makes by force his merit known
    And lives to clutch the golden keys,[2]   10
    To mould a mighty state's decrees,
And shape the whisper of the throne;

And moving up from high to higher,
    Becomes on Fortune's crowning slope
    The pillar of a people's hope,   15
The centre of a world's desire;

1. According to his son, Tennyson composed this poem while walking in the Strand and Fleet Street, London.
2. "Keys of office of State"—Tennyson.

Yet feels, as in a pensive dream,
 When all his active powers are still,
 A distant dearness in the hill,
A secret sweetness in the stream,   20

The limit of his narrower fate,
 While yet beside its vocal springs
 He play'd at counsellors and kings,
With one that was his earliest mate;

Who ploughs with pain his native lea   25
 And reaps the labour of his hands,
 Or in the furrow musing stands;
'Does my old friend remember me?'

65

Sweet soul, do with me as thou wilt;
 I lull a fancy trouble-tost
 With 'Love's too precious to be lost,
A little grain shall not be spilt.'

And in that solace can I sing,   5
 Till out of painful phases wrought
 There flutters up a happy thought,
Self-balanced on a lightsome wing:[1]

Since we deserved the name of friends,
 And thine effect so lives in me,   10
 A part of mine may live in thee
And move thee on to noble ends.

1. Lines 7–8: Cf. Section 48, lines 15–16.

66

You thought my heart too far diseased;[1]
 You wonder when my fancies play
 To find me gay among the gay,
Like one with any trifle pleased.

The shade by which my life was crost,   5
 Which makes a desert in the mind,
 Has made me kindly with my kind,
And like to him whose sight is lost;

Whose feet are guided thro' the land,
 Whose jest among his friends is free,   10
 Who takes the children on his knee,
And winds their curls about his hand:

1. The poet is addressing a friend, per-   Section 21. "Diseased": sunk in gloom.
haps one of the imagined speakers in

He plays with threads,² he beats his chair
   For pastime, dreaming of the sky;
   His inner day can never die,   15
His night of loss is always there.

2. Makes cats'-cradles to amuse children.

67

When on my bed the moonlight falls,
   I know that in thy place of rest
   By that broad water of the west,¹
There comes a glory on the walls;

Thy marble bright in dark appears,   5
   As slowly steals a silver flame
   Along the letters of thy name,
And o'er the number of thy years.

The mystic glory swims away;
   From off my bed the moonlight dies;   10
   And closing eaves of wearied eyes
I sleep till dusk is dipt in gray:

And then I know the mist is drawn
   A lucid veil from coast to coast,
   And in the dark church like a ghost   15
Thy tablet glimmers to the dawn.²

1. The Severn River at Clevedon.
2. "I myself did not see Clevedon till years after the burial of A. H. H. ... and then in later editions of *In Memo-* *riam* I altered the word 'chancel' ... to 'dark church' "—Tennyson. "Tablet": Hallam's commemorative marker on the wall of the church above the vault.

68

When in the down I sink my head,
   Sleep, Death's twin-brother, times my breath;
   Sleep, Death's twin-brother, knows not Death,
Nor can I dream of thee as dead:

I walk as ere I walk'd forlorn,   5
   When all our path was fresh with dew,
   And all the bugle breezes blew
Reveillée to the breaking morn.

But what is this? I turn about,
   I find a trouble in thine eye,   10
   Which makes me sad I know not why,
Nor can my dream resolve the doubt:

But ere the lark hath left the lea
   I wake, and I discern the truth;
   It is the trouble of my youth   15
That foolish sleep transfers to thee.

69

I dream'd there would be Spring no more,
    That Nature's ancient power was lost:
    The streets were black with smoke and frost,
They chatter'd trifles at the door:

I wander'd from the noisy town,   5
    I found a wood with thorny boughs:
    I took the thorns to bind my brows,
I wore them like a civic crown:

I met with scoffs, I met with scorns
    From youth and babe and hoary hairs: 10
    They call'd me in the public squares
The fool that wears a crown of thorns:[1]

They call'd me fool, they call'd me child:
    I found an angel of the night;
    The voice was low, the look was bright;   15
He look'd upon my crown and smiled:

He reach'd the glory of a hand,
    That seem'd to touch it into leaf:
    The voice was not the voice of grief,
The words were hard to understand.   20

1. Lines 9–12: Cf. Section 21, lines 5–20.

70

I cannot see the features right,
    When on the gloom I strive to paint
    The face I know; the hues are faint
And mix with hollow masks of night;

Cloud-towers by ghostly masons wrought,   5
    A gulf that ever shuts and gapes,
    A hand that points, and palled shapes[1]
In shadowy thoroughfares of thought;

And crowds that stream from yawning doors,
    And shoals of pucker'd faces drive;   10
    Dark bulks that tumble half alive,
And lazy lengths on boundless shores;

Till all at once beyond the will
    I hear a wizard music roll,
    And thro' a lattice on the soul   15
Looks thy fair face and makes it still.[2]

1. Pale, as if shrouded.
2. Falling into that half-conscious state which precedes sleep, the speaker strives unsuccessfully to summon to memory the image of Hallam's face (lines 1–12). Only after full sleep has come and the conscious will has ceased to function, however, does the vision clearly emerge, unbidden, from the well of the unconscious (lines 12–16).

71[1]

Sleep, kinsman thou to death and trance
    And madness, thou hast forged at last
    A night-long Present of the Past
In which we went thro' summer France.

Hadst thou such credit with the soul?   5
    Then bring an opiate trebly strong,
    Drug down the blindfold sense of wrong
That so my pleasure may be whole;

While now we talk as once we talk'd
    Of men and minds, the dust of change,   10
    The days that grow to something strange,
In walking as of old we walk'd

Beside the river's wooded reach,
    The fortress, and the mountain ridge,
    The cataract flashing from the bridge,   15
The breaker breaking on the beach.

1. In this section the poet describes a dream which had its basis in a real event. In the summer of 1830 Hallam and Tennyson had traveled through the Pyrenees to Spain on an undergraduate political mission. Tennyson subsequently turned what he saw to good poetic use, as in the visual imagery of stanza 4 of this section. Much of the remarkable imagery of several other poems, among them *The Lotos-Eaters* and *Oenone*, also derived from Tennyson's recollections of that trip.

72

Risest thou thus, dim dawn, again,[1]
    And howlest, issuing out of night,
    With blasts that blow the poplar white,[2]
And lash with storm the streaming pane?

Day, when my crown'd estate begun   5
    To pine in that reverse of doom,
    Which sicken'd every living bloom,
And blurr'd the splendour of the sun;

Who usherest in the dolorous hour
    With thy quick tears that make the rose   10
    Pull sideways, and the daisy close
Her crimson fringes to the shower;

Who might'st have heaved a windless flame
    Up the deep East, or, whispering, play'd
    A chequer-work of beam and shade   15
Along the hills, yet look'd the same.

As wan, as chill, as wild as now;
    Day, mark'd as with some hideous crime,

1. The first anniversary of Hallam's death, September 15, 1834.   2. I.e., the wind exposes the white undersides of the poplar leaves.

When the dark hand struck down thro' time,
And cancell'd nature's best: but thou,   20

Lift as thou may'st thy burthen'd brows
    Thro' clouds that drench the morning star,
    And whirl the ungarner'd sheaf afar,
And sow the sky with flying boughs,

And up thy vault with roaring sound   25
    Climb thy thick noon, disastrous day;
    Touch thy dull goal of joyless gray,
And hide thy shame beneath the ground.

73

So many worlds, so much to do,
    So little done, such things to be,
    How know I what had need of thee,
For thou wert strong as thou wert true?

The fame is quench'd that I foresaw,   5
    The head hath miss'd an earthly wreath:
    I curse not nature, no, nor death;
For nothing is that errs from law.

We pass; the path that each man trod
    Is dim, or will be dim, with weeds: 10
    What frame is left for human deeds
In endless age? It rests with God.

O hollow wraith of dying fame,
    Fade wholly, while the soul exults,
    And self-infolds the large results   15
Of force that would have forged a name.

74

As sometimes in a dead man's face,
    To those that watch it more and more,
    A likeness, hardly seen before,
Comes out—to some one of his race:

So, dearest, now thy brows are cold,   5
    I see thee what thou art, and know
    Thy likeness to the wise below,[1]
Thy kindred with the great of old.

But there is more than I can see,
    And what I see I leave unsaid,   10
    Nor speak it, knowing Death has made
His darkness beautiful with thee.

1. I.e., the wise men of the ages past.

75

I leave thy praises unexpress'd
   In verse that brings myself relief,
   And by the measure of my grief
I leave thy greatness to be guess'd;

What practice howsoe'er expert   5
   In fitting aptest words to things,
   Or voice the richest-toned that sings,
Hath power to give thee as thou wert?

I care not in these fading days[1]
   To raise a cry that lasts not long,   10
   And round thee with the breeze of song
To stir a little dust of praise.

Thy leaf has perish'd in the green,
   And, while we breathe beneath the sun,
   The world which credits what is done   15
Is cold to all that might have been.

So here shall silence guard thy fame;
   But somewhere, out of human view,
   Whate'er thy hands are set to do
Is wrought with tumult of acclaim.   20

1. The poet's characterization of his own age, which he considers hostile to poetry.

76

Take wings of fancy, and ascend,
   And in a moment set thy face
   Where all the starry heavens of space
Are sharpen'd to a needle's end;[1]

Take wings of foresight; lighten thro'   5
   The secular abyss to come,[2]
   And lo, thy deepest lays are dumb
Before the mouldering of a yew;[3]

And if the matin songs,[4] that woke
   The darkness of our planet, last,   10
   Thine own shall wither in the vast,
Ere half the lifetime of an oak.

Ere these[5] have clothed their branchy bowers
   With fifty Mays, thy songs are vain;
   And what are they when these remain   15
The ruin'd shells of hollow towers?

1. Lines 1–4: "So distant in void space that all our firmament would appear to be a needle-point thence"—Tennyson. Cf. the cosmic perspective in Dante Gabriel Rossetti's *The Blessed Damozel*, lines 25–36.
2. "The ages upon ages to be"—Tennyson.
3. The yew lives to a great age.
4. "The great early poets"—Tennyson.
5. I.e., the oak and the yew.

77

What hope is here for modern rhyme
    To him, who turns a musing eye
    On songs, and deeds, and lives, that lie
Foreshorten'd in the tract of time?[1]

These mortal lullabies of pain   5
    May bind a book, may line a box,
    May serve to curl a maiden's locks;
Or when a thousand moons shall wane

A man upon a stall may find,
    And, passing, turn the page that tells   10
    A grief, then changed to something else
Sung by a long-forgotten mind.

But what of that? My darken'd ways
    Shall ring with music all the same;
    To breathe my loss is more than fame,   15
To utter love more sweet than praise.

1. Lines 1–4: As one casts the mind's eye backward, the perspective of time increasingly contracts the "songs, and deeds, and lives" of even the greatest poets of the past. What hope can there be, therefore, for "modern rhyme," specifically these poems?

78[1]

Again at Christmas did we weave
    The holly round the Christmas hearth;
    The silent snow possess'd the earth,
And calmly fell our Christmas-eve:

The yule-clog[2] sparkled keen with frost,   5
    No wing of wind the region swept,
    But over all things brooding slept
The quiet sense of something lost.

As in the winters left behind,
    Again our ancient games had place,   10
    The mimic picture's breathing grace,[3]
And dance and song and hoodman-blind.[4]

Who show'd a token of distress?
    No single tear, no mark of pain:
    O sorrow, then can sorrow wane?   15
O grief, can grief be changed to less?

1. This section, which describes the second Christmas after Hallam's death, is the initial lyric of Part III of the poem. Cf. Sections 28–30 (the first Christmas) for some indication of the spiritual progression which has occurred in Part II. Cf. also Section 105 (the third Christmas).
2. The Yule log.
3. Perhaps charades.
4. Blind man's bluff.

O last regret, regret can die!
No—mixt with all this mystic frame,
Her deep relations are the same,
But with long use her tears are dry.   20

79[1]

'More than my brothers are to me,'—
Let this not vex thee, noble heart!
I know thee of what force thou art
To hold the costliest love in fee.[2]

But thou and I are one in kind,   5
As moulded like in Nature's mint;
And hill and wood and field did print
The same sweet forms in either mind.

For us the same cold streamlet curl'd
Thro' all his eddying coves; the same   10
All winds that roam the twilight came
In whispers of the beauteous world.

At one dear knee we proffer'd vows,
One lesson from one book we learn'd,
Ere childhood's flaxen ringlet turn'd   15
To black and brown on kindred brows.

And so my wealth resembles thine,
But he[3] was rich where I was poor,
And he supplied my want the more
As his unlikeness fitted mine.   20

1. In this section Tennyson addresses his
brother Charles. In line 1 the poet
quotes himself, Section 9, line 20.
2. In possession.
3. I.e., Hallam.

80

If any vague desire should rise,
That holy Death ere Arthur died
Had moved me kindly from his side,
And dropt the dust on tearless eyes;

Then fancy shapes, as fancy can,   5
The grief my loss in him had wrought,
A grief as deep as life or thought,
But stay'd[1] in peace with God and man.

I make a picture in the brain;
I hear the sentence that he speaks;   10

1. Held fast.

He bears the burthen of the weeks
But turns his burthen into gain.

His credit thus shall set me free;
     And, influence rich to soothe and save,
     Unused example from the grave   15
Reach out dead hands to comfort me.

81

Could I have said while he was here,[1]
     'My love shall now no further range;
     There cannot come a mellower change,
For now is love mature in ear.'

Love, then, had hope of richer store: 5
     What end is here to my complaint?
     This haunting whisper makes me faint,
'More years had made me love thee more.'

But Death returns an answer sweet:
     'My sudden frost was sudden gain,   10
     And gave all ripeness to the grain,
It might have drawn from after-heat.'[2]

1. I.e., "I wish I could have said. . . ." 2. Lines 9–12: In the metaphor of grain ripened by an unexpected frost, the poet suggests a rudimentary acceptance of his friend's death and even takes some small measure of consolation in it.

82

I wage not any feud with Death
     For changes wrought on form and face;
     No lower life that earth's embrace
May breed with him, can fright my faith.[1]

Eternal process moving on,   5
     From state to state the spirit walks;
     And these[2] are but the shatter'd stalks,
Or ruin'd chrysalis of one.[3]

Nor blame I Death, because he bare
     The use of virtue out of earth: 10
     I know transplanted human worth
Will bloom to profit, otherwhere.

For this alone on Death I wreak
     The wrath that garners[4] in my heart;
     He put our lives so far apart   15
We cannot hear each other speak.

1. Lines 1–4: Cf. Section 73, lines 7–8. 2. The physical changes wrought by death. 3. Lines 5–8: The poet further develops the metaphor of Section 81. "Chrysalis": the hard case in which a butterfly is enclosed while it passes through its pupal stage. Thus the spirit, in evolving from lower to higher stages, sheds its body as the butterfly sheds its pupal case. 4. Is stored.

83

Dip down upon the northern shore,[1]
  O sweet new-year delaying long;[2]
  Thou doest expectant nature wrong;
Delaying long, delay no more.

What stays thee from the clouded noons,[3]   5
  Thy sweetness from its proper place?
  Can trouble live with April days,
Or sadness in the summer moons?

Bring orchis, bring the foxglove spire,
  The little speedwell's[4] darling blue,   10
  Deep tulips dash'd with fiery dew,
Laburnums, dropping-wells of fire.[5]

O thou, new-year, delaying long,
  Delayest the sorrow in my blood,
  That longs to burst a frozen bud   15
And flood a fresher throat with song.

1. England.
2. The poet is invoking spring. Cf. the first spring song, Section 38.
3. English winter days are more often than not abundantly "clouded."
4. A small spring flower.
5. Laburnum blossoms are brilliant yellow.

84

When I contemplate all alone
  The life that had been thine below,
  And fix my thoughts on all the glow
To which thy crescent would have grown;

I see thee sitting crown'd with good,   5
  A central warmth diffusing bliss
  In glance and smile, and clasp and kiss,
On all the branches of thy blood;

Thy blood, my friend, and partly mine;
  For now the day was drawing on,   10
  When thou should'st link thy life with one[1]
Of mine own house, and boys of thine

Had babbled 'Uncle' on my knee;
  But that remorseless iron hour
  Made cypress of her orange flower,[2]   15
Despair of Hope, and earth of thee.

I seem to meet their least desire,
  To clap their cheeks, to call them mine.
  I see their unborn faces shine
Beside the never-lighted fire.   20

1. Tennyson's older sister Emily, to whom Hallam had been engaged.
2. Orange blossoms traditionally symbolize weddings, cypresses death.

I see myself an honour'd guest,
    Thy partner in the flowery walk
    Of letters, genial table-talk,
Or deep dispute, and graceful jest;

While now thy prosperous labour fills   25
    The lips of men with honest praise,
    And sun by sun the happy days
Descend below the golden hills

With promise of a morn as fair;
    And all the train of bounteous hours   30
    Conduct by paths of growing powers,
To reverence and the silver hair;

Till slowly worn her earthly robe,
    Her lavish misson richly wrought,
    Leaving great legacies of thought,   35
Thy spirit should fail from off the globe;

What time mine own might also flee,
    As link'd with thine in love and fate,
    And, hovering o'er the dolorous strait
To the other shore, involved in thee,   40

Arrive at last the blessed goal,
    And He that died in Holy Land
    Would reach us out the shining hand,
And take us as a single soul.

What reed was that on which I leant?   45
    Ah, backward fancy, wherefore wake
    The old bitterness again, and break
The low beginnings of content.

85[1]

This truth came borne with bier and pall,
    I felt it, when I sorrow'd most,
    'Tis better to have loved and lost,
Than never to have loved at all[2]—

O true in word, and tried in deed,   5
    Demanding, so to bring relief
    To this which is our common grief,
What kind of life is that I lead;

1. Turning away from excessive manifestations of grief, the poet addresses this section to a new friend, Edmund Lushington, who married Tennyson's younger sister, Cecilia, on October 10, 1842. The marriage is celebrated in the Epilogue to *In Memoriam*. A few commentators have argued that Section 85 is the turning point of the poem.
2. Lines 3–4: Cf. Section 27, lines 15–16.

And whether trust in things above
    Be dimm'd of sorrow, or sustain'd;   10
    And whether love for him have drain'd
My capabilities of love;

Your words have virtue such as draws
    A faithful answer from the breast,
    Thro' light reproaches, half exprest,   15
And loyal unto kindly laws.

My blood an even tenor kept,
    Till on mine ear this message falls,
    That in Vienna's fatal walls
God's finger touch'd him, and he slept.   20

The great Intelligences fair[3]
    That range above our mortal state,
    In circle round the blessed gate,
Received and gave him welcome there;

And led him thro' the blissful climes,   25
    And show'd him in the fountain fresh
    All knowledge that the sons of flesh
Shall gather in the cycled times.[4]

But I remain'd, whose hopes were dim,
    Whose life, whose thoughts were little worth,   30
    To wander on a darken'd earth,
Where all things round me breathed of him.

O friendship, equal-poised control,
    O heart, with kindliest motion warm,
    O sacred essence, other form,   35
O solemn ghost, O crowned soul!

Yet none could better know than I,
    How much of act at human hands
    The sense of human will demands[5]
By which we dare to live or die.   40

Whatever way my days decline,
    I felt and feel, tho' left alone,
    His being working in mine own,
The footsteps of his life in mine;

A life that all the Muses deck'd   45
    With gifts of grace, that might express

3. Angels.
4. I.e., the time yet to come.
5. "Yet I know that the knowledge that
we have free will demands from us ac-
tion"—Tennyson.

All-comprehensive tenderness,
All-subtilising intellect:

And so my passion hath not swerved
    To works of weakness, but I find   50
    An image comforting the mind,
And in my grief a strength reserved.

Likewise the imaginative woe,
    That loved to handle spiritual strife,
    Diffused the shock thro' all my life,   55
But in the present broke the blow.

My pulses therefore beat again
    For other friends that once I met;
    Nor can it suit me to forget
The mighty hopes that make us men.   60

I woo your love: I count it crime
    To mourn for any overmuch;
    I, the divided half of such
A friendship as had master'd Time;

Which masters Time indeed, and is   65
    Eternal, separate from fears:
    The all-assuming[6] months and years
Can take no part away from this:

But Summer on the steaming floods,
    And Spring that swells the narrow brooks,   70
    And Autumn, with a noise of rooks,
That gather in the waning woods,

And every pulse of wind and wave
    Recalls, in change of light or gloom,
    My old affection of the tomb,   75
And my prime passion in the grave:

My old affection of the tomb,
    A part of stillness, yearns to speak:
    'Arise, and get thee forth and seek
A friendship for the years to come.   80

'I watch thee from the quiet shore;
    Thy spirit up to mine can reach;
    But in dear words of human speech
We two communicate no more.'

6. All-destroying.

And I, 'Can clouds of nature⁷ stain 85
 The starry clearness of the free?
 How is it? Canst thou feel for me
Some painless sympathy with pain?'

And lightly does the whisper fall;
 ' 'Tis hard for thee to fathom this; 90
 I triumph in conclusive bliss,
And that serene result of all.'⁸

So hold I commerce with the dead;
 Or so methinks the dead would say;
 Or so shall grief with symbols play 95
And pining life be fancy-fed.

Now looking to some settled end,
 That these things pass, and I shall prove
 A meeting somewhere, love with love,
I crave your pardon, O my friend; 100

If not so fresh, with love as true,
 I, clasping brother-hands, aver
 I could not, if I would, transfer
The whole I felt for him to you.

For which be they that hold apart 105
 The promise of the golden hours?
 First love, first friendship, equal powers,
That marry with the virgin heart.

Still mine, that cannot but deplore,
 That beats within a lonely place, 110
 That yet remembers his embrace,
But at his footstep leaps no more,

My heart, tho' widow'd, may not rest
 Quite in the love of what is gone,
 But seeks to beat in time with one 115
That warms another living breast.

Ah, take the imperfect gift I bring,
 Knowing the primrose yet is dear,
 The primrose of the later year,
As not unlike to that of Spring. 120

7. Human nature.
8. Lines 89–92: "Think of me as having reached the final goal of bliss, and as triumphing in the 'one far-off divine event/To which the whole creation moves' "—Hallam Tennyson. Cf. the Epilogue, final stanza.

86[1]

Sweet after showers, ambrosial air,
  That rollest from the gorgeous gloom[2]
  Of evening over brake and bloom
And meadow, slowly breathing bare

The round of space, and rapt below   5
  Thro' all the dewy-tassell'd wood,
  And shadowing down the horned flood[3]
In ripples, fan my brows and blow

The fever from my cheek, and sigh
  The full new life that feeds thy breath   10
  Throughout my frame, till Doubt and Death,
Ill brethren, let the fancy fly

From belt to belt of crimson seas
  On leagues of odour streaming far,
  To where in yonder orient star[4]   15
A hundred spirits whisper 'Peace.'

1. This poem, one of the most notable nature lyrics of *In Memoriam*, was written at Barmouth in 1839. Cf. Sections 38, 83. Subsequently Tennyson told his son that it embodied "pre-eminently his sense of the joyous peace in Nature" (*Memoir*, I, 313).

2. A west wind, Tennyson noted; customarily the clearing wind after a rain.
3. The river wound between two craggy hills.
4. "Any rising star is here intended"— Tennyson.

87[1]

I past beside the reverend walls
  In which of old I wore the gown;
  I roved at random thro' the town,
And saw the tumult of the halls;

And heard once more in college fanes   5
  The storm their high-built organs make,
  And thunder-music, rolling, shake
The prophet blazon'd on the panes;

And caught once more the distant shout,
  The measured pulse of racing oars   10
  Among the willows; paced the shores
And many a bridge, and all about

The same gray flats again, and felt
  The same, but not the same; and last
  Up that long walk of limes I past[2]   15
To see the rooms in which he dwelt.

1. In this section the poet revisits in imagination Trinity College, Cambridge, where as undergraduates he and Hallam first met.
2. Trinity Avenue.

Another name was on the door:
  I linger'd; all within was noise
  Of songs, and clapping hands, and boys
That crash'd the glass and beat the floor;   20

Where once we held debate, a band
  Of youthful friends, on mind and art,
  And labour, and the changing mart,
And all the framework of the land;[3]

When one would aim an arrow fair,   25
  But send it slackly from the string;
  And one would pierce an outer ring,
And one an inner, here and there;

And last the master-bowman, he,
  Would cleave the mark. A willing ear   30
  We lent him. Who, but hung to hear
The rapt oration flowing free

From point to point, with power and grace
  And music in the bounds of law,
  To those conclusions when we saw   35
The God within him light his face,

And seem to lift the form, and glow
  In azure orbits heavenly-wise;
  And over those ethereal eyes
The bar of Michael Angelo.[4]   40

3. Lines 21–24: The "Apostles," or the Cambridge Conversazione Society, an undergraduate discussion group to which Hallam and Tennyson belonged.

4. Like Michelangelo, Hallam had "a broad bar of frontal bone over the eyes" —Tennyson.

88

Wild bird, whose warble, liquid sweet,[1]
  Rings Eden thro' the budded quicks,[2]
  O tell me where the senses mix,
O tell me where the passions meet,

Whence radiate: fierce extremes employ   5
  Thy spirits in the darkening leaf,
  And in the midmost heart of grief
Thy passion clasps a secret joy:

And I—my harp would prelude woe—
  I cannot all command the strings;   10
  The glory of the sum of things
Will flash along the chords and go.

1. The nightingale.   2. Hedgerows of hawthorn.

89

Witch-elms that counterchange the floor
    Of this flat lawn with dusk and bright;[1]
    And thou, with all thy breadth and height
Of foliage, towering sycamore;

How often, hither wandering down,   5
    My Arthur found your shadows fair,
    And shook to all the liberal air
The dust and din and steam of town:

He brought an eye for all he saw;
    He mixt in all our simple sports;   10
    They pleased him, fresh from brawling courts
And dusty purlieus of the law.[2]

O joy to him in this retreat,
    Immantled in ambrosial dark,
    To drink the cooler air, and mark   15
The landscape winking thro' the heat:

O sound to rout the brood of cares,
    The sweep of scythe in morning dew,
    The gust that round the garden flew,
And tumbled half the mellowing pears!   20

O bliss, when all in circle drawn
    About him, heart and ear were fed
    To hear him, as he lay and read
The Tuscan poets[3] on the lawn:

Or in the all-golden afternoon   25
    A guest, or happy sister, sung,
    Or here she brought the harp and flung
A ballad to the brightening moon:

Nor less it pleased in livelier moods,
    Beyond the bounding hill to stray,   30
    And break the livelong summer day
With banquet in the distant woods;

Whereat we glanced from theme to theme,
    Discuss'd the books to love or hate,
    Or touch'd the changes of the state,   35
Or threaded some Socratic dream;[4]

1. Lines 1–2: The poet is describing the lawn at Somersby checkered by sun and the shadows of elms.
2. Lines 11–12: After Cambridge Hallam had read law in the Inner Temple.
3. Dante and Petrarch, Hallam's favorites among the Italian poets.
4. One of the Platonic dialogues in which Socrates is the chief speaker.

But if I praised the busy town,
    He loved to rail against it still,
    For 'ground in yonder social mill
We rub each other's angles down,   40

'And merge' he said 'in form and gloss
    The picturesque of man and man.'
    We talk'd: the stream beneath us ran,
The wine-flask lying couch'd in moss,

Or cool'd within the glooming wave;   45
    And last, returning from afar,
    Before the crimson-circled star
Had fall'n into her father's grave,[5]

And brushing ankle-deep in flowers,
    We heard behind the woodbine veil   50
    The milk that bubbled in the pail,
And buzzings of the honied hours.

5. Lines 47–48: "Before Venus, the evening star, had dipped into the sunset. The planets, according to Laplace [*Mécanique Celeste*, 1799–1825], were evolved from the sun"—Tennyson. Thus the poet alludes again to the nebular hypothesis. Cf. Section 3, line 8.

90

He tasted love with half his mind,
    Nor ever drank the inviolate spring
    Where nighest heaven, who first could fling
This bitter seed among mankind;

That could the dead, whose dying eyes   5
    Were closed with wail, resume their life,
    They would but find in child and wife
An iron welcome when they rise:

'Twas well, indeed, when warm with wine,
    To pledge them with a kindly tear,
    To talk them o'er, to wish them here,   10
To count their memories half divine;

But if they came who past away,
    Behold their brides in other hands;
    The hard heir strides about their lands,   15
And will not yield them for a day.

Yea, tho' their sons were none of these,
    Not less the yet-loved sire would make
    Confusion worse than death, and shake
The pillars of domestic peace.   20

Ah dear, but come thou back to me:
  Whatever change the years have wrought,
  I find not yet one lonely thought
That cries against my wish for thee.

91

When rosy plumelets tuft the larch,
  And rarely pipes the mounted thrush;
  Or underneath the barren bush
Flits by the sea-blue bird of March;[1]

Come, wear the form by which I know   5
  Thy spirit in time among thy peers;[2]
  The hope of unaccomplish'd years
Be large and lucid round thy brow.

When summer's hourly-mellowing change
  May breathe, with many roses sweet,   10
  Upon the thousand waves of wheat,
That ripple round the lonely grange;

Come: not in watches of the night,
  But where the sunbeam broodeth warm,
  Come, beauteous in thine after form,   15
And like a finer light in light.

1. The kingfisher.   2. The poet addresses Hallam.

92[1]

If any vision should reveal
  Thy likeness, I might count it vain
  As but the canker of the brain;
Yea, tho' it spake and made appeal

To chances where our lots were cast   5
  Together in the days behind,
  I might but say, I hear a wind
Of memory murmuring the past.

Yea, tho' it spake and bared to view
  A fact within the coming year;   10
  And tho' the months, revolving near,
Should prove the phantom-warning true,

1. Some authorities suggest that in this section Tennyson deals with the belief that communication between the living and the souls of the dead can be established by spiritualism. The poet rejects the notion, they point out, as but "the canker of the brain" (line 3). Other commentators disagree. Spiritualism, in the table-rapping sense, is nowhere suggested, they argue; the poet fears only that the vision of Hallam which he has asked for above (Section 91) may be self-induced, a psychic trick caused by his own memory "murmuring the past" (line 8). The belief in spiritualism, with its crude trappings of mediums, trances, and table-rapping, was not uncommon in Victorian England. Cf. Browning's emphatic rejection of the concept in *Mr. Sludge, The Medium.*

They might not seem thy prophecies,
    But spiritual presentiments,
    And such refraction of events   15
As often rises ere they rise.[2]

93
I shall not see thee. Dare I say
    No spirit ever brake the band
    That stays him from the native land
Where first he walk'd when claspt in clay?

No visual shade of some one lost,   5
    But he, the Spirit himself, may come
    Where all the nerve of sense is numb;
Spirit to Spirit, Ghost to Ghost.[1]

O, therefore from thy sightless range
    With gods in unconjectured bliss   10
    O, from the distance of the abyss
Of tenfold-complicated change,

Descend, and touch, and enter; hear
    The wish too strong for words to name;
    That in this blindness of the frame[2]   15
My Ghost may feel that thine is near.

2. "The heavenly bodies are seen above the horizon, by refraction, before they actually rise"—Tennyson.
1. Lines 1–8: No spirit can be apprehended by the senses (Section 92); spirit can be perceived only spiritually. "This spiritual state is described in [94]"—Hallam Tennyson.
2. The human body.

94
How pure at heart and sound in head,
    With what divine affections bold
    Should be the man whose thought would hold
An hour's communion with the dead.

In vain shalt thou, or any, call   5
    The spirits from their golden day,
    Except, like them, thou too canst say,
My spirit is at peace with all.

They haunt the silence of the breast,
    Imaginations calm and fair,   10
    The memory like a cloudless air,
The conscience as a sea at rest:

But when the heart is full of din,
    And doubt beside the portal waits,
    They can but listen at the gates,   15
And hear the household jar within.

95[1]

By night we linger'd on the lawn,
    For underfoot the herb was dry;
    And genial warmth; and o'er the sky
The silvery haze of summer drawn;

And calm that let the tapers burn   5
    Unwavering: not a cricket chirr'd:
    The brook alone far-off was heard,[2]
And on the board the fluttering urn:[3]

And bats went round in fragrant skies,
    And wheel'd or lit the filmy shapes   10
    That haunt the dusk, with ermine capes
And woolly breasts and beaded eyes;[4]

While now we sang old songs that peal'd
    From knoll to knoll, where, couch'd at ease,
    The white kine glimmer'd, and the trees   15
Laid their dark arms about the field.

But when those others, one by one,
    Withdrew themselves from me and night,
    And in the house light after light
Went out, and I was all alone,   20

A hunger seized my heart; I read
    Of that glad year which once had been,[5]
    In those fall'n leaves which kept their green,
The noble letters of the dead:

And strangely on the silence broke   25
    The silent-speaking words, and strange
    Was love's dumb cry defying change
To test his worth; and strangely spoke

The faith, the vigour, bold to dwell
    On doubts that drive the coward back,   30
    And keen thro' wordy snares to track
Suggestion to her inmost cell.

1. This section, in which the speaker's soul achieves the mystic communion with the soul of Hallam which had been anticipated in Sections 90–94, is one of the notable climaxes—most commentators say *the* climax—of the poem. Almost all the themes, symbols, and images of *In Memoriam* are focused in this section, and in embodying his mystical trance in verse Tennyson climbs to a poetic height only seldom reached.
2. "It was a marvelously still night, and I asked my brother Charles to listen to the brook, which we had never heard so far off before"—Tennyson.
3. A tea-urn.
4. Night-moths, sometimes called ermine moths.
5. The whole time of their friendship.

So word by word, and line by line,
    The dead man touch'd me from the past,
    And all at once it seem'd at last   35
The living soul was flash'd on mine,

And mine in this was wound, and whirl'd
    About empyreal heights of thought,
    And came on that which is,[6] and caught
The deep pulsations of the world,   40

Aeonian music[7] measuring out
    The steps of Time—the shocks of Chance—
    The blows of Death. At length my trance
Was cancell'd, stricken thro' with doubt.[8]

Vague words! but ah, how hard to frame   45
    In matter-moulded forms of speech,[9]
    Or ev'n for intellect to reach
Thro' memory that which I became:

Till now the doubtful dusk reveal'd
    The knolls once more where, couch'd at ease,   50
    The white kine glimmer'd, and the trees
Laid their dark arms about the field:

And suck'd from out the distant gloom
    A breeze began to tremble o'er
    The large leaves of the sycamore,   55
And fluctuate all the still perfume,

And gathering freshlier overhead,
    Rock'd the full-foliaged elms, and swung
    The heavy-folded rose, and flung
The lilies to and fro, and said   60

6. "The Absolute Reality"—Hallam Tennyson. In the late 1870s Tennyson altered lines 36–39. From the first edition of *In Memoriam* (1850), and throughout numerous subsequent printings, they had read:

His living soul was flash'd on mine

And Mine in *his* was wound, and whirl'd
    About empyreal heights of thought,
    And came on that which is, . . .
    [*Italics added*]

The reasons for the revision are unclear: "The first reading, 'his living soul,' troubled me, as perhaps giving the wrong impression," Tennyson wrote enigmatically in the notes to the Eversley Edition. The effect of the alteration, however, is somewhat to depersonalize the experience and to make it more abstract. "With ref-erence to the later reading, my father would say: 'Of course the greater Soul may include the less.' He preferred, however, for fear of giving a wrong impression, the vague and more abstract later reading; and his further comment was: 'I have often had the feeling of being whirled up and rapt into the Great Soul'"
—Hallam Tennyson.

7. The "music" of the everlasting eons.

8. Lines 41–44: "The trance came to an end in a moment of critical doubt, but the doubt was dispelled by the glory of the dawn of the 'boundless day,' line 64"—Tennyson.

9. Lines 45–46: Ordinary language, because it is designed to express material experience, is incapable of carrying the burden of the meaning of this mystic, immaterial experience.

'The dawn, the dawn,' and died away;
    And East and West, without a breath,
    Mixt their dim lights, like life and death,
To broaden into boundless day.

96

You[1] say, but with no touch of scorn,
    Sweet-hearted, you, whose light-blue eyes
    Are tender over drowning flies,
You tell me, doubt is Devil-born.

I know not: one indeed I knew[2]   5
    In many a subtle question versed,
    Who touch'd a jarring lyre at first,
But ever strove to make it true:

Perplext in faith, but pure in deeds,
    At last he beat his music out.   10
    There lives more faith in honest doubt,
Believe me, than in half the creeds.

He fought his doubts and gather'd strength,
    He would not make his judgment blind,
    He faced the spectres of the mind   15
And laid them: thus he came at length

To find a stronger faith his own;
    And Power was with him in the night,
    Which makes the darkness and the light,
And dwells not in the light alone,   20

But in the darkness and the cloud,
    As over Sinaï's peaks of old,
    While Israel made their gods of gold,
Altho' the trumpet blew so loud.[3]

1. A woman of simple faith, perhaps Emily Sellwood, Tennyson's future wife. Cf. the woman described in Section 33.
2. Identified by Tennyson as Hallam, though the description in the following lines also fits the poet as well.
3. Lines 21–24: The image and Biblical allusion make specific the generalized maxim expressed in lines 11–12. When God appeared to Moses on Mount Sinai the Israelites below could neither see nor hear Him because He was hidden in "thunders and lightnings, and a thick cloud upon the mount, and the voice of a trumpet exceeding loud" (Exodus xix.16–25). "The stronger faith of Moses —found in the darkness of the cloud through commune with the Power therein dwelling—is of a higher order than the creeds of those who walk by sight rather than by insight"—Hallam Tennyson.

97

My love has talk'd with rocks and trees;[1]
   He finds on misty mountain-ground
   His own vast shadow glory-crown'd;
My love sees himself in all he sees.

Two partners of a married life—
   I look'd on these and thought of thee[2]
   In vastness and in mystery,
And of my spirit as of a wife.

These two—they dwelt with eye on eye,
   Their hearts of old have beat in tune,
   Their meetings made December June
Their every parting was to die.

Their love has never past away;
   The days she never can forget
   Are earnest[3] that he loves her yet,
Whate'er the faithless people say.

Her life is lone, he sits apart,
   He loves her yet, she will not weep,
   Tho' rapt in matters dark and deep
He seems to slight her simple heart.

He thrids the labyrinth of the mind,
   He reads the secret of the star,
   He seems so near and yet so far,
He looks so cold: she thinks him kind.

She keeps the gift of years before,
   A wither'd violet is her bliss:
   She knows not what his greatness is,
For that, for all, she loves him more.

For him she plays, to him she sings,
   Of early faith and plighted vows;
   She knows but matters of the house,
And he, he knows a thousand things.

Her faith is fixt and cannot move,
   She darkly feels him great and wise,
   She dwells on him with faithful eyes,
'I cannot understand: I love.'

1. The poet personifies his love.   3. Proof.
2. I.e., Hallam.

98[1]

You leave us: you will see the Rhine,
  And those fair hills I sail'd below,
  When I was there with him; and go
By summer belts of wheat and vine

To where he breathed his latest breath,   5
  That City. All her splendour seems
  No livelier than the wisp that gleams
On Lethe in the eyes of Death.

Let her great Danube rolling fair
  Enwind her isles, unmark'd of me: 10
  I have not seen, I will not see
Vienna; rather dream that there,

A treble darkness, Evil haunts
  The birth, the bridal; friend from friend
  Is oftener parted, fathers bend   15
Above more graves, a thousand wants

Gnarr[2] at the heels of men, and prey
  By each cold hearth, and sadness flings
  Her shadow on the blaze of kings:
And yet myself have heard him say,   20

That not in any mother town
  With statelier progress to and fro
  The double tides of chariots flow
By park and suburb under brown

Of lustier leaves; nor more content,   25
  He told me, lives in any crowd,
  When all is gay with lamps, and loud
With sport and song, in booth and tent,

1. In this poem Tennyson addresses his brother Charles, who journeyed up the Rhine on his wedding trip in 1836. Tennyson and Hallam had toured the Rhine Valley in 1832, and Hallam had died in Vienna in 1833. Here, as elsewhere, Tennyson's poetic purposes required him to take some liberties with chronology of both year and season. Since Charles's wedding trip took place in May 1836, fidelity to literal chronology would have required that Section 99 precede, not follow, this section. For 99 records the second anniversary of Hallam's death, or September 15, *1835*, almost a year earlier than the wedding trip. Moreover, although the wedding took place in May and the journey up the Rhine immedi-

ately thereafter, some of the details of Section 98 suggest that the time was mid- to late summer ("summer belts of wheat and vine," line 4). By making this section a summer poem, however, Tennyson preserves the integrity of the seasonal cycle upon which much of the structure of *In Memoriam* depends. The movement now is forward, from the summer of this section, through the autumn of 99, to the Third Christmas of 104–5, and to the paean to the new year in 106 with its affirmation and suggestion of fresh starts and new beginnings. The way of the soul is not necessarily the way of literal chronology.
2. "Snarl"—Tennyson.

Imperial halls, or open plain;
    And wheels the circled dance, and breaks   30
    The rocket molten into flakes
Of crimson or in emerald rain.

99

Risest thou thus, dim dawn, again,[1]
    So loud with voices of the birds,
    So thick with lowings of the herds,
Day, when I lost the flower of men;

Who tremblest thro' thy darkling red   5
    On yon swoll'n brook that bubbles fast
    By meadows breathing of the past,
And woodlands holy to the dead;

Who murmurest in the foliaged eaves
    A song that slights the coming care,[2]   10
    And Autumn laying here and there
A fiery finger on the leaves;

Who wakenest with thy balmy breath
    To myriads on the genial earth,
    Memories of bridal, or of birth,   15
And unto myriads more, of death.

O wheresoever those may be,
    Betwixt the slumber of the poles,[3]
    To-day they count as kindred souls;
They know me not, but mourn with me.   20

1. September 15, 1835, the second anniversary of Hallam's death. Cf. Section 72, line 1ff. See also note 1, Section 98.
2. The coming of winter.
3. "The ends of the axis of the earth, which move so slowly that they seem not to move, but slumber"—Tennyson.

100[1]

I climb the hill: from end to end
    Of all the landscape underneath,
    I find no place that does not breathe
Some gracious memory of my friend;

No gray old grange, or lonely fold,   5
    Or low morass and whispering reed,

1. Sections 100–3 record the feelings engendered in the poet by the move of the Tennyson family from the familiar surroundings of Somersby, Lincolnshire, to High Beech, Epping Forest, not far north of London. The move occurred in 1837, two years after the second anniversary of Hallam's death, the subject of Section 99 immediately preceding. But, again, Tennyson's poetic purpose is served by a disregard of literal chronology. "A Farewell to Old Scenes," as one commentator calls them, Sections 100–3 serve not only as a closing to Part III of the poem but also as a poetically appropriate transition to the new affirmative tone of Part IV. See note 1, Section 98.

Or simple stile from mead to mead,
Or sheepwalk up the windy wold;

Nor hoary knoll of ash and haw
    That hears the latest linnet trill,   10
    Nor quarry trench'd along the hill
And haunted by the wrangling daw;

Nor runlet tinkling from the rock;
    Nor pastoral rivulet that swerves
    To left and right thro' meadowy curves,   15
That feed the mothers of the flock;

But each has pleased a kindred eye,
    And each reflects a kindlier day;
    And, leaving these, to pass away,
I think once more he seems to die.   20

101

Unwatch'd, the garden bough shall sway,
    The tender blossom flutter down,
    Unloved, that beech will gather brown,
This maple burn itself away;

Unloved, the sun-flower, shining fair,   5
    Ray round with flames her disk of seed,
    And many a rose carnation feed
With summer spice the humming air;

Unloved, by many a sandy bar,
    The brook shall babble down the plain,   10
    At noon or when the lesser wain[1]
Is twisting round the polar star;

Uncared for, gird the windy grove,
    And flood the haunts of hern and crake;[2]
    Or into silver arrows break   15
The sailing moon in creek and cove;

Till from the garden and the wild
    A fresh association blow,
    And year by year the landscape grow
Familiar to the stranger's child;   20

As year by year the labourer tills
    His wonted glebe,[3] or lops the glades;

1. The constellation of Ursa Minor, or the Little Dipper, which revolves around the North Star.
2. "Hern": heron. "Crake": corncake, a common European marsh bird.
3. Strictly, land attached to a parsonage; but here perhaps generally, a field.

And year by year our memory fades
From all the circle of the hills.

102

We leave the well-beloved place
    Where first we gazed upon the sky;
    The roofs, that heard our earliest cry,
Will shelter one of stranger race.

We go, but ere we go from home,   5
    As down the garden-walks I move,
    Two spirits of a diverse love[1]
Contend for loving masterdom.

One whispers, 'Here thy boyhood sung
    Long since its matin song,[2] and heard   10
    The low love-language of the bird
In native hazels tassel-hung.'

The other answers, 'Yea but here
    Thy feet have stray'd in after hours
    With thy lost friend among the bowers,   15
And this hath made them trebly dear.'

These two have striven half the day,
    And each prefers his separate claim,
    Poor rivals in a losing game,
That will not yield each other way.   20

I turn to go: my feet are set
    To leave the pleasant fields and farms;
    They mix in one another's arms
To one pure image of regret.

1. "First, the love of native place; second, this enhanced by the memory of A. H. H."—Tennyson.
2. Tennyson's early poetry.

103[1]

On that last night before we went
    From out the doors where I was bred,
    I dream'd a vision of the dead,
Which left my after-morn content.

1. This section is an allegory, although it is also set in the framework of a literal event, namely, the Tennyson family's departure from Somersby. Emblematically, life is conceived as a voyage down a river to the sea, which represents eternity. Both structurally and esthetically this is one of the most significant sections of the poem. Being the final section of Part III, it is situated at a crucial position; it contains—in a sense, sums up—almost all the themes and symbols introduced in *In Memoriam*; it records the poet's release from most of the spiritually debilitating influences of his grief (the dream leaves him "content"—line 4); and in it Tennyson comes to an important conclusion regarding his role as nineteenth-century poet in general and elegist of Arthur Henry Hallam in particular. Tennyson himself took some pains to explain some of the more obscure symbols in this section (see following notes).

Methought I dwelt within a hall,
    And maidens with me:[2] distant hills
    From hidden summits fed with rills
A river sliding by the wall.[3]

The hall with harp and carol rang.
    They sang of what is wise and good   10
    And graceful. In the centre stood
A statue veil'd,[4] to which they sang;

And which, tho' veil'd, was known to me,
    The shape of him I loved, and love
    For ever: then flew in a dove   15
And brought a summons from the sea:[5]

And when they learnt that I must go
    They wept and wail'd, but led the way
    To where a little shallop lay
At anchor in the flood below;   20

And on by many a level mead,
    And shadowing bluff that made the banks,
    We glided winding under ranks
Of iris, and the golden reed;

And still as vaster grew the shore   25
    And roll'd the floods in grander space,
    The maidens gather'd strength and grace
And presence, lordlier than before;[6]

And I myself, who sat apart
    And watch'd them, wax'd in every limb;   30
    I felt the thews of Anakim,[7]
The pulses of a Titan's[8] heart;

As one would sing the death of war,
    And one would chant the history
    Of that great race, which is to be.   35
    And one the shaping of a star;[9]

2. "They are the Muses, poetry, arts—all that made life beautiful here, which we hope will pass with us beyond the grave"—Tennyson. The maidens also stand for Tennyson's aspirations for his own poetry.
3. Lines 6–8: "*Hidden summits*: the divine. *River*: life"—Tennyson. Cf. the garden and water imagery in *The Poet's Mind* (1830).
4. Hallam, who personified the three virtues extolled by the maidens above (lines 10–11).
5. "Eternity"—Tennyson. Cf. *Crossing the Bar*.
6. Lines 25–28ff: Tennyson describes the passage down the ever-broadening river as "the great progress of the age, as well as the opening of another world."
7. Biblical giants, sons of Anak. Cf. Numbers xiii.33; Deuteronomy ix.2.
8. The Titans were primeval giants of Greek mythology.
9. Lines 33–36: "The great hopes of humanity and science"—Tennyson. On "the great race that is to be" see the Epilogue, lines 128–44.

Until the forward-creeping tides
    Began to foam, and we to draw
    From deep to deep,¹ to where we saw
A great ship lift her shining sides.   40

The man we loved was there on deck,
    But thrice as large as man he bent
    To greet us. Up the side I went,
And fell in silence on his neck:

Whereat those maidens with one mind   45
    Bewail'd their lot; I did them wrong:
    'We served thee here,' they said, 'so long,
And wilt thou leave us now behind?'

So rapt I was, they could not win
    An answer from my lips, but he   50
    Replying, 'Enter likewise ye
And go with us:' they enter'd in.²

And while the wind began to sweep
    A music out of sheet and shroud,
    We steer'd her toward a crimson cloud   55
That landlike slept along the deep.

1. I.e., from the river to the sea, from this life to eternal life. Cf. *Crossing the Bar.*
2. Lines 41–52: In the dream Hallam bids the maidens board the ship and pass with the poet to the other world. Thus, as Tennyson wrote of this passage, poetry, the arts, "everything that made life beautiful here, we may hope may pass on with us beyond the grave." Thus, too, the passage suggests, the poet's elegy has found favor with the spirit of his dead friend, Hallam.

104

The time draws near the birth of Christ;¹
    The moon is hid, the night is still;
    A single church below the hill²
Is pealing, folded in the mist.

A single peal of bells below,   5
    That wakens at this hour of rest
    A single murmur in the breast,
That these are not the bells I know.

Like strangers' voices here they sound,
    In lands where not a memory strays,   10
    Nor landmark breathes of other days,
But all is new unhallow'd ground.³

1. The third Christmas after Hallam's death and thus, according to the fictive time established within *In Memoriam*, 1835. In literal, biographical time, however, the Christmas being described is that of 1837, for the setting of this lyric is High Beech. See note 1, Section 98.
This section begins Part IV of *In Memoriam.* Cf. Sections 28, 30, 78.
2. Waltham Abbey Church, according to Tennyson.
3. "High Beech, Epping Forest"—Tennyson.

105

To-night ungather'd let us leave
This laurel, let this holly stand:
We live within the stranger's land
And strangely falls our Christmas-eve.[1]

Our father's dust is left alone   5
And silent under other snows:
There in due time the woodbine blows,
The violet comes, but we are gone.

No more shall wayward grief abuse[2]
The genial hour with mask and mime;   10
For change of place, like growth of time,
Has broke the bond of dying use.

Let cares that petty shadows cast,
By which our lives are chiefly proved,
A little spare the night I loved,   15
And hold it solemn to the past.

But let no footstep beat the floor,
Nor bowl of wassail mantle warm;
For who would keep an ancient form
Thro' which the spirit breathes no more?   20

Be neither song, nor game, nor feast;
Nor harp be touch'd, nor flute be blown;
No dance, no motion, save alone
What lightens in the lucid east

Of rising worlds by yonder wood.[3]   25
Long sleeps the summer in the seed;
Run out your measured arcs, and lead
The closing cycle rich in good.[4]

1. I.e., their new surroundings still seem
foreign, unfamiliar. Cf. "sadly," Section
30, line 4; "calmly," Section 78, line 4.
2. "In the old sense—wrong"—Tenny-
son.

3. Lines 23–25: "The scintillating motion
of the stars that rise"—Tennyson.
4. Lines 27–28: Cf. the Epilogue, lines
132–44.

106

Ring out, wild bells, to the wild sky,
The flying cloud, the frosty light:
The year is dying in the night;
Ring out, wild bells, and let him die.

Ring out the old, ring in the new,   5
Ring, happy bells, across the snow:
The year is going, let him go;
Ring out the false, ring in the true.

Ring out the grief that saps the mind,
  For those that here we see no more;
  Ring out the feud of rich and poor,
Ring in redress to all mankind.

Ring out a slowly dying cause,
  And ancient forms of party strife;
  Ring in the nobler modes of life,
With sweeter manners, purer laws.

Ring out the want, the care, the sin,
  The faithless coldness of the times;
  Ring out, ring out my mournful rhymes,
But ring the fuller minstrel in.[1]

Ring out false pride in place and blood,
  The civic slander and the spite;
  Ring in the love of truth and right,
Ring in the common love of good.

Ring out old shapes of foul disease;
  Ring out the narrowing lust of gold;
  Ring out the thousand wars of old,
Ring in the thousand years of peace.[2]

Ring in the valiant man and free,
  The larger heart, the kindlier hand;
  Ring out the darkness of the land,
Ring in the Christ that is to be.[3]

1. A restatement of the poet's resolve to direct his art to nobler ends than merely purveying grief. Cf. the first note 1, Section 103; Prologue, lines 41–44.
2. Cf. Revelations xx.
3. A time in the future, Tennyson wrote, "when Christianity without bigotry will triumph [and] the controversies of creeds should have vanished" (*Memoir*, I, 326).

107

It is the day when he was born,[1]
  A bitter day that early sank
  Behind a purple-frosty bank
Of vapour, leaving night forlorn.

The time admits not flowers or leaves
  To deck the banquet. Fiercely flies
  The blast of North and East, and ice
Makes daggers at the sharpen'd eaves,

And bristles all the brakes and thorns
  To yon hard crescent, as she hangs
  Above the wood which grides[2] and clangs
Its leafless ribs and iron horns[3]

1. February 1, 1838, which would have been Hallam's twenty-seventh birthday.
2. Grates.
3. Ice-encrusted branches.

Together, in the drifts that pass[4]
To darken on the rolling brine
That breaks the coast. But fetch the wine,   15
Arrange the board and brim the glass;

Bring in great logs and let them lie,
To make a solid core of heat;
Be cheerful-minded, talk and treat
Of all things ev'n as he were by;   20

We keep the day. With festal cheer,
With books and music, surely we
Will drink to him, whate'er he be,
And sing the songs he loved to hear.

4. Fine snow squalls which fall into the sea. Perhaps, also, drifts of dark clouds.

108

I will not shut me from my kind,
And, lest I stiffen into stone,
I will not eat my heart alone,
Nor feed with sighs a passing wind:

What profit lies in barren faith,   5
And vacant yearning, tho' with might
To scale the heaven's highest height,
Or dive below the wells of Death?

What find I in the highest place,
But mine own phantom chanting hymns?   10
And on the depths of death there swims
The reflex of a human face.

I'll rather take what fruit may be
Of sorrow under human skies:
'Tis held that sorrow makes us wise,   15
Whatever wisdom sleep with thee.[1]

1. Lines 15–16: As Tennyson originally wrote it, line 16 reads, "Yet how much wisdom sleeps with thee." Upon reading the manuscript of *In Memoriam*, Tennyson's friend James Spedding advised the poet, "You might give the thought a turn of this kind: 'The wisdom that died with you is lost forever, but out of the loss itself some other wisdom may be gained.'"—Hallam Tennyson. Tenny-son apparently agreed with Spedding's suggestion and changed his original line to the form which appears here, the major effect of which is to put more emphasis on the thought embodied in line 15. But never one to abandon an idea once conceived, Tennyson used precisely his original line in a subsequent section of the poem. See Section 113, lines 1–2.

109
Heart-affluence in discursive talk
From household fountains never dry;[1]

1. Lines 1–2: I.e., the fountains of Hallam's talk never dried because they sprang from his inexhaustible genius within.

The critic clearness of an eye,
That saw thro' all the Muses' walk;[2]

Seraphic intellect and force   5
    To seize and throw the doubts of man;
    Impassion'd logic, which outran
The hearer in its fiery course;

High nature amorous of the good,
    But touch'd with no ascetic gloom;   10
    And passion pure in snowy bloom
Thro' all the years of April blood;

A love of freedom rarely felt,
    Of freedom in her regal seat
    Of England; not the schoolboy heat,   15
The blind hysterics of the Celt;

And manhood fused with female grace
    In such a sort, the child would twine
    A trustful hand, unask'd, in thine,
And find his comfort in thy face;   20

All these have been, and thee mine eyes
    Have look'd on: if they look'd in vain,
    My shame is greater who remain,
Nor let thy wisdom make me wise.[3]

2. I.e., philosophy and literature.   16, and of the last line of the Prologue.
3. Cf. the echo of Section 108, lines 15–

110

Thy converse drew us with delight,
    The men of rathe and riper years:[1]
    The feeble soul, a haunt of fears
Forgot his weakness in thy sight.

On thee the loyal-hearted hung,   5
    The proud was half disarm'd of pride,
    Nor cared the serpent[2] at thy side
To flicker with his double tongue.

The stern were mild when thou wert by,
    The flippant put himself to school   10
    And heard thee, and the brazen fool
Was soften'd, and he knew not why;

While I, thy nearest, sat apart,
    And felt thy triumph was as mine;

1. "Rathe": from Old English *hreath*,   2. The liar or dissimulator.
"early." Thus, both young and old men.

And loved them more, that they were thine, 15
The graceful tact, the Christian art;

Nor mine the sweetness or the skill,
But mine the love that will not tire,
And, born of love, the vague desire
That spurs an imitative will. 20

111

The churl in spirit, up or down
Along the scale of ranks, thro' all,
To him who grasps a golden ball,[1]
By blood a king, at heart a clown;

The churl in spirit, howe'er he veil 5
His want in forms for fashion's sake,
Will let his coltish nature break
At seasons thro' the gilded pale:

For who can always act? but he,
To whom a thousand memories call, 10
Not being less but more than all
The gentleness he seem'd to be,

Best seem'd the thing he was, and join'd
Each office of the social hour
To noble manners, as the flower 15
And native growth of noble mind;

Nor ever narrowness or spite,
Or villain[2] fancy fleeting by,
Drew in[3] the expression of an eye,
Where God and Nature met in light; 20

And thus he bore without abuse
The grand old name of gentleman,
Defamed by every charlatan,
And soil'd with all ignoble use.

1. The golden orb held by a king and symbolic of rule.
2. Churlish, ignoble.
3. Contracted.

112

High wisdom holds my wisdom less,
That I, who gaze with temperate eyes
On glorious insufficiencies,
Set light by narrower perfectness.[1]

1. Lines 1–4: "*High wisdom* is ironical. 'High wisdom' [e.g., some hypothetical worldly-wise friend] has been twitting the poet that although he gazes with calm and indulgent eyes on unaccomplished greatness, yet he makes light of narrower natures more perfect in their own small way"—Hallam Tennyson. *Glorious insufficiencies*: "unaccomplished greatness such as Arthur Hallam's"—Tennyson. *Set Light by*: underestimate. The poet's answer to "high wisdom" is contained in stanzas 2–4.

But thou, that fillest all the room 5
    Of all my love, art reason why
    I seem to cast a careless eye
On souls, the lesser lords of doom.²

For what wert thou?³ some novel power
    Sprang up for ever at a touch, 10
    And hope could never hope too much,
In watching thee from hour to hour,

Large elements in order brought,
    And tracts of calm from tempest made,
    And world-wide fluctuation sway'd 15
In vassal tides that follow'd thought.

2. "Those that have free will, but less intellect"—Tennyson.
3. I.e., Hallam, who, the poet claims in the following lines of this section and Section 113, had an intellect of such great potential as to be inestimable.

113

'Tis held that sorrow makes us wise;
    Yet how much wisdom sleeps with thee¹
    Which not alone had guided me,
But served the seasons that may rise;

For can I doubt, who knew thee keen 5
    In intellect, with force and skill
    To strive, to fashion, to fulfil—
I doubt not what thou wouldst have been:

A life in civic action warm,
    A soul on highest mission sent, 10
    A potent voice of Parliament,
A pillar steadfast in the storm,

Should licensed boldness gather force,
    Becoming, when the time has birth,
    A lever to uplift the earth 15
And roll it in another course,

With thousand shocks that come and go,
    With agonies, with energies,
    With overthrowings and with cries
And undulations to and fro. 20

1. Lines 1–2: Cf. the significant variation of Section 108, lines 15–16.

114¹

Who loves not Knowledge? Who shall rail
    Against her beauty? May she mix

1. In this section Tennyson develops an important theme which he had already touched on several times in *In Memoriam* and which he also developed in other poems: the distinction between knowledge and wisdom. See especially the Prologue, stanzas 5, 6, and 7, and Sections 36 and 37. See also *Locksley Hall*, lines 134–44, and *The Ancient Sage*, lines 37–46.

With men and prosper! Who shall fix
Her pillars?[2] Let her work prevail.

But on her forehead sits a fire: 5
She sets her forward countenance
And leaps into the future chance,
Submitting all things to desire.

Half-grown as yet, a child, and vain—
She cannot fight the fear of death.   10
What is she, cut from love and faith,
But some wild Pallas from the brain

Of Demons?[3] Fiery-hot to burst
All barriers in her onward race
For power. Let her know her place;   15
She is the second, not the first.

A higher hand must make her mild,
If all be not in vain; and guide
Her footsteps, moving side by side
With wisdom, like the younger child: 20

For she is earthly of the mind,
But Wisdom heavenly of the soul.
O, friend, who camest to thy goal
So early, leaving me behind,

I would the great world grew like thee,   25
Who grewest not alone in power
And knowledge, but by year and hour
In reverence and in charity.

2. The metaphor rests upon an allusion to the Pillars of Hercules, believed by the ancients to be the limits of the knowable world.
3. Lines 12–13ff: According to Greek myth, Pallas Athene sprang from the brain of Zeus, father of gods. By means of both metaphor and personification (Knowledge is consistently feminine, "she") throughout this section Tennyson elaborates the Pallas myth, but he does so only to make a crucial distinction. Whereas the Greek Pallas was the goddess of Wisdom, sprung from the brain of Zeus, our modern Athene is not the genuine goddess but rather "some *wild* Pallas," the goddess of Knowledge only, who has burst from "the brain of Demons" (lines 12–13). In Tennyson's view she is therefore "the second, not the first" (line 16); she must be guided, that is, by Wisdom, for our modern Pallas "is earthly of the mind," but Wisdom is "heavenly of the soul" (lines 21–22). Thus the poet again expresses all but directly one of his major fears for his age: with its unbounded humanistic faith in the primacy of knowledge, in its "onward race/For power" over matter (lines 14–15), and in its emphasis on man's rational faculties, it tends to minimize, if not exclude, the qualities of soul, heart, and intuition. Cf. the Prologue, lines 21–32.

115[1]

Now fades the last long streak of snow,
Now burgeons every maze of quick[2]

1. Another spring song, this section may be compared with Sections 38, 83, and 91.
2. Tangled, budding hedgerows.

About the flowering squares,[3] and thick
By ashen roots the violets blow.

Now rings the woodland loud and long,   5
    The distance takes a lovelier hue,
    And drown'd in yonder living blue
The lark becomes a sightless song.

Now dance the lights on lawn and lea,
    The flocks are whiter down the vale,   10
    And milkier every milky sail
On winding stream or distant sea;

Where now the seamew pipes, or dives
    In yonder greening gleam,[4] and fly
    The happy birds, that change their sky   15
To build and brood; that live their lives

From land to land; and in my breast
    Spring wakens too; and my regret
    Becomes an April violet,
And buds and blossoms like the rest.   20

3. Fields.   4. The sea.

116

Is it, then, regret for buried time
    That keenlier in sweet April wakes,
    And meets the year, and gives and takes
The colours of the crescent prime?[1]

Not all: the songs, the stirring air,   5
    The life re-orient out of dust,
    Cry thro' the sense to hearten trust
In that which made the world so fair.

Not all regret: the face will shine
    Upon me, while I muse alone;   10
    And that dear voice, I once have known,
Still speak to me of me and mine:

Yet less of sorrow lives in me
    For days of happy commune dead;
    Less yearning for the friendship fled,   15
Than some strong bond which is to be.

1. 'Growing spring"—Tennyson.

117

O days and hours, your work is this
    To hold me from my proper place,
    A little while from his embrace,
For fuller gain of after bliss:

That out of distance might ensue   5
    Desire of nearness doubly sweet;
    And unto meeting when we meet,
Delight a hundredfold accrue,

For every grain of sand that runs,
    And every span of shade that steals,   10
    And every kiss of toothed wheels,
And all the courses of the suns.[1]

1. Lines 9–12: However his time on earth may be measured, by the hourglass, the sundial, clocks, or the movement of the stars, its only function will be to increase the speaker's joy in his ultimate heavenly reunion with Hallam. Cf. the previous description of that anticipated meeting, Section 47, lines 6–16.

118[1]

Contemplate all this work of Time,
    The giant labouring in his youth;
    Nor dream of human love and truth,
As dying Nature's earth and lime;[2]

But trust that those we call the dead   5
    Are breathers of an ampler day
    For ever nobler ends. They say,
The solid earth whereon we tread

In tracts of fluent heat began,[3]
    And grew to seeming-random forms,   10
    The seeming prey of cyclic storms,[4]
Till at the last arose the man;

1. In this section, thematically one of the most important in the poem, Tennyson returns to a subject he had dealt with earlier, notably in Sections 55 and 56: the implications of recent scientific discoveries for contemporary religious and moral creeds. Here he disavows the pessimistic conclusions he had reached in the earlier sections and concludes that the evidence upon which contemporary theories of geology and evolutionary development are based affords no cause for despair over the ultimate extinction of the human race (as he had concluded in Section 56). On the contrary, modern scientific discoveries themselves give some hope for believing in the reality of human progress. Sections 55 and 56 had been written under the influence largely of Lyell's *Principles of Geology*, but Section 118 shows evidence of Tennyson's having read some of the more optimistic scientific works of his age as well, among them Chambers's *Vestiges of the Natural History of Creation* and Herschel's *Discourses on Natural Philosophy*.
2. Two of the perishable organic ingredients of the human body.
3. Lines 7–9: The allusion is to the nebular hypothesis of Laplace, who in the *Mécanique Celeste* (1799–1825) theorized that our solar system has been formed from out of an original gaseous nebula, the matter in which, as it gradually cooled, compacted into an incandescent sun and the cooler planets that revolved around it.
4. I.e., storms which last through entire cosmic ages. Taken together, lines 10 and 11 are obscure. Presumably Tennyson alludes to those primeval geologic forces (metaphorically, "storms") which shaped the contours of the earth after it had been formed (e.g., the cooling of the crust and the consequent thrusting up of mountains in "seeming random" forms, or the violent action of earthquakes or volcanoes as described by Lyell). Whatever the specific allusion, clearly in lines 7–12 Tennyson is reflecting the theories of the creation and development of the earth and of man as many of the thoughtful scientists of his age (whom the poet identifies only as "they" in line 7) had come to see them: the earth was not necessarily God-created, they argued, but the passive result of natural cosmic forces (metaphorically, the "prey" of those forces); and man arose not through any act of special creation by a Deity but only when natural laws had created an environment propitious to his existence.

Who throve and branch'd from clime to clime,
  The herald of a higher race,[5]
  And of himself in higher place,   15
If so he type this work of time

Within himself, from more to more;[6]
  Or, crown'd with attributes of woe
  Like glories, move his course, and show
That life is not as idle ore,   20

But iron dug from central gloom,
  And heated hot with burning fears,
  And dipt in baths of hissing tears,
and batter'd[7] with the shocks of doom

To shape and use. Arise and fly   25
  The reeling Faun,[8] the sensual feast;
  Move upward,[9] working out the beast,
And let the ape and tiger die.[1]

5. Lines 13–14: Presumably Tennyson is saying that the human race, once in existence, will progress to increasingly higher forms of being; but the precise meaning is obscure.
6. Lines 16–17: Man will progress, that is, *if* he understands the necessity for emulating in his moral universe the pattern of progressive development for which nature has furnished the archetypes in the physical universe. Cf. lines 25–28. "Type" (line 16) has the force of *represent, or emulate*.
7. Beaten into shapes.

8. A mythic creature—part man, part beast—who represents man's sensual, libidinous nature.
9. I.e., from the merely sensual to the moral planes of life.
1. "Ape": symbolic of the subhuman portions of man's phylogenetic inheritance. "Tiger": symbolic of man's amoral, natural cruelty, also a part of his racial inheritance. Both must be repressed ("die") if man is to progress morally and become "the herald of a higher race" (line 14).

119[1]

Doors, where my heart was used to beat
  So quickly, not as one that weeps
  I come once more; the city sleeps;
I smell the meadow in the street;

I hear a chirp of birds; I see   5
  Betwixt the black fronts long-withdrawn
  A light-blue lane of early dawn,
And think of early days and thee,

And bless thee, for thy lips are bland,
  And bright the friendship of thine eye;   10
  And in my thoughts with scarce a sigh
I take the pressure of thine hand.

1. In this section the speaker again stands before Hallam's house in Wim- pole Street. Cf. Section 7.

120[1]

I trust I have not wasted breath:
    I think we are not wholly brain,
    Magnetic mockeries;[2] not in vain,
Like Paul with beasts, I fought with Death;[3]

Not only cunning casts in clay:[4]   5
    Let Science prove we are, and then
    What matter Science unto men,
At least to me? I would not stay.[5]

Let him, the wiser man[6] who spring
    Hereafter, up from childhood shape   10
    His action like the greater ape,
But I was *born* to other things.[7]

1. This section continues Tennyson's attack on scientific materialism begun in Section 118. The spiritual and the material, he argues, function in different realms; the former does not grow out of the latter.
2. Soulless mechanisms controlled by electrical ("magnetic") forces. Contemporary biologists had recently theorized that impulses generated in the brain were translated into muscular action by means of minute electrical impulses traveling along the nerves.
3. " 'If after the manner of men I have fought with beasts at Ephesus, what advantageth it me?' (I Cor. xv.32)"—Tennyson.
4. I.e., bodies without souls.
5. I.e., "I would not heed, or believe." But one critic paraphrases the sentence as "I would kill myself."
6. The man who heeds the materialistic scientist. The epithet "wiser" is therefore sarcastic.
7. Lines 9–12: "Spoken ironically against mere materialism, not against evolution" —Tennyson.

121[1]

Sad Hesper o'er the buried sun[2]
    And ready, thou, to die with him,
    Thou watchest all things ever dim
And dimmer, and a glory done:

The team is loosen'd from the wain,   5
    The boat is drawn upon the shore;
    Thou listenest to the closing door,
And life is darken'd in the brain.

Bright Phosphor, fresher for the night,[3]
    By thee the world's great work is heard   10
    Beginning, and the wakeful bird;
Behind thee comes the greater light:

The market boat is on the stream,
    And voices hail it from the brink;
    Thou hear'st the village hammer clink,   15
And see'st the moving of the team.

1. Tennyson composed this section at Shiplake, where he and Emily Sellwood were married.
2. The evening star, which shines after sunset.
3. The morning star, which shines at dawn.

Sweet Hesper-Phosphor, double name
    For what is one, the first, the last,[4]
    Thou, like my present and my past,[5]   20
Thy place is changed; thou art the same.

4. "The evening star is also the morning star, death and sorrow brighten into death and hope"—Tennyson. *Hesper* and *Phosphor* are two names for the same planet, Venus. At some periods of the year Venus rises as the morning star, at others as the evening star. The remarkable development of the patterns of imagery and metaphor in this section depend in part, too, upon the recognition that Venus, whether under the name *Phosphor* or *Hesper*, is the planet of love.

5. If Phosphor symbolizes the poet's past and Hesper his present, both are made one in love.

122[1]

Oh, wast thou with me, dearest, then,
    While I rose up against my doom,[2]
    And yearn'd to burst the folded gloom,
To bare the eternal Heavens again,

To feel once more, in placid awe,   5
    The strong imagination roll
    A sphere of stars about my soul,
In all her motion one with law;

If thou wert with me and the grave
    Divide us not, be with me now,[3]   10
    And enter in at breast and brow,
Till all my blood, a fuller wave,

Be quicken'd with a livelier breath,
    And like an inconsiderate boy,
    As in the former flash of joy,   15
I slip the thoughts of life and death;

And all the breeze of Fancy blows,
    And every dew-drop paints a bow,[4]
    The wizard lightnings deeply glow,
And every thought breaks out a rose.   20

1. What specific past event the poet may have had in mind by his references to "then," "again," and "once more" (lines 1, 4, 5) has caused critics to disagree sharply over the proper reading of this section. Perhaps the most likely reference is to the mystic trance Tennyson described in Section 95, when the poet felt "the living soul" of Hallam "flash'd" on his own.

2. "That of grief"—Tennyson.
3. Cf. Section 50, lines 1, 5, 9, 13.
4. Each dewdrop reflects a small rainbow.

123[1]

There rolls the deep where grew the tree.
O earth, what changes hast thou seen!

1. In this section Tennyson again turns the findings of contemporary geology to poetic use. His imagination seizes upon the incessant processes of erosion of land masses by water, sedimentation, and uplifting of sea bottoms ("the interchange of sea and land," as Lyell calls it) as emblematic of the ceaseless change in the material world of becoming, which flows "from form to form, and nothing stands" (line 6). To this he contrasts the permanence of the spiritual world of being (stanza 3).

> There where the long street roars, hath been
> The stillness of the central sea.[2]
>
> The hills are shadows, and they flow   5
> From form to form, and nothing stands:
> They melt like mist, the solid lands,
> Like clouds they shape themselves and go.
>
> But in my spirit will I dwell,
> And dream my dream, and hold it true;   10
> For tho' my lips may breathe adieu,
> I cannot think the thing farewell.[3]

124

> That which we dare invoke to bless;
> Our dearest faith; our ghastliest doubt;
> He, They, One, All; within, without;
> The Power in darkness whom we guess;[1]
>
> I found Him not in world or sun,   5
> Or eagle's wing, or insect's eye;
> Nor thro' the questions men may try,
> The petty cobwebs we have spun:[2]
>
> If e'er when faith had fall'n asleep,
> I heard a voice 'believe no more'   10
> And heard an ever-breaking shore
> That tumbled in the Godless deep;
>
> A warmth within the breast would melt
> The freezing reason's colder part,
> And like a man in wrath the heart   15
> Stood up and answer'd 'I have felt.'[3]
>
> No, like a child in doubt and fear:
> But that blind clamour[4] made me wise;
> Then was I as a child that cries,
> But, crying, knows his father near;[5]   20

2. "Balloonists say that even in a storm the middle sea is noiseless"—Tennyson.
3. Lines 11–12: Cf. Section 57, lines 15–16.
1. Lines 1–4: We sense the Eternal Spirit both inside us and outside, in moments of both doubt and faith. Line 4: Cf. the Prologue, line 24.
2. Lines 5–8: The speaker rejects the argument from design (i.e., that the existence of design in nature proves the existence of a Designer) as well as other rational arguments for the existence of God. Cf. Browning's attack on "natural theology" in *Caliban upon Setebos*.
3. Lines 13–16: A quintessential statement of Tennyson's belief that spiritual reality can be apprehended only through the heart, not through the reason.
4. I.e., the "clamour" of the emblems of materialism described in lines 10–12 above.
5. Lines 17–20: Cf. the image of the crying child in this passage and the very different use to which the poet puts the same image in Section 54, lines 17–20.

And what I am beheld again
  What is, and no man understands;
  And out of darkness came the hands
That reach thro' nature, moulding men.

125

Whatever I have said or sung,   5
  Some bitter notes my harp would give,
  Yea, tho' there often seem'd to live
A contradiction on the tongue,

Yet Hope had never lost her youth;
  She did but look through dimmer eyes;   10
  Or Love but play'd with gracious lies,
Because he[1] felt so fix'd in truth:

And if the song were full of care,
  He breathed the spirit of the song;
  And if the words were sweet and strong   15
He set his royal signet there;

Abiding with me till I sail
  To seek thee on the mystic deeps,[2]
  And this electric force,[3] that keeps
A thousand pulses dancing, fail.   20

1. I.e., Love.
2. Lines 13–14: The metaphor of death in these lines may be contrasted to that in *Crossing the Bar.*
3. Tennyson concedes to the neurologists of his age that nerve force is exerted by means of small electric currents. Such materialistic explanations, however, take into account neither man's soul nor the reality of love (as also argued in Section 124 above, lines 13–16).

126

Love is and was my Lord and King,[1]
  And in his presence I attend
  To hear the tidings of my friend,
Which every hour his couriers bring.

Love is and was my King and Lord,   5
  And will be, tho' as yet I keep
  Within his court on earth, and sleep
Encompass'd by his faithful guard,

And hear at times a sentinel
  Who moves about from place to place,   10
  And whispers to the worlds of space,
In the deep night, that all is well.

1. The metaphor of love as king is anticipated in the previous section, line 12.

127

And all is well, tho' faith and form[1]
   Be sunder'd in the night of fear;
   Well roars the storm to those that hear
A deeper voice across the storm,

Proclaiming social truth shall spread,   5
   And justice, ev'n tho' thrice again
   The red fool-fury of the Seine
Should pile her barricades with dead.[2]

But ill for him that wears a crown,
   And him, that lazar,[3] in his rags: 10
   They tremble, the sustaining crags;
The spires of ice are toppled down,

And molten up, and roar in flood;
   The fortress crashes from on high,
   The brute earth lightens to the sky,   15
And the great Aeon[4] sinks in blood,

And compass'd by the fires of Hell;
   While thou, dear spirit, happy star,
   O'erlook'st the tumult from afar,
And smilest, knowing all is well.   20

1. Cf. Section 33, stanza 3. The "forms" are those religious creeds through which faith was formally expressed in past ages but which, in Tennyson's time, have been "sunder'd" from faith by the inroads of skepticism and determinism. Tennyson's reading of the ills of his age in this section and others is remarkably similar to the views habitually expressed by another social and political conservative, Thomas Carlyle (see the essay *Characteristics*).
2. Lines 6–8: Possibly an allusion to the three French revolutions of 1789, 1830, and 1848, though there is evidence that this lyric was written some time before 1848.
3. A diseased person, usually a leper.
4. The vast period covered by modern history.

128

The love that rose on stronger wings,
   Unpalsied when he met with Death,
   Is comrade of the lesser faith
That sees the course of human things.

No doubt vast eddies in the flood   5
   Of onward time shall yet be made,
   And throned races may degrade;[1]
Yet O ye mysteries of good,

Wild Hours that fly with Hope and Fear,
   If all your office had to do   10
   With old results that look like new;[2]
If this were all your mission here,

1. I.e., races now in power may degenerate.
2. With change, that is, but not progress.

To draw, to sheathe a useless sword,
To fool the crowd with glorious lies,
To cleave a creed in sects and cries,   15
To change the bearing of a word,

To shift an arbitrary power,
To cramp the student at his desk,
To make old bareness picturesque
And tuft with grass a feudal tower;   20

Why then my scorn might well descend
On you and yours. I see in part
That all, as in some piece of art,
Is toil coöperant to an end.[3]

3. Lines 22–24: Cf. the Epilogue, lines 141–44.

129
Dear friend, far off, my lost desire,
So far, so near in woe and weal;
O loved the most, when most I feel
There is a lower and a higher;

Known and unknown; human, divine;   5
Sweet human hand and lips and eye;
Dear heavenly friend that canst not die,
Mine, mine, for ever, ever mine;

Strange friend, past, present, and to be;
Loved deeplier, darklier understood;   10
Behold, I dream a dream of good,
And mingle all the world with thee.[1]

1. Lines 11–12: Tennyson's wife re-
marked that the "two faiths" of this sec-
tion (faith in the individual immortality
of Hallam and in the progress of the
human race) "are in reality the same.
The thought of [Hallam] as human and
divine mingles with all great thoughts as
to the destiny of the world (cf. [cxxx])"
(Eversley, p. 264).

130
Thy voice is on the rolling air;
I hear thee where the waters run;
Thou standest in the rising sun,
And in the setting thou art fair.

What art thou then? I cannot guess;   5
But tho' I seem in star and flower
To feel thee some diffusive power,
I do not therefore love thee less:

My love involves the love before;
My love is vaster passion now;   10
Tho' mix'd with God and Nature thou,
I seem to love thee more and more.

Far off thou art, but ever nigh;
   I have thee still, and I rejoice;
   I prosper, circled with thy voice;   15
I shall not lose thee tho' I die.

131[1]

O living will[2] that shalt endure
   When all that seems shall suffer shock,
   Rise in the spiritual rock,[3]
Flow thro' our deeds and make them pure,

That we may lift from out of dust   5
   A voice as unto him that hears,
   A cry above the conquer'd years
To one that with us works, and trust,

With faith that comes of self-control,
   The truths that never can be proved   10
   Until we close with all we loved,
And all we flow from, soul in soul.

1. "Yes, it is true that there are moments when the flesh is nothing to me, when I feel and know the flesh to be the vision, God and the Spiritual the only real and true. Depend upon it, the Spiritual *is* the real: it belongs to one more than the hand and the foot. You may tell me that my hand and my foot are only imaginary symbols of my existence, I could believe you; but you never, never can convince me that the *I* is not an eternal reality, and that the Spiritual is not the true and real part of me"—Tennyson.
2. Human free will.
3. "And did all drink the same spiritual drink; for they drank of that spiritual Rock that followed them: and that Rock was Christ" (I Corinthians x.4).

[EPILOGUE][1]

O true and tried, so well and long,
   Demand not thou a marriage lay;
   In that it is thy marriage day
Is music more than any song.

Nor have I felt so much of bliss   5
   Since first he told me that he loved
   A daughter of our house;[2] nor proved
Since that dark day[3] a day like this;

Tho' I since then have number'd o'er
   Some thrice three years:[4] they went and came,   10
   Remade the blood and changed the frame,
And yet is love not less, but more;

1. Though perhaps written several years later, the Epilogue gives the impression of having been written on the wedding day of Edmund Lushington and Cecilia Tennyson, the poet's youngest sister, which was October 10, 1842. As Tennyson himself pointed out, *In Memoriam* "begins with a funeral and ends with a marriage—begins with death and ends with promise of a new life. . . ." In spite of the poet's defense of the Epilogue, however, some critics have argued that it has at best only minimal poetic merit and fails to harmonize with the high solemnity of the sections which have just preceded it.
2. Lines 6–7: The "he" is Hallam, and Tennyson's reference is to the engagement of Hallam to the eldest Tennyson sister, Emily, which was of course sundered by Hallam's death.
3. The day of Hallam's death.
4. I.e., 1833 to 1842.

No longer caring to embalm
    In dying songs a dead regret,
    But like a statue solid-set,   15
And moulded in colossal calm.

Regret is dead, but love is more
    Than in the summers that are flown,
    For I myself with these have grown
To something greater than before;   20

Which makes appear the songs I made
    As echoes out of weaker times,
    As half but idle brawling rhymes,
The sport of random sun and shade.

But where is she, the bridal flower,   25
    That must be made a wife ere noon?
    She enters, glowing like the moon
Of Eden on its bridal bower:

On me she bends her blissful eyes
    And then on thee; they meet thy look   30
    And brighten like the star that shook
Betwixt the palms of paradise.

O when her life was yet in bud,
    He too foretold the perfect rose.[5]
    For thee she grew, for thee she grows   35
For ever, and as fair as good.

And thou art worthy; full of power;
    As gentle; liberal-minded, great,
    Consistent; wearing all that weight
Of learning lightly like a flower.   40

But now set out: the noon is near,
    And I must give away the bride;
    She fears not, or with thee beside
And me behind her, will not fear.

For I that danced her on my knee,   45
    That watch'd her on her nurse's arm,[6]
    That shielded all her life from harm
At last must part with her to thee;

Now waiting to be made a wife,
    Her feet, my darling, on the dead;   50

5. Lines 33–34: I.e., Hallam foresaw when she was yet a child that Cecilia would grow into a beautiful woman.

6. Lines 45–46: Tennyson was eight years older than Cecilia.

Their pensive tablets round her head,[7]
And the most living words of life

Breathed in her ear. The ring is on,
    The 'wilt thou' answer'd, and again
    The 'wilt thou' ask'd, till out of twain   55
Her sweet 'I will' has made you one.

Now sign your names,[8] which shall be read,
    Mute symbols of a joyful morn,
    By village eyes as yet unborn;
The names are sign'd, and overhead   60

Begins the clash and clang that tells
    The joy to every wandering breeze;
    The blind wall rocks, and on the trees
The dead leaf trembles to the bells.

O happy hour, and happier hours   65
    Await them. Many a merry face
    Salutes them—maidens of the place,
That pelt us in the porch with flowers.

O happy hour, behold the bride
    With him to whom her hand I gave.   70
    They leave the porch, they pass the grave
That has to-day its sunny side.

To-day the grave is bright for me,
    For them the light of life increased,
    Who stay to share the morning feast,   75
Who rest to-night beside the sea.

Let all my genial spirits advance
    To meet and greet a whiter sun;
    My drooping memory will not shun
The foaming grape of eastern France.   80

It circles round, and fancy plays,
    And hearts are warm'd and faces bloom,
    As drinking health to bride and groom
We wish them store of happy days.

Nor count me all to blame if I   85
    Conjecture of a stiller guest,
    Perchance, perchance, among the rest,
And, tho' in silence, wishing joy.[9]

7. Lines 50–51: Cecilia stands before the church altar over the remains of those buried below the chancel and surrounded by memorial tablets to the dead.

8. In the parish register.
9. Lines 86–88. The "stiller guest" is the spirit of Hallam.

But they must go, the time draws on,
  And those white-favour'd horses wait;
  They rise,[1] but linger; it is late;
Farewell, we kiss, and they are gone.   90

A shade falls on us like the dark
  From little cloudlets on the grass,
  But sweeps away as out we pass   95
To range the woods, to roam the park,

Discussing how their courtship grew,
  And talk of others that are wed,
  And how she look'd, and what he said,
And back we came at fall of dew.   100

Again the feast, the speech, the glee,
  The shade of passing thought, the wealth
  Of words and wit, the double health,
The crowning cup, the three-times-three,

And last the dance;—till I retire: 105
  Dumb is that tower which spake so loud,
  And high in heaven the streaming cloud,
And on the downs a rising fire:

And rise, O moon, from yonder down,
  Till over down and over dale   110
  All night the shining vapour sail
And pass the silent-lighted town,

The white-faced halls, the glancing rills,
  And catch at every mountain head,
  And o'er the friths that branch and spread   115
Their sleeping silver thro' the hills;

And touch with shade the bridal doors,
  With tender gloom the roof, the wall;
  And breaking let the splendour fall   120
To spangle all the happy shores

By which they rest, and ocean sounds,
  And, star and system rolling past,
  A soul shall draw from out the vast
And strike his being into bounds,

And, moved thro' life of lower phase,   125
  Result in man,[2] be born and think,

1. From the wedding feast.
2. Lines 123–26: A child will be conceived on their wedding night, and the embryo will repeat, throughout its prenatal period, all the evolutionary stages of the human race from the lowest animal phases to the highest human form.

And act and love, a closer link
Betwixt us and the crowning race

Of those that, eye to eye, shall look
    On knowledge; under whose command   130
    Is Earth and Earth's, and in their hand
Is Nature like an open book;

No longer half-akin to brute,
    For all we thought and loved and did,
    And hoped, and suffer'd, is but seed   135
Of what in them is flower and fruit;[3]

Whereof the man, that with me trod
    This planet, was a noble type
    Appearing ere the times were ripe,
That friend of mine who lives in God,   140

That God, which ever lives and loves,
    One God, one law, one element,
    And one far-off divine event,
To which the whole creation moves.[4]

3. Lines 126–36: In this passage Tennyson again asserts his belief not only in human development but in the progress of the race to ever higher forms, and he anticipates some far-off time when man will in fact have evolved into a species "no longer half-akin to brute" (line 133). Here, as in the lines immediately above, the poet reflects the concepts put forward by Chambers in the *Vestiges of the Natural History of Creation*.
4. Lines 143–44: Cf. Section 54, lines 14–15; Section 55, lines 9–28.

Backgrounds and Sources

ROBERT H. ROSS

The Three Faces of *In Memoriam*

In the 120 years since its publication *In Memoriam* has evoked varied responses from many different kinds of readers, from the straightforward tribute of the widowed Queen Victoria ("Next to the Bible 'In Memoriam' is my comfort," she told Tennyson after the death of the Prince Consort) to the intricate explications of some modern critics. Like any long, complex poem, it invites reading and analysis from several points of view. Not the least interesting dimension of the poem is the autobiographical. *In Memoriam* is an intensely personal poem, "the concentrated diary of a man confessing himself," as T. S. Eliot observed. Indeed, Tennyson himself, who was one of the most reticent public literary figures in Victorian England, lived uneasily with the suspicion that in charting "the way of the soul" through *In Memoriam* he had laid himself open to the charge of making public, poetic capital out of his private, subjective grief.

And so, perhaps, he had; or so, from his point of view, it must have seemed. In any event, his deep misgivings over the propriety of exposing his private grief to the public gaze are woven early and late into the very fabric of *In Memoriam*. The poet's debate with himself is joined almost at the outset of the poem:

> I sometimes hold it half a sin
>   To put in words the grief I feel:
>   For words, like Nature, half reveal
> And half conceal the Soul within.
>
> But, for the unquiet heart and brain,
>   A use in measured language lies;
>   A sad mechanic exercise,
> Like dull narcotics, numbing pain.   (5:1–8)

Subsequently Tennyson embodies his own arguments against himself in the voices of three imagined adversaries who put the case against him in the accents of his own time. Their accusations are uncomfortably personal. To luxuriate in such an excess of grief is unmanly, the first charges. Worse, the poet is self-consciously posturing, the second adds:

> He loves to make parade of pain
> That with his piping he may gain
> The praise that comes to constancy.   (21:10–12)

93

To put even the best possible light on it, says the third more sternly, the poet is out of step with his age. The mid-nineteenth century, witness to the almost daily marvels produced by the march of mind, is a time for doing, not repining. Surely it is not the hour to indulge in "private sorrow's barren song" or "to sicken and to swoon" over personal grief like a romantic maiden (21: 14, 17). Examples could be multiplied from first to last. Tennyson's debate with himself hovers palpably in the background of even the last section of *In Memoriam* to be written, the Prologue, where the poet's closing prayer for forgiveness seems inevitably to imply some self-imputed guilt for, among other things, having borne his private grief into the public forum.

> Forgive my grief for one removed,
> Thy creature, whom I found so fair. . . .
>
> Forgive these wild and wandering cries,
> Confusions of a wasted youth.   (37–38, 41–42)

Perhaps only Tennyson could have succeeded in laying before the public a long poem exploring every nuance of his personal, private sorrow while in the selfsame poem conducting an extended debate with himself over the propriety of his doing so. That is not to impugn Tennyson's poetic sincerity; it is only to suggest, in yet another context, the now-familiar premise that Tennyson's was ever a uniquely divided sensibility. Some of the poet's subsequent commentaries on *In Memoriam* serve to underscore the observation. In one of them he felt compelled, characteristically, to warn his readers against interpreting his poem too exclusively as a personal confession. *In Memoriam* "is a poem, *not* an actual biography," he wrote. "The different moods of sorrow as in a drama are dramatically given. . . . 'I' is not always the author speaking of himself, but the voice of the human race speaking through him" (*Memoir*, I, 304).

After Tennyson's "not always"—which in itself admits of some ambiguities—many readers are prepared to insert the mental reservation "but usually." For in spite of the poet's disclaimer, the confessional quality of *In Memoriam* seems overwhelming. In many of the 131 sections of the poem "the way of the soul" seems not so much the universalized way of Everyman's soul as the unique, personal way of Alfred Tennyson's. Even the structure of the poem is essentially autobiographical. To be sure, Tennyson exercises a good deal of chronological poetic license; his fictive time (the temporal order he imposed upon events in the poem) is not identical to real time (the order in which events actually occurred). Organized around the three Christmas lyrics (28, 78, 104), the poem is constructed as if to span a period of three years, whereas in actuality the events Tennyson describes took place over a period of about nine years. Nevertheless, from beginning to end—from Section 9, describing the return of Hallam's body to England (which occurred in December 1833), to the Epilogue, celebrating the marriage of Tennyson's sister Cecilia (which occurred in October 1842)—the structure of the poem is delineated by lyrics or groups of lyrics which had their genesis in some very real, clearly identifiable events in Tennyson's life during the years following the death of Hallam.

But for all its confessional, private qualities, *In Memoriam* also has an important public dimension. It is, as Jerome Buckley remarks, "a kind of Victorian *Essay on Man*." Of all the major Victorian poets Tennyson is perhaps most unmistakably a man of his time. Somewhere in *In Memoriam* most of the philosophical, religious, and ethical issues which shook the mid-Victorian age—and to an astonishing degree shaped the Victorian poetic temper—are refracted through the sensibility of Tennyson. But they emerge not as intellectual abstractions, rather—since *In Memoriam* is a poem, not a metaphysical tract—as felt spiritual dilemmas. It is not impossible, therefore, that a perceptive modern reader of *In Memoriam* may be brought to sense something of the immense significance that such issues bore for Victorian minds and hearts, for in this elegy the devastating spiritual dislocations of the age find full poetic voice.

Among the public issues of his day Tennyson was particularly well read in the field of science. Thomas Henry Huxley roundly declared him to be "the first poet since Lucretius who has understood the drift of science." For all its overstatement, the dictum implies an important distinction. Tennyson was of course no paleontologist, geologist, or astronomer; neither his interest nor his knowledge was that of the professional scientist. His expertise was rather that of the thoughtful, well-informed layman. But the general "drift" of science—its premises, assumptions, modes of arguing, implications—these things he surely understood and, what is more important for a poet, felt. The tenets, hypotheses, and assumptions of the new science became a fixed part of Tennyson's intellectual equipment and profoundly permeated his poetic consciousness. A. C. Bradley's comment gets more precisely to the heart of the matter than Huxley's: excepting Shelley in part, he wrote, "Tennyson is the only one of our great poets whose attitude towards the sciences of Nature was what a modern poet's attitude ought to be, . . . the only one to whose *habitual way of seeing, imagining, or thinking* it makes any real difference that Laplace, or for that matter Copernicus, ever lived" (italics added). And so as Tennyson, in the elegiac tradition, universalized his individual grief over Hallam dead, it was inevitable that he should have done so in full awareness of the metaphysical, religious, and ethical dilemmas being forced upon thoughtful Victorians by the recent findings and hypotheses in such scientific fields as geology, astronomy, paleontology, evolution, and the Higher Criticism.

That is not to say that because Tennyson is vitally concerned with the public issues of another day than ours *In Memoriam* necessarily becomes for the modern reader merely a historical period piece, a literary artifact which tells us much about the concerns of the Victorian age but little about our own. To claim that *In Memoriam* is perhaps *the* Victorian poem is not to claim that it is *only* a Victorian poem. Many of the questions Tennyson ponders, as Basil Willey points out, are neither "local nor ephemeral; they are universal in that they are those which beset a sensitive and meditative mind in any age. Has man an immortal soul? Is there any meaning in life? any purpose or design in the world-process? any evidence in Nature, in philosophy or in the human heart for a beneficent Providence?"

Although *In Memoriam* undeniably yields up its fullest experiences to the reader who will take the trouble to reconstruct some of its Victorian contexts, some modern readers still seem surprised to discover that Tennyson's journey through his own nineteenth-century wasteland is neither unfamiliar nor as remote from the twentieth-century experience as they might have supposed. Several critics of our own time have pointed the way to that conclusion. Tennyson's religious faith, as it finally develops at the end of *In Memoriam*, "is frequently not far removed from Kierkegaardian 'existentialism,' " Jerome Buckley suggests. Tennyson "is our true precursor," Arthur J. Carr asserts. "He shows and hides, as if in embryo, a master theme of Joyce's *Ulysses*. . . . He forecasts Yeats's interest in the private myth. He apprehended in advance of Aldous Huxley the uses of mysticism to castigate materialistic culture. . . . At some crucial points Tennyson is a modern poet, and there are compelling reasons why we should try to comprehend him." And many years ago T. S. Eliot remarked that the most intense poetic experience in *In Memoriam* lies in the quality not of its faith but of its doubt. "*In Memoriam* is a poem of despair," he reminded us, "though of despair of a religious kind." Tennyson himself was quite aware of the power of some of the darker moods of his elegy. Long after *In Memoriam* had suffered the fate of a "classic" and had become a treasure trove of text and quotation for Victorian sermonizers, ethical preceptors, and Anglican divines, Tennyson confessed to a friend that the Prologue to his poem, that paean to faith triumphant, was "too hopeful"—"more than I am myself," he added. Tennyson's struggle with the *néant*, even though it is embodied in the archetypal Victorian poem, has its clear and present analogues to the modern human condition.

Finally, in spite of all of its extra-poetical dimensions, *In Memoriam* is quintessentially a poem. Even Tennyson wearied of the Victorian message hunters, those too-assiduous practitioners of the moral esthetic, who insisted on reading a poem as if it were a sermon on morality, a text on theology, or a source document in intellectual history. "They are always speaking of me as if I were a writer of philosophical treatises," he complained to his son. Tennyson of all poets felt in the deep heart's core the ineffaceable difference between poetry and philosophy, poetry and biography, poetry and homiletics. Even at its simplest, he well knew, the poet's task is formidable. At its most difficult, as in the supremely crafted Section 95 of *In Memoriam*, for instance, it borders on the impossible. For in that lyric the poet's job is nothing less than to use the resources of language in such a way as to describe and make actual to a reader an incorporeal, almost inchoate, mystical vision. Tennyson recognized the difficulty of expressing the inexpressible:

> Vague words! but ah, how hard to frame
> In matter-moulded forms of speech,
> Or e'en for intellect to reach
> Thro' memory that which I became.   (45–48)

But section 95, the most masterful lyric in the poem, stands testimony to his achievement.

Even in less lofty lyrics of *In Memoriam*, as in those where he makes use of the abstract concepts of the new science, for example, Tennyson shows himself to be far from the "writer of philosophical treatises" that some of his more literal-minded contemporaries took him for. Whatever else a poet does or fails to do, he cannot rest content with versified metaphysics or morality, however exalted the thoughts he expresses. The poet not only tells a reader *what* he believes; he also brings his reader to understand how it *feels* to believe that. And so with Tennyson. Even when he seems most the man of his times, the secular *vates* with the mantle of prophecy upon him, he characteristically approaches the public issues of his day "not in the manner of a thinker," as Basil Willey observes, "but in the manner of a well-informed modern poet: that is, in the manner of one who, though not ignorant of what the specialists are saying, cares for their results only insofar as they are felt in the blood, and felt along the heart, affecting there the innermost quality of living."

GEORGE O. MARSHALL, JR.

In Memoriam (1850) †

The year 1850—Tennyson's *annus mirabilis*—was marked by three major events, all interconnected. Edward Moxon published *In Memoriam* on June 1; Tennyson married Emily Sellwood on June 13; and the Queen appointed him Poet Laureate on November 19. The publication of *In Memoriam* served a double purpose in making the marriage possible: it relieved Emily's doubts about the state of Tennyson's soul, and the prospect of its financial success gave Tennyson confidence enough to assume the responsibilities of a family. The Laureateship was a fitting tribute to England's greatest living poet.

The new volume was more successful than could have been anticipated. Under Tennyson's new agreement with Moxon he paid all the expenses and gave the publisher one-third of the profits and five per cent on gross sales.[1] The published price was six shillings a copy. Although only 5,000 copies were printed for the first edition, two more editions were called for before the year was out and 60,000 copies were sold within a few months. There were nineteen regularly numbered editions plus two others: after the three in 1850 there were two in 1851, one in 1855, 1856, 1859, 1860, 1861, two in 1862, two in 1863, 1864, two in 1865, 1866, 1867, 1869, and 1870. The poem's continued popularity is reflected by various editions in 1880, 1885, 1889, two in 1900, four in 1901, two in 1902, one in 1903, one in 1905, and so on.

The volume was bound in deep purple cloth boards with the title in gilt across the spine. The Prologue, dated 1849, is on pp. v-vii. Opposite the first page is "IN MEMORIAM/A.H.H./OBIIT MDCCCXXXIII." The main part of the poem, which is divided into 129 numbered sections of varying numbers of stanzas, occupies pp. 1-201. The Epilogue is on pp. 203-210. Of the 2868 lines in the poem, 44 are in the Prologue, 2680 are in the main body of the poem, and 144 are in the Epilogue. Two sections added since the first edition bring the total to 131 sections. Section LIX ("O Sorrow, wilt thou live with me") was inserted in the fourth edition (1851), and Section XXXIX ("Old warder of these buried bones") was added in the 1870 edition. On the title-page was: "IN MEMORIAM. / LONDON: / EDWARD MOXON, DOVER STREET. / 1850."

† From *A Tennyson Handbook* (New York, Twayne Publishing Co., 1963), pp. 118–24. The author's footnotes have been renumbered.

1. Charles Tennyson, *Alfred Tennyson*, p. 247.

Although Tennyson's name was not in the book, his authorship was soon discovered. The manuscript was given to Trinity College, Cambridge, with the stipulation that it would not be copied and that manuscript variations from the published versions would never be published. The manuscript is open in the exhibit case at "Ring out, wild bells, to the wild sky."[2]

The poem was first printed in March, 1850, entitled *Fragments of an Elegy*, and distributed to a few friends. Tennyson's future wife suggested *In Memoriam* for its title. It is written in a single metre, lines of iambic tetrameter rhyming abba. Tennyson's use of this metrical form in this poem has caused it to be known as the "*In Memoriam* stanza." He had previously used the metre in three poems in the 1842 volume, *The Blackbird*, "Love thou thy land," and "You ask me, why, though ill at ease," and in *To—,: After Reading a Life and Letters*, published in *The Examiner*, March 24, 1849. He later used it in his epilogue *To the Queen* (1851) and in two poems in the 1889 volume, *To the Marquis of Dufferin and Ava* and *To Ulysses*. Although Tennyson thought that he had invented the metre, it had previously been used by Lord Herbert of Cherbury, Ben Jonson, and Sir Philip Sidney.

The subject of the elegy is Arthur Henry Hallam, the son of the historian Henry Hallam. Tennyson and Hallam had become immediately attracted to each other when they met at Trinity College, Cambridge. They were both members of the Apostles, an undergraduate discussion group at Cambridge, in which Hallam was regarded as the greatest personality. Gladstone, who had been at Eton with Hallam, regarded him as the coming great man of the age. His contemporaries, in fact, seem to have been unanimous in their anticipation of his future greatness.[3]

But Hallam's early death kept him from fulfilling what his friends regarded as his great promise. He died in Vienna on September 15, 1833, while travelling with is father. A frequent visitor at the Tennyson home in Somersby, he had become engaged to the poet's sister Emily. He and Tennyson had been abroad together twice, visiting the Pyrenees in 1830 and touring the Rhineland in 1832. The personal element is greater in *In Memoriam* than it is in any of the other great English elegies.

In Memoriam is only one of Tennyson's poems inspired or greatly influenced by Hallam's death. Before 1850 Tennyson had given vent to his feelings in such poems as *Ulysses*, *Tithonus*, *The Two Voices*, and "Break, break, break," and was later to enshrine his friendship with Hallam with many references and in the moving

2. Eleanor B. Mattes, *In Memoriam: The Way of a Soul*, p. xvi:
3. The most accessible edition of Hal-
lam's literary remains is *The Writings of Arthur Hallam*, ed. T. H. Vail Motter (New York, 1943).

In the Valley of Cauteretz (1864). Tennyson never forgot. His niece Agnes Weld records that "In after years he would frequently talk to me about the friends of his youth, especially Arthur Hallam, of whom he spoke as of one who had died but yesterday."[4]

Tennyson's prostration at Hallam's death is rather hard for modern readers to understand. Their bewilderment is increased by the many seemingly unduly tender phrases of *In Memoriam*. But their friendship was not as unusual as it now seems. A biographer of Lord Houghton has expressed the situation well:

> Modern commentators on *In Memoriam* and students of the Cambridge phase of Tennyson's life have written of the relationship with Arthur Hallam as though it were, in its day, unique. This is mistaken. The unique quality of the friendship lay squarely in the fact that one of the two friends was a major English poet, who has immortalised it in his finest series of lyrics. Seen in the perspective of Cambridge at that day, and particularly of the Trinity set to which they both belonged, the relationship falls into place as one among many such close mutual affections.[5]

Tennyson began writing his short elegies in the winter after Hallam's death.[6] He was involved with the composition sporadically until the complete poem was published. He wrote part of the poem in Lincolnshire, London, Essex, Gloucestershire, Wales, or anywhere else he happened to be during this period of his wandering around England. Many of the sections have been dated, both as to place and time of composition. Notes to the *Eversley Edition* furnish Tennyson's own comments on the circumstances under which some parts were written. All editions date the Prologue 1849. The Epilogue was obviously written after October 14, 1842, as it celebrates the marriage of the poet's sister Cecilia to Edmund Lushington on that date.

The poem should be considered in the light of Tennyson's own statement about its nature:

> It must be remembered that this is a poem, *not* an actual biography. It is founded on our friendship, on the engagement of Arthur Hallam to my sister, on his sudden death at Vienna, just before the time fixed for their marriage, and on his burial at Clevedon Church. The poem concludes with the marriage of my youngest sister Cecilia. It was meant to be a kind of *Divina Commedia*, ending with happiness. The sections were written at many different places, and as the phases of our intercourse came to my memory and suggested them. I did not write them with any view of weaving them into a whole, or for publication, until I found

4. *Glimpses of Tennyson and of Some of His Relations and Friends*, p. 51.
5. James Pope-Hennessy, *Monckton-Milnes: The Years of Promise*, 1809–
1851, p. 17.
6. Hallam Tennyson prints in *Memoir*, I, 107, lines he identifies as the germ of the poem.

that I had written so many. The different moods of sorrow as in a drama are dramatically given, and my conviction that fear, doubts, and suffering will find answer and relief only through Faith in a God of Love. 'I' is not always the author speaking of himself, but the voice of the human race speaking thro' him. After the Death of A. H. H., the divisions of the poem are made by First Xmas Eve (Section XXVIII.), Second Xmas (LXXVIII.), Third Xmas Eve (CV. and CV. etc.).[7]

Composed under such circumstances, it is a wonder that *In Memoriam* has any unity. Like *Maud* (1855), it is really a series of poems, with each poem expressing a nuance in the changing grief of the poet.[8] The form must have been influenced by sonnet sequences, which are more flexible metrically, but which Tennyson compensates for by having varying numbers of stanzas in the sections.

The time of the poem is supposed to cover approximately three years. We can accept Tennyson's division of the poem into parts separated by the Christmases. Although there have been many attempts definitely to date all of the action in the poem, none has been successful in eliminating all inconsistencies. These inconsistencies seem to indicate that the poet did not wish the "way of the soul" to be tied down to a calendar.[9]

One of the most remarkable things about *In Memoriam* was its popularity with Tennyson's contemporaries. It seemed to be such a satisfactory answer to the problems of existence, especially those raised by the struggle between religion and science, that the Victorians clasped it to their bosoms to supplement the consolation offered by the Bible. This wholehearted acceptance of its teachings went from the highest to the lowest. Prince Albert's admiration for *In Memoriam* was one of the reasons that Tennyson was appointed Poet Laureate.[1] And Queen Victoria said to Tennyson when he visited her in April, 1862, after the death of the Prince Consort: "Next to the Bible 'In Memoriam' is my comfort."[2]

The poem furnished steady material for the clergy in England. Stanzas and phrases became so incorporated into the common consciousness that by the end of the century there was hardly any significant passage that had not become trite from excessive quotation. But its popularity has diminished with the present-day disregard of

7. *Memoir*, I, 304–305.
8. Herbert J. C. Grierson explains why Tennyson chose the form he did ("The Tennysons," in *The Cambridge History of English Literature*, ed. A. W. Ward and A. R. Waller, XIII, 30): "For each of Tennyson's shorter poems, at any rate —hence, perhaps, his preference of the idyll to the epic—is the expression of a single mood of feeling. . . . In his longer poems, *In Memoriam* and *Idylls of the King* . . . , the plan of construction finally adopted is a concession to this quality of the poet's genius."
9. There have been many separate books devoted to *In Memoriam*. A helpful recent one is Eleanor B. Mattes, *In Memoriam: The Way of a Soul*. The best of the earlier studies is A. C. Bradley, *Commentary on Tennyson's In Memoriam*.
1. *Memoir*, I, 334.
2. *Memoir*, I, 485.

the great soul-searching problems which concerned the Victorians. No longer does it serve the purpose of bolstering faith in the meaning of life. Like *The Princess* and *Maud*, it seems destined to be remembered in sections. Various passages are anthologized, some with great regularity, but seldom is the entire poem read.

* * *

Tennyson effected a compromise between science and religion before Darwin's *The Origin of Species* (1859) called out the main arguments. He had, however, availed himself of several other books whose influence can be seen in his poem. In 1837 he read Sir Charles Lyell's *Principles of Geology* (1830–1833). In October, 1843, he obtained a copy of J. F. W. Herschel's *A Preliminary Discourse on the Study of Natural Philosophy* (1830), which emphasized the progressive development of the human race, both in an existence after death and in succeeding generations on earth.[3] And he used Robert Chambers' *Vestiges of the Natural History of Creation* (1844), which postulated a superior race to come, of which outstanding individuals were to be considered heralds.[4] * * *

* * *

One of the reasons for the poem's popularity was that its spiritual basis was not circumscribed by any specific creed. It is a religious poem, but not specifically Christian, although Charles Kingsley and others thought it to be the noblest Christian poem of several centuries. T. S. Eliot suggests that it deserves to be called religious for another reason than that which made it seem religious to the author's contemporaries. "It is not religious because of the quality of its faith," says Eliot, "but because of the quality of its doubt. Its faith is a poor thing, but its doubt is a very intense experience."[5] And so it seems to the twentieth century, which regards Tennyson as much more pessimistic than his contemporaries thought him to be.

SIR CHARLES TENNYSON

[*In Memoriam*] †

1833

So for Alfred, with writing, revising and study, which was his normal routine of existence, the summer ebbed quietly away at

3. Eleanor B. Mattes, *In Memoriam: The Way of a Soul*, pp. 76, 87, n.8.
4. For Tennyson's indebtedness to the
† From *Alfred Tennyson* (New York, Macmillan, 1949), pp. 143–46. 149–52,

Vestiges see Mattes, pp. 76–87.
5. "In Memoriam," in *Essays Ancient and Modern*, p. 187.
168–70, 177–78, 239–43. 247–48. 253–54.

Somersby. Arthur passed there what time he could spare from his labours at Lincoln's Inn and the two friends spent many happy weeks together at the old Rectory—weeks which Alfred was to remember with piercing regret during the sixty years of life that remained to him. The spirit of them lives in *The Gardener's Daughter*, which was composed at that time. Long afterwards Tennyson told Browning that when he was writing it he felt his life to be in flower and that he wrote baskets full of similar poems, emanations of the same spirit. None of these survives, but there is evidence of the mood which created them in the many exquisite lines and passages which were composed for *The Gardener's Daughter* and discarded because the poet felt it to be complete without them.

This mood was, I think, largely due to a great emotional development which the poet had undergone during the past eighteen months. The eroticism of *The Gardener's Daughter*, though reticent according to modern standards, has a keener edge and a greater directness than any of Tennyson's earlier writings, and these qualities are even more apparent in the early drafts of the poem. No doubt Arthur's engagement to Emily, though it had not in any sense weakened the friendship between him and Alfred, had served to release in his friend emotions, which the exclusiveness of their early affection had tended to absorb. Indeed, I believe that, despite the brutal shock of Croker's article[1] and the clouds hanging over Somersby, those spring and summer months of 1833 were the happiest and fullest that Alfred had yet known. His ripened friendship with Arthur, Arthur's love for Emily, so understanding and so selfless, his own consciousness of growing power, combined to make of that short time the "glad year" for which he was to know such heart-hunger in the days to come.

The friends parted at Somersby towards the end of July, Alfred going to visit in Scotland and Arthur staying on for a while at the Rectory.

At the beginning of August Arthur was to go with his father on a Continental tour. Alfred came down to London from Scotland to see him off, and gave a supper in his lodgings at which Moxon and Leigh Hunt were present. Afterwards he recited glorious fragments of *The Gardener's Daughter*, and the party did not separate till half past four in the morning. The next day the friends went in a troop to see Rogers' famous Gallery of Paintings. In the library of the great man who had defended Alfred as "the most promising genius

1. John Wilson Croker had written an abusive review of Tennyson's *Poems* (1832) in the *Quarterly Review*, 49 (April 1833), 81–96. Tennyson was abnormally sensitive to public criticism, and although Croker's was only one of several hostile reviews he received in the early 1830s, the poet was deeply shocked by the ridicule heaped upon his work. The attack left Tennyson with deep—some say lasting—psychic scars; he never forgot Croker's abuse throughout his life [*Editor*].

of the time" they found a copy of Charles' little volume of 1830, but—as though to rub one more grain of salt into the *Quarterly* sore—no volume by Alfred. The Hallams started in the first week of August and reached Vienna at the end of the month. On September 6th Arthur wrote Alfred a cheerful and enthusiastic letter about the picture galleries there. On September 15th his father, coming back to their hotel (The Goldene Birn) in the afternoon, found his son lying dead in the arm-chair. The news was conveyed to Alfred in a letter from Arthur's uncle, Henry Elton.

At the request of a most afflicted family, I write to you because they are unequal, from the grief into which they have fallen, to do it themselves. Your friend, Sir, and my much loved Nephew, Arthur Hallam, is no more ... May that Being in whose hands are all the destinies of man, and who has promised to comfort all that mourn, pour the balm of consolation on all the families who are bowed by this unexpected dispensation. I have just seen Mr. Hallam, who begs that I will tell you that he will write himself as soon as his heart will let him.

This letter did not arrive till October 1st, when seventeen-year-old Matilda Tennyson, who had been for a dancing lesson to Spilsby, picked it up at the post-office and brought it back with her to Somersby. Strangely enough, one evening early in September, she and Mary had seen a tall figure, clothed in white from head to foot, pass down the lane in front of the Rectory. They followed it until it passed through the hedge, at a point where there was no gap, and disappeared. Matilda had been so awed by this experience that she ran home and burst into tears. Of course this had not been connected with Arthur in anyone's mind as nothing was yet known of his death.

Now Matilda, on reaching home with the unopened letter, went into the Gothic dining-room where Alfred was sitting at table, handed it to him and went on upstairs to take off her hat. He opened the letter, read it, rose and left the room. In a few moments he asked for Emily to be sent to him and broke the news to her alone.

The shock to all Arthur's friends was terrible. The Cambridge circle had for so long regarded him as their centre. With his vivacity, unselfishness and breadth of interests he touched all their lives at so many points, that they seemed almost to have lost a part of themselves. The letters which passed between them as the news reached one after another, and the references in memoirs and poems written years afterwards by Gladstone, Alford, Trench, Milnes and others, all show their deep affection for him as a friend and their profound admiration for his intellectual powers.

To both Alfred and Emily the blow was overwhelming. On Arthur's betrothed it fell at a moment when, after years of trial and disappointment, there seemed good prospect that their hopes would at last be crowned with marriage. For Alfred, a sudden and brutal stroke had annihilated in a moment a love "passing the love of women." The prop, round which his own growth had twined itself for four fruitful years, was suddenly removed. A lifelong prospect, founded on his own friendship and Emily's hoped-for union with his friend, was blotted out instantly and for ever.

During the first months of his sorrow waves of depression swept over him, so dark that he often longed for death. The sudden extinction of his friend, with all his infinite capacity for affection and his brilliant promise, struck at the very roots of his will to live. Could it really be that all this great spiritual treasure was annihilated: that all human love and all man's spiritual effort are but a momentary ripple on the ocean of eternity? Was the world wholly without purpose and man an irresponsible toy for the gigantic forces of Nature? If so, what value could there be in life? What was left but to curse God and die?

These months of suffering intensified the desire, which was to haunt the poet throughout his life, to find an answer to the great and insoluble questions, regarding the survival of the human spirit, the freedom of the human will, and the existence of a divine purpose guiding the universe. Now, under the first shock of his great grief man's fleeting existence seemed to have lost all meaning for him * * *. The wretched state of poor Edward, the fears about Charles and Septimus[2] and the disastrous reception of his own work added to his misery. But his deep-seated love of beauty and his desire to help his mother and Emily were strengthening influences. One of his friends wrote in the early winter: "Alfred, though much broken in spirit, is yet able to divert his thoughts from gloomy brooding and keep his mind in activity"; and at about the same time Trench and FitzGerald both reported that he was writing again and producing very fine new work, besides continuing steadily the revision of what he had already written.

By the end of the year he had already completed or sketched out, *The Two Voices* (originally called *Thoughts of a Suicide*), *Ulysses*, *St. Simeon Stylites*, *St. Agnes*, *Lancelot and Guinevere*, *Sir Galahad* and *The Beggar Maid*. He had also composed some of the most famous sections of *In Memoriam*, and had probably begun the first draft of the *Morte d'Arthur*.

On the last day of the year came a letter from Henry Hallam, saying that the ship which brought Arthur's body had arrived.

2. Three of Tennyson's six brothers. Edward, the youngest, was suffering intermittent periods of mental illness which, as they increased in intensity and dura- tion, eventually rendered him mad and required, at age nineteen, his permanent confinement [*Editor*].

It may remove some anxiety from the mind of yourself and others to know that the mortal part of our dearest Arthur will be interred at Clevedon on Friday. My first thought was not to write to you till all was over, but you may have been apprehensive for the safety of the vessel. I did not expect her arrival so soon. Use your discretion about telling your sister. Mrs. Hallam is very anxious to hear about her. If not too painful to her, Miss Tennyson will have the goodness to write. Do your utmost, my dear young friend, to support her and yourself. Give as little way to grief as you may, but I feel my own rather increases with time: yet I find also that both occupation and conversation are very serviceable. I fear the solitary life you both lead in the country is sadly unpropitious.

With this letter in his hand, Alfred Tennyson saw the sun go down on the year 1833.

* * *

1834–1835

As the year went on, Alfred began to recover slowly from the shock. As usual, he found relief in creative work and study, and the programme which he drew up for himself at this time and which included history, chemistry, botany, electricity, animal physiology, mechanics and theology, showed his determination to increase his capacity to grapple with the great philosophic and religious questions which were more and more absorbing to his thoughts. He had much besides to occupy his mind. The care of his mother and sisters and the business of the household fell entirely on him, for the eldest son was too erratic and tempestuous. Moreover, in July Frederick set out for Italy and the Mediterranean in search of sun and music, his most enduring passion.

* * *

Alfred's chief anxiety was, of course, for Emily. Old Mr. Hallam, whose heart ached with the thought that he might have made Arthur's short life happier had he been more helpful about his marriage, had announced his intention of allowing her three hundred pounds a year, and asked her to visit him at Molesey Park, where he was then living. This would be her first introduction to him, although it was more than two years since she had become engaged to Arthur. Emily felt the old man's belated kindness deeply and was eager to take advantage of it as soon as she could. "What is life to me?" she wrote. "If I die (which the Tennysons never do) the effort shall be made." She thought that Arthur's sister Ellen might prove the friend to remove in some degree the horrible feeling of desolation which was ever at her heart.

In the early summer there arrived copies of Arthur Hallam's literary remains, which his father had collected and edited with a short memoir. Alfred dutifully sent a copy of this to his grandfather with the following letter:

My dear Grandfather,
Mr. Hallam has sent me some copies of a work printed for private circulation amongst his friends containing the literary remains of his son, my ever lamented friend, Arthur Hallam. I thought it would not be unpleasing to you, as the Head of that family to which had he lived he would have been allied yet more closely than he was by the bonds of friendship, to receive a copy from me. I wish indeed that he had had more frequent opportunities of conversing with and seeing you. I am sure you could not have failed of loving and admiring the many excellent qualities for which his contemporaries esteemed him—but Life and Death are in the hands of God.
Mr. Hallam wrote to me some time ago to draw up a Memoir of his son's life and character—but at that time my heart seemed too crushed and all my energies too paralysed to permit me any compliance with his request, otherwise I had not been found wanting in the dearest office I could discharge to the memory of one whom I can never forget. . . .

*   *   *

All the year he had continued to work steadily at the revision of his published poems and had composed many new ones. Before starting for London he wrote to James Spedding offering to insert the corrections, on which he had decided, in James's copy of the volume of 1833, and sending him drafts of various new pieces. * * * He was making steady progress, too, with the early sections of *In Memoriam*, and the ship stanzas and the first Christmas section were already circulating among his friends. He had been encouraged by some signs of a friendlier disposition in the press. A favourable notice in the *Calcutta Journal* stimulated him to finish his "Sleeping Beauty," and in March the *Oxford Magazine* had published a short article expressing disapproval of the line taken by *Blackwood's* and the *Quarterly*. "If Alfred Tennyson is more laughed over than wept over," said the writer, "anyone can laugh —some eyes are naturally dry."

*   *   *

1836–1837

On the whole this seems to have been a time of comparative stagnation with Alfred. There is no mention of visits to London or meetings with friends and no record of any new poems completed, though no doubt he was working away intermittently at the elegies which were later to be united and completed in *In Memoriam*.

It was also a time of depression and unrest, for the idea of leaving Somersby was in all their minds and there were other unsettling influences. * * *

In the end, the decision to leave Somersby was precipitated by the desire of the Burton family to take over the Rectory. Beech Hill House at High Beech, Epping was chosen and the move entirely managed by Alfred, who could, when need arose, be most severely and economically practical. Not only did he carry through the business transaction, but every bit of furniture and equipment, including pots and pans and garden tools, was bought by him.

He was, on the whole, glad of the change, though it was to cause him much sadness. "A known landskip," he wrote to Emily Sellwood, after he had left Lincolnshire, "is to me an old friend that continually talks to me of my own youth and half-forgotten things, and indeed, does more for me than many an old friend that I know." Every corner of the little house and garden was endeared to him by poignant memories of childhood and boyhood, and of Arthur, and he knew in his heart that no other country could ever so wind itself into his affections as the high wolds, the green dyke-trenched fenland, the long ridged dunes and the magnificent rolling seas of Lincolnshire.

* * * He could not help feeling a sense of relief and hopefulness in thus breaking away from the past, with all its griefs and troubles. Once more there was conflict between his desire to seclude himself, to muse and brood and live in memory, and his sympathy with the broad stream of human life and human progress, towards which he felt himself at times irresistibly drawn.

This phase of his emotions is illustrated in the mystical poem which forms Section C.III of *In Memoriam* and describes a dream which visited the poet on the night before his departure from his old home, and which, he says, left his "aftermorn content." He dreamed that he was living in a great hall surrounded by maidens, singing of "what is wise and good and graceful." They sang to a veiled figure in the centre, which he realized to be Arthur. Then came a summons to the poet from the sea. The maidens wept and wailed at the thought of departure, but they led him to the river, down which they voyaged in a little boat. As the river widened, the maidens gradually gathered strength and grace and the poet, too, grew in spirit and stature till he felt

The thews of Anakim,
The pulses of a Titan's heart.

At last they reach the sea, where a great ship lifts her shining sides and from the deck Arthur, now grown to a figure of supernatural grandeur, bends to greet them. Alfred hastens up the side of the ship to fall on his friend's neck, leaving the maidens, who beg to be allowed to follow.

"We served thee here," they said, "so long,
And wilt thou leave us now behind?"

Arthur bids them enter the ship and the party steer together to the open sea.

* * *

1839–1840

On September 5th, 1840, Carlyle described him as follows:

A fine, large-featured, dim-eyed, bronze-coloured, shaggy-headed man is Alfred; dusty, smoky, free and easy; who swims outwardly and inwardly, with great composure in an articulate element as of tranquil chaos and tobacco smoke: great now and then when he does emerge: a most restful, brotherly, solid-hearted man.

In another letter, written when he had got to know Alfred better, he spoke of him "as one of the few British and foreign figures who are and remain beautiful to me, a true human soul ... I do not meet in these late decades such company over a pipe." Indeed, the only thing which he criticized in his new friend was his profession. He considered him a "life-guardsman spoilt by making poetry."

More important than all this social activity was Alfred's engagement to Emily Sellwood, which was recognized by the Sellwoods early in 1838. It has, I think, not been noticed before that the last date in the time sequence of *In Memoriam* is April, 1838—the April following the move from Somersby. The reference occurs in the two beautiful spring sections—C.XV and C.XVI, which open what Tennyson himself defined as the closing division of the poem, and lead straight on to its serenely triumphant conclusion. There is no mention of the engagement in these stanzas, but the reference to this springtime and the mood in which the poem closes, are strong evidence that he regarded it as having brought to an end the long period of depression following Arthur's death, and given him a new hope and a new purpose in life. I think that a good part of this last sequence of *In Memoriam* was probably written during the next two years.

He was now much more cheerful than at any time since Arthur's death and was composing more freely, though Milnes said that nothing would persuade him to write down what he composed. The first rush of lyrical inspiration, which had sustained him up to the beginning of 1835, had faded away and he was able to look at the world with more serenity and detachment. * * *

1850

The new year (the middle year of the century) was to end the time of grief, loneliness and disappointment through which Alfred had struggled so distressfully since Arthur Hallam's death, and to bring him prosperity, fame and, better than either of these, the foundation of a deep and lasting happiness. And it was to Arthur's spirit and his own consecration of their friendship that he was to owe this consummation.

Although there is no direct evidence, it seems that some time before the end of the year he had renewed correspondence with Emily Sellwood. The only indication of this is Hallam Tennyson's statement that he sent her two versions of the song "Sweet and Low," so that she might choose which should be inserted in the third edition of *The Princess*. This edition was published at the beginning of February, 1850, and must have gone to the printers before the end of the preceding year. I have in my possession the manuscript of an unpublished version of this song (which is quoted in Hallam Tennyson's *Memoir*) very beautifully written in the poet's hand, signed by him and dated November 24th, 1849. He very rarely signed or dated any manuscript, and I believe this to be the identical copy which he sent to Emily and November 24th the date on which it was sent.

The causes leading up to the renewal of relations between the lovers will probably never be exactly discovered. I do not think that he met either Emily or her father before the end of the year, for they had left Lincolnshire by this time and were living at Hale, in Surrey. He had only seen her once since they had parted in 1839 and that had been by accident. Thinking that he was in Italy, she had gone to visit Cecilia at Maidstone. On the first morning of her visit Alfred had walked into the house before breakfast and she had felt it her duty to leave as soon as possible. A very important factor was the reunion of Charles Tennyson with his wife, Louisa, Emily Sellwood's sister, which took place some time during the last half of 1849. Charles had for many years been quite free of the opium habit, and Louisa's mental health was now fully restored. As there had never been any doubt of their mutual affection, there was every reason for them to come together again and every prospect of their being able to settle down to a happy married life.

Alfred met Charles in London during the first half of December, and it seems likely that he then asked his brother to sound the Sellwoods about the possibility of a renewal of his engagement, which Charles very readily undertook to do. From the worldly point of view, the renewal was much easier to justify than ever before. Alfred had now an income of about five hundred pounds a year, including his pension. *The Princess* was still selling well and Moxon, to whom he showed the completed manuscript of *The Elegies* during this visit to London, was eager to publish them and offered an advance of three hundred pounds. Moxon's enthusiasm, and his own hopes in regard to Emily, decided Alfred to print *The Elegies*, though he had not yet definitely made up his mind about publication. He stayed in London till the end of January, but, with his usual shrinking from personal publicity, kept his new hopes and intentions secret from everyone. The friends who saw him during these weeks, had no idea of the impending change, though a letter from Fitz suggests that he thought him in unusually good spirits.

> I found A.T. in Chambers at Lincoln's Inn [he wrote in January], and recreated myself with a sight of his fine old mug and got out of him all his dear old stories and many new ones. I wish I could take 20 years off his shoulders and set him up in his youthful glory. He is the same magnanimous, kindly, delightful fellow as ever, uttering by far the finest prose sayings of any one.

His hesitation in deciding on the publication of *The Elegies* nearly led to the manuscript being lost altogether, for when he went down to Bonchurch in February, he accidentally left it in the London lodgings in Mornington Place, which he was vacating. This carelessness about his manuscript was, like his carelessness about writing down his poems, due in part to his feeling that they were living things, part of his own being, with a life quite independent of any visible existence. This was particularly true of *The Elegies*, which had been with him as an intimate record of his emotions for sixteen years, and enshrined so many of the thoughts and aspirations which he had discussed with Arthur during their five years of friendship. He had never contemplated weaving them into a whole, or publishing them, until he found how many he had written, but had jotted them down as they occurred to him, wherever he happened to be. Now, finding that the manuscript book was missing, he wrote to Coventry Patmore from Bonchurch with characteristic calm:

> My dear Coventry,
> I went up to my room yesterday to get my book of Elegies: you know what I mean, a long Butcher ledger-like book. I was going to read one or two to an artist here: I could not find it. I have some obscure remembrance of having lent it to you. If so, all is well. If not, will you go to my old chambers and institute a vigorous inquiry? I was coming up today on purpose to look after it, but as the weather is so furious I have yielded to the wishes of my friend here to stop till tomorrow. . . .

Patmore had considerable difficulty in gaining access to the room which Alfred had occupied, as it was now let to someone else. Indeed, the landlady stoutly refused him admittance, but he pushed past her, ran upstairs and, after some search, found the "butcher's book" at the back of the cupboard in which the poet had been used to keep his tea and bread and butter.

Even then Alfred does not seem to have made up his mind to immediate publication, but he had a few copies struck off by the printers and distributed to chosen friends, under the title *Fragments of an Elegy*. These contained ten sections less than the first published edition. Usually Tennyson circulated these privately printed copies some months before publication and gave them prolonged study, and that may have been his intention now, for Patmore told William Rossetti on March 21st that *The Elegies* would probably not be published till about Christmas.

All this time little progress seems to have been made towards a renewal of Alfred's engagement. There was probably still some reluctance on the part of the Sellwoods, largely on religious grounds. But these difficulties were soon to be resolved. Amongst the friends to whom Alfred sent copies of *The Elegies* was Drummond Rawnsley, now vicar of Shiplake-on-Thames. Catherine Rawnsley, Emily's cousin, who was most eager to bring the two lovers together again, obtained Alfred's leave to send Drummond's copy to Emily so that she might read it and return it to the poet. On April 1st Emily wrote Catherine a letter in which she set out a copy of a note which she had sent to Alfred. This, as will be seen, suggests that she was still far from a definite understanding with him.

April 1st, 1850.

My dearest Katie,

. . . Do you really think I should write a line with the Elegies, that is in a separate note, to say I have returned them? I am almost afraid, but since you say I am to do so I will, only I cannot say what I feel . . . You and Drummond are among the best and kindest friends I have in the world, and let me not be ungrateful, I have some very good and very kind. The longer I live the more I feel how blessed I am in this way. Now I must say goodbye—

Thy loving sister,
Emily

P.S. I thought I would write my note before the others came. Here it is, no beginning nor end, not a note at all, a sort of label only. "Katie told me the poems might be kept until Saturday. I hope I shall not have occasioned any inconvenience by keeping them to the limit of time; and if I have I must be forgiven, for I cannot willingly part from what is so precious. The thanks I would say for them and for the faith in me which has trusted them to me must be thought for me, I cannot write them. I have read the poems through and through and through and to me they were and they are ever more and more a spirit monument grand and beautiful, in whose presence I feel admiration and delight, not unmixed with awe. The happiest possible end to this labour of love! But think not its fruits shall so soon perish, for they are life in life, and they shall live, and as years go on be only the more fully known and loved and reverenced for what they are.

"So says a true seer. Can anyone guess the name of this seer? After such big words shall I put anything about my own little I? —that I am the happier for having seen these poems and that I hope I shall be the better too."

I cannot enter into things more particularly with him. I only hope he will not be vexed by this apology of a note.

Catherine followed up energetically the powerful effect made by the reading of Alfred's poem; and Charles Kingsley, a close friend of Drummond's and an ardent admirer of Alfred's work, who met Emily at the Shiplake rectory soon afterwards, added his strong pressure.

Just two months later, on the 1st of June, *In Memoriam* was published. Less than a fortnight afterwards, on June 13th, Alfred and Emily were married.

It is difficult to avoid the inference that the two events were closely connected, that the study of the poem finally removed Emily's scruples and those of her father, and that the decision to marry induced Alfred to give the order for publication.

* * *

The four months which passed since Alfred's marriage had not only brought him assurance of spiritual happiness and peace; they brought him also fame and a reasonable prospect of material prosperity. He had sent *In Memoriam* out into the world with even more than his usual reticence. Many of his friends—even Henry Hallam—were left in ignorance of the intended publication, and there had been a complete absence of preliminary announcements. Moreover, the plain little purple volume was issued anonymously, without anything to indicate its authorship. The title *In Memoriam*, suggested by Emily and surely a stroke of genius, held out no specious allurements to the reader. There was no indication as to the identity of the "A.H.H." who was mentioned in the sub-title, no publisher's blurb to explain why he had been judged worthy of such commemoration. No doubt Moxon took care to let literary London know who was in fact the author of the poem, but many reviews were written in ignorance of this.

In the circumstances it is surprising that from the very first *In Memoriam* was favourably received by the critics. John Forster led the way with an enthusiastic notice in *The Examiner* on June 8th. A week later came another in the *Atlas*. *Tait's* heralded it as the "creation of the first poet of the day," and Fraser's as "the noblest English Christian poem which several centuries have seen." Most of the critics, however, agreed that, owing to the unavoidable monotony of its subject and the method of presentation, *In Memoriam* could not hope to be popular. In this they were singularly at fault. Tennyson had 5,000 copies printed for the first edition, which was at his own risk, for he had made a new arrangement with Moxon under which he paid all the expenses and gave the publisher one-third of the profits and 5 per cent on gross sales, keeping the balance of the profits for himself. In this way he retained a firmer control over the printing and publishing arrangements and, of course, stood to benefit more by the success of the book, though he took all the risk of loss.

The change of policy was evidence of the poet's increased self-confidence and of his sound business instinct. It was fully justified by events, for the first 5,000 copies were sold out in a few weeks. A second edition had to be issued in the middle of July, a third at the end of November. In a few months no less than 60,000 copies had passed into circulation.

* * *

The overwhelming success of *In Memoriam* could not have come at a more opportune moment for Tennyson. Five weeks before its publication Wordsworth, the Poet Laureate, had died, and the literary world immediately began to cast about for a successor. Many candidates were put forward—such as Leigh Hunt, Henry Taylor, "Barry Cornwall," Charles Mackay, Elizabeth Barrett Browning and, with less confidence, her husband, Robert. Tennyson was, of course, amongst those mentioned, even before the publication of *In Memoriam*, but there does not seem to have been any strong party in his favour, for the success which he had achieved was still within a very limited sphere. When his name was suggested to the Under-Secretary of State for the Home Department, George Cornwall Lewis, a fine classical scholar who was to become editor of the *Edinburgh Review* two years later, Lewis expressed surprise that Tennyson should be considered at all, as he was so little known to the public.

There was one obvious course for the Government to adopt which would be sure to receive widespread approval: to offer the post to Samuel Rogers. Rogers' first popular success, "The Pleasures of Memory," had been published nearly sixty years before and he had been for forty years one of the leading figures in London Society, a discerning patron of literature and art, whose ardent ambition and refined taste had enabled him, with only moderate poetical endowments, to produce poems which achieved wide popularity while earning the respect of cultivated opinion. His appointment offered the Government an excellent solution of an embarrassing problem, and he was accordingly approached by the Prince Consort on behalf of the Queen at the beginning of May. But Rogers was eighty-seven years old and he refused on the score of age.

When his refusal became known, discussion broke out again, the two candidates most favoured by the press now being Elizabeth Browning and Leigh Hunt. Mrs. Browning's case was urged by H. F. Chorley of *The Athenaeum*, who strongly opposed the claims made on behalf of Tennyson, on the ground that he was already in receipt of a State pension and that the very small amount of money available for the support of literature ought to be distributed as widely as possible. Mrs. Browning's claim he pressed particularly on the ground that a woman would be the most suitable holder of the office under a female Sovereign. Leigh Hunt had no scruple in urging his own claims. His autobiography, which was published in June, included a long discussion as to his suitability and set out the arguments which might be advanced against him on religious and political grounds. He made it clear that if these arguments were not considered valid, he thought himself very well fitted for the position and would be glad to accept it.

The extraordinary effect produced on lovers of poetry by *In Memoriam* during the summer and autumn, introduced a completely new factor. Amongst the greatest admirers of the poem was the Prince Consort. On October 2nd an inquiry about Tennyson's personal character was addressed by the Prime Minister (Lord John Russell) to Rogers, and on November 5th a letter was written to the poet from Windsor Castle offering him the Laureateship. The offer came as a complete surprise to him. Living in happy seclusion with Emily at Tent Lodge, he had heard little of the controversy, which had been going on since Rogers' refusal in the spring, and, in spite of the considerable extent to which his claims had been canvassed, he had absolutely no idea that he was likely to be selected. It must, therefore, be considered a curious and entertaining coincidence that, the night before the Royal letter reached him, he dreamed that Prince Albert came and kissed him on the cheek, and that he commented to himself in his dream, "Very kind, but very German."

He took the whole day to consider the offer, writing two letters, one of acceptance and one of refusal, and making up his mind to decide which he would send after discussing the question at dinner with his friends. Their advice was for acceptance, and next day the acceptance was sent.

*   *   *

ALFRED, LORD TENNYSON

[On *In Memoriam:* Extract from a Letter
by Tennyson to Emily Sellwood, 1839]†

"Why has God created souls knowing they would sin and
suffer?" a question unanswerable. Man is greater than all animals
because he is capable of moral good and evil, tho' perhaps dogs and
elephants, and some of the higher mammalia have a little of this
capability. God might have made me a beast: but He thought good
to give me power, to set Good and Evil before me that I might
shape my own path. The happiness, resulting from this power well
exercised, must in the end exceed the mere physical happiness of
breathing, eating, and sleeping like an ox. Can we say that God pre-
fers higher happiness in some to a lower happiness in all? It is a
hard thing that if I sin and fail I should be sacrificed to the bliss of
the Saints. Yet what reasonable creature, if he could have been askt
beforehand, would not have said, "Give me the metaphysical power;
let me be the lord of my decisions; leave physical quietude and dull
pleasure to lower lives." All souls methinks would have answered
thus, and so had men suffered by their own choice, as now by the
necessity of being born what they are, but there is no answer to
these questions except in a great *hope* of universal good: and even
then one might ask, why has God made one to suffer more than
another, why is it not meted equally to all? Let us be silent, for we
know nothing of these things, and we trust there is One who knows
all. God cannot be cruel. If he were, the heart could only find relief
in the wildest blasphemies, which would cease to be blasphemies.
God must be all powerful, else the soul could never deem Him
worthy of her highest worship. Let us leave it therefore to God, as
to the wisest. Who knows whether revelation be not itself a veil to
hide the glory of that Love which we could not look upon without
marring our sight, and our onward progress? If it were proclaimed
as a truth "No man shall perish: all shall live, after a certain time
shall have gone by, in bliss with God" such a truth might tell well
with one or two lofty spirits, but would be the hindrance of the
world.

* * *

At first the reviews of [*In Memoriam*] were not on the whole

---

† From Hallam, Lord Tennyson, *Alfred,
Lord Tennyson: A Memoir* (New York,
Macmillan, 1897), I, 170–71, 298, 300–1,
312–14, 321–24. After Tennyson's death
his son Hallam wrote and published this
Memoir. The "I" in the book is there-
fore Hallam, except, of course, in those
passages where he is quoting the words
of his father. The author's footnotes
have been omitted.

sympathetic. One critic in a leading journal, for instance, considered that "a great deal of poetic feeling had been wasted," and "much shallow art spent on the tenderness shown to an Amaryllis of the Chancery Bar." Another referred to the poem as follows: "These touching lines evidently come from the full heart of the widow of a military man." However, men like Maurice and Robertson thought that the author had made a definite step towards the unification of the highest religion and philosophy with the progressive science of the day; and that he was the one poet who "through almost the agonies of a death-struggle" had made an effective stand against his own doubts and difficulties and those of the time, "on behalf of those first principles which underlie all creeds, which belong to our earliest childhood, and on which the wisest and best have rested through all ages; that all is right; that darkness shall be clear; that God and Time are the only interpreters; that Love is King; that the Immortal is in us; that, which is the keynote of the whole, 'All is well, tho' Faith and Form be sundered in the night of Fear.'" Scientific leaders like Herschel, Owen, Sedgwick and Tyndall regarded him as a champion of Science, and cheered him with words of genuine admiration for his love of Nature, for the eagerness with which he welcomed all the latest scientific discoveries, and for his trust in truth. Science indeed in his opinion was one of the main forces tending to disperse the superstition that still darkens the world.

* * *

"It must be remembered," writes my father, "that this is a poem, *not* an actual biography. It is founded on our friendship, on the engagement of Arthur Hallam to my sister, on his sudden death at Vienna, just before the time fixed for their marriage, and on his burial at Clevedon Church. The poem concludes with the marriage of my youngest sister Cecilia. It was meant to be a kind of *Divina Commedia*, ending with happiness. The sections were written at many different places, and as the phases of our intercourse came to my memory and suggested them. I did not write them with any view of weaving them into a whole, or for publication, until I found that I had written so many. The different moods of sorrow as in a drama are dramatically given, and my conviction that fear, doubts, and suffering will find answer and relief only through Faith in a God of Love. 'I' is not always the author speaking of himself, but the voice of the human race speaking thro' him. After the Death of A. H. H., the divisions of the poem are made by First Xmas Eve (Section xxviii.), Second Xmas (lxxviii.), Third Xmas Eve (civ. and cv. etc.). I myself did not see Clevedon till years after the burial of A. H. H. Jan. 3rd, 1834, and then in later editions of 'In Memoriam' I altered the word 'chancel,' which was the word used by Mr. Hallam in his Memoir, to 'dark church.' As to the localities

in which the poems were written, some were written in Lincoln-
shire, some in London, Essex, Gloucestershire, Wales, anywhere
where I happened to be."

"And as for the metre of 'In Memoriam' I had no notion till
1880 that Lord Herbert of Cherbury had written his occasional
verses in the same metre. I believed myself the originator of the
metre, until after 'In Memoriam' came out, when some one told me
that Ben Jonson and Sir Philip Sidney had used it. * * *"

* * *

"Personality," as far as our intelligence goes, is the widest definition
and includes "Mind," "Self-consciousness," "Will," "Love" and
other attributes of the Real, the Supreme, "the High and Lofty
One that inhabiteth Eternity Whose name is Holy."

* * *

Everywhere throughout the Universe he saw the glory and
greatness of God, and the science of Nature was particularly dear to
him. Every new fact which came within his range was carefully
weighed. As he exulted in the wilder aspects of Nature (see for
instance sect. xv.) and revelled in the thunderstorm; so he felt a joy
in her orderliness; he felt a rest in her steadfastness, patient progress
and hopefulness; the same seasons ever returned; the same stars
wheeled in their courses; the flowers and trees blossomed and the
birds sang yearly in their appointed months; and he had a trium-
phant appreciation of her ever-new revelations of beauty. One of
the "In Memoriam" poems, written at Barmouth, gives preemi-
nently his sense of the joyous peace in Nature, and he would quote
it in this context along with his Spring and Bird songs:

[Here Hallam Tennyson quotes Section 86 of *In Memoriam*.]

But he was occasionally much troubled with the intellectual prob-
lem of the apparent profusion and waste of life and by the vast
amount of sin and suffering throughout the world, for these seemed
to militate against the idea of the Omnipotent and All-loving Father.

No doubt in such moments he might possibly have been heard to
say what I myself have heard him say: "An Omnipotent Creator
Who could make such a painful world is to me *sometimes* as hard
to believe in as to believe in blind matter behind everything. The
lavish profusion too in the natural world appals me, from the
growths of the tropical forest to the capacity of man to multiply,
the torrent of babies."

"I can almost understand some of the Gnostic heresies, which
only after all put the difficulty one step further back":

> O me! for why is all around us here
> As if some lesser god had made the world,

But had not force to shape it as he would,
Till the High God behold it from beyond
And enter it, and make it beautiful?

After one of these moods in the summer of 1892 he exclaimed: "Yet God *is* love, transcendent, all-pervading! We do not get *this* faith from Nature or the world. If we look at Nature alone, full of perfection and imperfection, she tells us that God is disease, murder and rapine. We get this faith from ourselves, from what is highest within us, which recognizes that there is not one fruitless pang, just as there is not one lost good."

* * *

I need not enlarge upon his faith in the Immortality of the Soul as he has dwelt upon that so fully in his poems. "I can hardly understand," he said, "how any great, imaginative man, who has deeply lived, suffered, thought and wrought, can doubt of the Soul's continuous progress in the after-life." His poem of "Wages" he liked to quote on this subject.

He more than once said what he has expressed in "Vastness": "Hast Thou made all this for naught! Is all this trouble of life worth undergoing if we only end in our own corpse-coffins at last? If you allow a God, and God allows this strong instinct and universal yearning for another life, surely that is in a measure a presumption of its truth. We cannot give up the mighty hopes that make us men."

* * *

I have heard him even say that he "would rather know that he was to be lost eternally than not know that the whole human race was to live eternally"; and when he speaks of "faintly trusting the larger hope" he means by "the larger hope" that the whole human race would through, perhaps, ages of suffering, be at length purified and saved, even those who now "better not with time"; so that at the end of "The Vision of Sin" we read

God made Himself an awful rose of dawn.

Letters were not unfrequently addressed to him asking what his opinions were about Evolution, * * *

Of Evolution he said: "That makes no difference to me, even if the Darwinians did not, as they do, exaggerate Darwinism. To God all is present. He sees present, past, and future as one."

* * *

In the poem "By an Evolutionist," written in 1888 when he was dangerously ill, he defined his position; he conceived that the further science progressed, the more the Unity of Nature, and the purpose hidden behind the cosmic process of matter in motion and changing forms of life, would be apparent. Someone asked him whether it was not hard to account for genius by Evolution. He put aside the question, for he believed that genius was the greatest mystery to itself.

To Tyndall he once said, "No evolutionist is able to explain the mind of Man or how any possible physiological change of tissue can produce conscious thought." Yet he was inclined to think that the theory of Evolution caused the world to regard more clearly the "Life of Nature as a lower stage in the manifestation of a principle which is more fully manifested in the spiritual life of man, with the idea that in this process of Evolution the lower is to be regarded as a means to the higher."

In "Maud" he spoke of the making of man:

As nine months go to the shaping an infant ripe for his birth,
So many a million of ages have gone to the making of man:
He now is first, but is he the last?

The answer he would give to this query was: "No, mankind is as yet on one of the lowest rungs of the ladder, although every man has and has had from everlasting his true and perfect being in the Divine Consciousness."

* * *

ELEANOR B. MATTES

The Challenge of Geology to Belief in Immortality and a God of Love†

i

As far as "the way of the soul" was concerned, the year 1837 brought Tennyson an experience more crucial to the further development of *In Memoriam* than either the moment of mystical union with Hallam or the departure from Somersby; for "during some months" of that year he was "deeply immersed in . . . Lyell's Geology."[1]

† From *In Memoriam: The Way of a Soul* (New York, Exposition Press, 1951), pp. 55–61, 73–86, 111–25.
1. *Memoir*, I 162. Lyell's *Principles of Geology* was in its fourth edition by 1835, but the schedule of studies that Tennyson set for himself after publishing the *Poems* of 1832 apparently did not include geology (*ibid.*, I, 124). Edward Fitzgerald and John Sterling also read Lyell's *Geology* for the first time in 1837

(William Aldis Wright, ed., *Letters and Literary Remains of Edward Fitzgerald* [London and New York, the Macmillan Co., 1889], I, 40; and Thomas Carlyle, *The Life of John Sterling* [London, Chapman and Hall, 1870], p. 181). So the book may have received some special review or other notice in that year, which drew it to the attention of Tennyson and his friends.

Charles Lyell's *Principles of Geology*, which appeared in three volumes from 1830–1833, proved revolutionary not only to the geologic theories of the period but to religious thought as well. On the basis of studies made by his predecessors and his own geologic observations over a number of years, Lyell sought to demonstrate that the present state of the earth is wholly the result of natural forces like wind and water erosion, rock faulting, and sedimentation, operating over long periods of time. This hypothesis challenged Cuvier's theory that various catastrophic disturbances were responsible for the present configurations of the earth. In his second volume Lyell then proceeded to explain that the continual physical changes which geology revealed pointed to the certain extinction of species after species throughout the earth's history, as they found themselves unable to cope with the new conditions they encountered.

None of Lyell's conclusions were actually new. James Hutton, in his *Theory of the Earth*, published in 1795, had asserted that one can account for all the past changes of the earth's surface by reference to natural forces still in operation. And the French naturalist Buffon had insisted upon the inevitable extinction of man and all his works.

But Hutton's *Theory of the Earth* had no popular sale like that of Lyell's *Geology*, and Buffon had few English readers. The whole situation in England was, moreover, markedly different from that in France, where the astronomer Laplace is said to have brushed aside Napoleon's question as to where the Creator figured in his nebular theory, with the reply, "Sire, I have no need of that hypothesis." In England, in the early 1830's, the official Church of England theology was predominantly rationalist, and the outstanding scientists were also religious men, so that there had been no serious questioning of the eighteenth-century assumption that science is the handmaid of religion, since it leads men to appreciate "the Power, Wisdom, and Goodness of God as manifested in the Creation."[2] And as late as 1837, when the distinguished geologist Adam Sedgwick was Chairman of the British Association (for the advancement of scientific research), he concluded its annual meeting by declaring that if he found his science "interfere in any of its tenets with the representations of doctrines of Scripture, he would dash it to the ground."[3]

Lyell, although he by no means shared Sedgwick's sentiments, was no iconoclast, and he therefore did everything possible to con-

2. The Earl of Bridgewater left £8,000 in 1829 to subsidize various works on this theme. See Notice prefixed to William Whewell, *Astronomy and General Physics Considered with Reference to Natural Theology* (London, Pickering, 1836), p. ix; for Whewell's *Astronomy and General Physics* is Treatise III in the series of Bridgewater Treatises financed by this subsidy.

3. Caroline Fox, *Memories of Old Friends, Being Extracts from the Journals and Letters of Caroline Fox from 1835 to 1871* (Philadelphia, J. B. Lippincott and Co., 1882), p. 25.

ceal the disturbing religious implications of his theories. He found that most churchmen were willing to accept almost any description of the *manner* of God's activity in the universe, so long as the *fact* of such divine activity was affirmed. He accordingly cloaked and minimized the revolutionary nature of his conclusions, as he disclosed in a confidential statement of his strategy:

> If you don't triumph over them, but compliment the liberality and candour of the present age, the bishops and enlightened saints will join us in despising both the ancient and modern physico-theologians. . . . I give you my word that full *half* of my history and comments was cut out, and even many facts; because . . . I . . . felt that it was anticipating twenty or thirty years of the

march of honest feeling to declare it undisguisedly.[4]
And those who read to the end of the *Principles of Geology* might well have any uncomfortable doubts allayed by its eloquent, pious conclusion:

> In vain do we aspire to assign limits to the works of creation in *space*, whether we examine the starry heavens, or that world of minute animalcules which is revealed to us by the microscope. We are prepared, therefore, to find that in *time* also, the confines of the universe lie beyond the reach of mortal ken. But in whatever direction we pursue our researches, whether in time or space, we discover everywhere the clear proofs of a Creative Intelligence, and of His foresight, wisdom, and power.[5]

For Tennyson, however, such a conclusion—if he read it—did not gloss over the shocking implications that he sensed in Lyell's descriptions of geologic process. He had never been interested in the deist's Master Mind, nor convinced that His existence and wisdom could be demonstrated from the wonders of nature. When the Apostles at Cambridge had asked: "Is an intelligible First Cause deducible from the phenomena of the Universe?" he had voted "no."[6] And when he looked through a microscope at the minute life it revealed he said: "Strange that these wonders should draw some men to God and repel others. No more reason in one than in the other."[7] But in the early sections of *In Memoriam* he had assumed, with Wordsworth, that nature does testify to immortality, and had repeatedly affirmed the eternal quality of love. Lyell's conclusions challenged both these premises, the first directly, the second implicitly; and the next phase of *In Memoriam* was the recording of Tennyson's reaction to this shock.

4. Mrs. (Katherine) Lyell, ed., *Life, Letters and Journals of Sir Charles Lyell* (London, J. Murray, 1881), I, 271.
5. Charles Lyell, *Principles of Geology, Being an Attempt to Explain the Former Changes of the Earth's Surface, by Reference to Causes Now in Operation* (1st ed.; London, 1830–33), III, 384.
6. *Memoir*, I, 44, n. 1.
7. *Ibid.*, I, 102.

ii

Writing a hundred years earlier than Lyell, Joseph Butler had challenged the supposed "reasonableness" of natural religion by pointing out that nature by no means shares the solicitous concern for every creature which the New Testament ascribes to God, since "of the numerous Seeds of Vegetables and Bodies of Animals, which are adapted and put in the Way, to improve to such a Point or State of natural Maturity and Perfection, we do not see perhaps that one in a million actually does."[8] And Tennyson, who must have read Butler's *Analogy of Religion* at Cambridge if not before,[9] may have been indebted to this thought in section 55 of *In Memoriam*:

> Are God and Nature then at strife,
> That Nature lends such evil dreams?
> So careful of the type she seems,
> So careless of the single life;
>
> That I, considering everywhere
> Her secret meaning in her deeds,
> And finding that of fifty seeds
> She often brings but one to bear,
>
> I falter where I firmly trod.   (55:5–13)

But it was almost certainly his reading in the *Principles of Geology* that led Tennyson to write section 56.

Lyell's second volume has this disconcerting quotation[1] on its title page: "The inhabitants of the globe, like all the other parts of it, are subject to change. It is not only the individual that perishes, but whole species."[2] The volume then presents an accumulation of evidence which leads relentlessly to the conclusion that

... the reader has only to reflect on what we have said of the habitations and the stations of organic beings in general, and to consider them in relation to those effects ... resulting from the ingneous and aqueous causes now in action, and he will immediately perceive that, amidst the vicissitudes of the earth's surface, species cannot be immortal, but must perish one after the other, like the individuals which compose them.[3]

Section 56 of *In Memoriam* takes up the assumption of section 55 and gives it the drastic revision required by Lyell's findings:

> "So careful of the type?" but no.
> From scarped cliff and quarried stone

8. Butler, *op. cit.*, p. 146.
9. See n. 13, Chapter IV, above.
1. From John Playfair's *Illustrations of* the Huttonian Theory.
2. Charles Lyell, *op. cit.*, II, title page.
3. *Ibid.*, II, 168–69.

> She cries, "A thousand types are gone;
> I care for nothing, all shall go.
>
> "Thou makest thine appeal to me:
> I bring to life, I bring to death:
> The spirit does but mean the breadth:
> I know no more." (56:1–8)

It states in specific and personal terms what these findings imply for man's hope of immortality:

> And he, shall he,
> Man, her last work, who seem'd so fair,
> Such splendid purpose in his eyes, (56:8–10)
> . . . .
> Be blown about the desert dust,
> Or seal'd within the iron hills?
> No more? . . . (56:19–21)

and the lines echo Lyell's conclusion " 'that none of the works of a mortal being can be eternal.' . . . And even when they have been included in rocky strata, . . . they must nevertheless eventually perish, for every year some portion of the earth's crust is shattered by earthquakes or melted by volcanic fire, or ground to dust by the moving waters on the surface."[4] It recognizes that Lyell's theory of natural laws operating ruthlessly throughout the earth's history is incompatible with belief that God is love and love is the law of creation (56:13–14). And it suggests that a horrible mockery and self-delusion permeates the entire structure of Western civilization, in which men build churches to worship a God of love whom nature disproves, and fight for supposedly eternal values like truth and justice, which die with the species that cherishes them.

It is easy to see how the whole fabric of assurance that Tennyson had woven in the earlier-written sections seemed destroyed by his reading of Lyell. The arguments for immortality he found in Wordsworth, and Isaac Taylor's confident assertions that the departed retain their affections for their earthly friends in their new spheres of life, took for granted a benevolent Nature and a loving God, which all Lyell's evidence seemed to deny. And, although Tennyson could long for his dead friend's "voice to soothe and bless" (56:26), as it had always done while Hallam lived, he could find no actual rebuttal to Lyell in what he remembered of Hallam's religious views or in the *Remains*.

Tennyson could not, however, accept such a dismal conception of man as a transient phenomenon on the earth's surface, who vainly believes in an immortality and a God of love that ruthless nature

4. *Ibid.*, II, 271.

belies. So he closed this disturbed section 56 by asserting that the questions raised by Lyell's findings must remain unanswered until he could penetrate "behind the veil" (56:28). One cannot state the exact meaning or certain source of this allusive phrase.[5] But Tennyson was seeking refuge in the position that the so-called realities of the physical world hide as much as they reveal of the truth, which man can have full access to only at death, when the "veil" of finite, mortal limitations is withdrawn.

iii

When Tennyson came to write section 123, Lyell's findings were still vivid in his mind, and the first stanza,

> There rolls the deep where grew the tree.
> O earth, what changes hast thou seen!
> There where the long street roars hath been
> The stillness of the central sea.   (123:1–4)

is a poetic summary of descriptions like the following:

> ... seas and lakes have since been filled up, the lands whereon the forests grew have disappeared or changed their form, the rivers and currents which floated the vegetable masses can no longer be traced. ...[6]

> ... how constant an interchange of sea and land is taking place

5. J. D. Yohannan ("Tennyson and Persian Poetry," *Modern Language Notes*, LVII [1942], 88–89; also "Reply" [to W. D. Paden], *Modern Language Notes*, LVIII [1943], 656) maintained that Tennyson's source for the phrase "behind the veil" was most probably a similar phrase in Persian poetry. W. D. Paden ("Correspondence: Tennyson and Persian Poetry Again," *Modern Language Notes*, LVIII [1943], 654) rejected this source in favor of Leviticus 16:2 and Hebrews 6:19–20. The image of the veil is also very common in Shelley's poetry: *e.g.*, "The veil of mortal frailty" ("Queen Mab"), "The veil of life and death" ("Mont Blanc"), "the veil . . . of things which seem" ("Prometheus Unbound").
It seems most likely, however, that when Tennyson used the phrase he had in mind the myth of the veiled statue of Truth at Sais, which one might unveil only at the cost of one's life. Hallam no doubt met this myth in Schiller's 'Das verschleierte Bild zu Sais," since he translated another poem of Schiller's only a few pages from "Das verschleierte Bild" (see Motter's note to line 8 "After First Meeting Emily Tennyson," *Writings*, p. 83). He alluded to it in a sonnet to Emily Tennyson, when he asked: "Art thou not She/ Who in my Sais-temple wast a light/ Behind all veils of thought, and fantasy . . . ?" (*ibid.*). And in discussing Cicero he wrote: ". . . he brought with him a thousand worldly prepossessions, which were to him as the veil of the temple at Sais, hiding impenetrably, 'that which was, and had been, and was to be' " (*ibid.*, p. 154). Tennyson therefore probably came to the image by way of Hallam. At any rate, he used it with obvious reference to the veiled-statue legend in the prologue of the essay on "Ghosts," intended to be read to the Apostles, which opens: "He who has the power of speaking of the spiritual world . . . speaks of life and death, and the things after death. He lifts the veil, but the form behind it is shrouded in deeper obscurity" (*Memoir*, I, 497). And the allusion reappears in Maud: "For the drift of the Maker is dark, an Isis hid by the veil" (Eversley, IV, 159). Bradley (*op. cit.*, p. 153) cited the parallel between this line of *Maud* and *In Memoriam* 56:28.
6. Lyell, *op. cit.*, I, 2.

on the face of our globe. In the Mediterranean alone, many flourishing inland towns, and a still greater number of ports, now stand where the sea rolled its waves since the era when civilized nations first grew up in Europe. It we could compare with equal accuracy the ancient and actual state of all the islands and continents, we should probably discover that millions of our race are now supported by lands situated where deep seas prevailed in earlier ages.[7]

At this time, however, Tennyson could borrow word pictures from Lyell without being distressed by his theories, and he concluded 123 on a note very different from that of 56.—But this is anticipating a later phase of his spiritual journey.

ELEANOR B. MATTES

Further Reassurances in Herschel's *Natural Philosophy* and Chamber's *Vestiges of Creation*

i

Tennyson continued to add to the elegies in the early 1840's, since Edward Lushington stated that by Christmas of 1841 "the number of the memorial poems had rapidly increased since I had seen the poet"[1]—about a year before[2]—and specifically mentioned that sections 6 and 51 were new to him. But there was apparently no plan to publish these elegies as yet, for in 1842 Tennyson broke his "ten years' silence" with two volumes of short poems, some of them revisions of published pieces, some of them poems written during the ten-year period.

There are few clues to the chronological development of the elegies after Lushington saw them. But, since the present Lord Tennyson owns a manuscript of *In Memoriam* which seems to represent the poem as it existed some time between 1841 and 1845,[3] a comparison of the number of sections in this manuscript with the number in the "trial issue" Tennyson had printed in March, 1850, gives some idea of his work upon the elegies during the intervening years.

Lord Tennyson's manuscript lacks the Prologue, sections 118, 123–127, 129–131, and the Epilogue, all of which are included in

7. *Ibid.*, I, 255.
1. *Memoir*, I, 202.
2. *Ibid.*, I, 201–2. But the chronology in

Lushington's reminiscences is vague and inexact.
3. See Appendix, p. 112.

the trial issue, and also lacks sections 7–8, 96–97, 119–121, 128, which were added to the first edition. In this shorter form the elegies brought to its conclusion that part of Tennyson's speculations which was concerned with his relation to Hallam, and traced his progress from despondent preoccupation with the past, in the early sections, to confident anticipation of the future, in section 117.

> O days and hours, your work is this
>   To hold me from my proper place,
>   A little while from his embrace,
> For fuller gain of after bliss:
>
> That out of distance might ensue
>   Desire of nearness doubly sweet;
>   And unto meeting when we meet,
> Delight a hundredfold accrue.   (117:1–8)

Such a statement hardly fulfilled the Apostles' expectation of a message for the age, however, although, coming from a man in his prime, it would interest the psychiatrist. Furthermore, Tennyson had stated[4] but had not resolved the most urgent religious problem of the day; how to reconcile God and geology—Divine Purpose and the inexorable rise and extinction of species which geologic evidence revealed. For, while section 114 points to a possible solution in the proper subordination of knowledge to wisdom, it has no actual answer to the questions raised in section 56.[5] The sections which appear in the trial issue of *In Memoriam,* but not in Lord Tennyson's manuscript, and so are presumably late, remedy these omissions, broadening "the way of the soul.

ii

Of these later sections, 123 and 124 affirm that the heart's or spirit's witness to man's cherished beliefs (especially in immortality) is proof against the counter-evidence of science to which the reason points in refutation of them. This was a line or argument against the implications of Lyell's findings which, as indicated above, Carlyle and perhaps also J. C. Hare may have suggested to Tennyson.

Section 130 rests on the quite different premise that nature and God are essentially one, and it represents nature as the medium which gave Tennyson a sense of Hallam's presence and the assurance that death could not sever their relations:

4. In section 56.

5. Sections 123 and 124, which do have an answer, are not included in Lord Tennyson's manuscript. In the preceding chapter, I departed from my customary procedure by considering these probably late sections out of their chronological order, because of their relation to the philosophic position of 114, and because there is no evidence that they were prompted by any later influence upon Tennyson's thought.

Thy voice is on the rolling air;
   I hear thee where the waters run;
   Thou standest in the rising sun,
And in the setting thou art fair.

What art thou then? I cannot guess;
   But tho' I seem in star and flower
   To feel thee some diffusive power,
I do not therefore love thee less:

   . . . .
   Tho' mix'd with God and Nature thou,
I seem to love thee more and more.

Far off thou art, but ever nigh;
   I have thee still, and I rejoice;
   I prosper, circled with thy voice;
I shall not lose thee tho' I die.

(130:1–8, 11–16)

These lines closely reproduce the conclusion of Shelley's *Adonais*, a poem Tennyson greatly admired;[6] specifically, they echo *Adonais* XLII:

He is made one with Nature: there is heard
His voice in all her music, from the moan
Of thunder, to the song of night's sweet bird;
He is a presence to be felt and known
In darkness and in light, from herb and stone,
Spreading itself wheree'er that Power may move
Which has withdrawn his being to its own. . . .[7]

iii

Although Tennyson in certain moods responded to Wordsworth's and Shelley's romanticist view of nature, yet Lyell's *Geology* had too vividly depicted a nature "red in tooth and claw" for him to embrace pantheism consistently at this time. And, although he grasped at Carlyle's assertions that man's intuitive belief in God and immortality is more valid than the scientific evidence which challenges it, he was not prepared wholly to dismiss this evidence. For he himself had a lively interest in science, and he also appreciated its hold upon his contemporaries. It is therefore easy to see why he would be receptive to answers to his questionings which

6. Shelley was highly esteemed by Tennyson's Cambridge contemporaries, especially by Hallam, who in 1829 arranged for the publication in England of *Adonais*, which had until then appeared only in Italy. Tennyson said to Frederick Locker-Lampson in 1869: "Nobody admires Shelley more than I once did" (*Memoir*, II, 70); and his son stated that *Adonais* was one of the poems he particularly valued (*ibid.*, II, 285).
7. Bradley (*op. cit.*, p. 235) noted the resemblance of section 130 to *Adonais* XLII and XLIII.

found religious meaning in, rather than in spite of, the natural proc-
esses science described, and especially receptive if he met with such
answers in the writings of scientists and of their popularisers, as he
apparently did in 1843 and 1844 or 1845.

Tennyson seems to have come into possession of J. F. W. Her-
schel's *A Preliminary Discourse on the Study of Natural Philosophy*
in October, 1843,[8] although it first appeared in 1830. And in
November, 1844, he asked his friend and publisher Moxon to
obtain for him *Vestiges of the Natural History of Creation*, which
the *Examiner* had enthusiastically reviewed.[9] Herschel's book, the
first of a series of discourses on the "objects and advantages of the
study of the principal departments of human knowledge,"[1] pre-
sented clearly and simply the reasons for studying the physical sci-
ences, the basic principles and methods involved in such study, and
the chief subject matter included. Robert Chambers' *Vestiges of
Creation*, published anonymously,[2] professed to be "the first at-
tempt to connect the natural sciences into a history of creation,"
beginning with the formation of the solar systems, and tracing the
mutations of the earth's surface and the development of life
revealed by geologic evidence, up to the appearance of the "adult
Caucasian"—the present highest form of organic life.

In these popular treatises Tennyson could and apparently did
find a religious interpretation of the scientific findings they describe.
For, although Herschel's volume preceded the *Principles of Geol-
ogy*, both it and *Vestiges of Creation* refer to "development" and
interpret it as an aspect of progress.

The *Discourse on Natural Philosophy* has a section on geology
which mentions the wearing away of old continents and the build-
ing up of new ones, but for Herschel this cast no doubt upon man's
immortality, which he wrote of confidently in the opening pages of
his book, asking:

> Is it wonderful that a being so constituted should first encourage
> a hope, and by degrees acknowledge an assurance, that his intel-
> lectual existence will not terminate with the dissolution of his
> corporeal frame but rather that, in a future state of being . . .
> endowed with acuter senses, and higher faculties, he shall drink

8. A copy of this *Discourse* (London,
1830), inscribed "A. Tennyson. 2 M.C.B.
Temple. Oct., '43," and having under-
scorings, presumably by Tennyson, was
sold in the William Harris Arnold
Collection at the Anderson Galleries,
November 10–11, 1924. Professor Ri-
chard L. Purdy drew this fact to my at-
tention. I have been unable to locate the
volume, however, as the Poetry Book-
shop, to whom it was sold, resold it but
has no record of the purchaser.

9. *Memoir*, I, 222–23. For reference to
this review in the *Examiner*, see Fitzger-
ald, *Letters and Literary Remains*, I,
148.
1. Quoted from the "Advertisement" ap-
pended to the 1832 edition.
2. For fear its divergence from currently
accepted, orthodox views of Creation
would injure Chambers' literary reputa-
tion or bring his publishing firm into dis-
repute.

deep at that fountain of beneficent wisdom for which the slight taste obtained on earth has given him so keen a relish?[3]

The development revealed in the history of the human species seemed to him equally valid ground for optimism, leading him to comment:

> ... we cannot fail to be struck with the rapid *rate of dilatation* which every degree upward of the scale, so to speak, exhibits, and which, in an estimate of averages, gives an immense preponderance to the present over every former condition of mankind, and, for aught we can see to the contrary, will place succeeding generations in the same degree of superior relation to the present that this holds to those passed away.[4]

The whole outlook of the volume would, in fact, be reassuring to Tennyson. For Herschel denied emphatically that the study of science leads men "to doubt the immortality of the soul," insisting that instead it leaves the mind "open and free to every impression of a higher nature which it is susceptible of receiving, ... encouraging, rather than suppressing, every thing that can offer a prospect or a hope beyond the present obscure and unsatisfactory state."[5] And he concluded his introductory apologia with a thought which to Tennyson must immediately have suggested Hallam and their relations: namely, that

> the observation of the calm, energetic regularity of nature, the immense scale of her operations, and the certainty with which her ends are attained, tends, irresistibly, to tranquillise and re-assure the mind. ... And this it does ... by calling upon us for the exercise of those powers and faculties by which we are susceptible of the comprehension of so much greatness, and which forms, as it were, a link between ourselves and the best and noblest benefactors of our species, with whom we hold communion in thoughts and participate in discoveries which have raised them above their fellow-mortals, and brought them nearer to their Creator.[6]

Vestiges of Creation was not so simply reassuring to religious faith as Herschel's *Discourse on Natural Philosophy*. For, while it affirmed, very early in the exposition, "that there is a First Cause to which all others are secondary and ministrative, a primitive almighty will, of which these [physical] laws are merely the mandates,"[7] it premised that "the organic creation is ... the result of natural laws"[8] rather than of any direct act of God. Secondly, it repre-

3. J. F. W. Herschel, *A Preliminary Discourse on the Study of Natural Philosophy* (Vol. I in the Rev. Dionysius Lardner's "The Cabinet of Natural Philosophy," London, Longman, Rees, Orme, Brown & Green, 1831), p. 7.
4. *Ibid.*, pp. 67–68.
5. *Ibid.*, pp. 7–8.
6. *Ibid.*, pp. 16–17.
7. [Robert Chambers], *Vestiges of the Natural History of Creation* (New York, Wiley and Putnam, 1945), p. 25.
8. *Ibid.*, p. 117.

sented man as a part of "the animal scale"[9]—the paragon of animals—and so a part of the vast process of organic development which geologic evidence reveals. Thirdly, it pointed out that "the individual, as far as the present sphere of Being is concerned, is to the Author of Nature a consideration of inferior moment. Everywhere we see the arrangements for the species perfect; the individual is left, as it were, to take his chance amidst the mêlée of the various laws affecting him."[1] This conception of the mutual relation of God, man, and nature was clearly at variance with Christian teaching. It repudiated the biblical account of a Divine creative act: it was incompatible with the doctrine of man's fall from an originally perfect state: most serious of all, it ran counter to the Gospels' message of a loving God who marks the fall of every sparrow and watches over each of His children with tender care.

Many readers, therefore, found *Vestiges of Creation* disturbing and irreligious. Edward Fitzgerald asked his friend Bernard Barton: "How do you like Vestiges of Creation?—Are you all turned infidels—or Atheists, as Mrs. Turly was minded to become?"[2] And Fanny Kemble, while she was reading it in 1847, reported a very unfavorable first reaction: "The book is extremely disagreeable to me, though my ignorance and desire for knowledge combined give it, when treating of facts, a thousand times more interest than the best of novels for me; but its conclusions are utterly revolting to me. . . ."[3]

There was nothing in the *Vestiges of Creation* to shock Tennyson, however. He had never been a biblicist. As early as in his college days he had been attracted by the theory "that the 'development of the human body might possibly be traced from the radiated, vermicular, molluscous and vertebrate organisms.' "[4] Furthermore, in reading Lyell he had already confronted the geologic indications that man, not only as individual but also as species, is subject to the processes of extinction which the onward and upward surge of nature makes inevitable.

The disturbing features in *Vestiges of Creation* were, therefore, already familiar to Tennyson, and it contained counter-reassurances, and suggested a meaning and purpose underlying the seemingly ruthless sweep of development, which were not to be found in Lyell's presentation. For it proposed that the very vastness of space and time which astronomy and geology disclose points to the fragmentary character of whatever natural processes man can see, and

9. *Ibid.*, p. 151.
1. *Ibid.*, p. 281.
2. In a letter of December 29, 1844 (Barton, *op. cit.*, p. 102).
3. Letter of November 14, 1847, in Frances Ann Kemble, *Records of Later Life* (London, Richard Bentley & Son, 1882), III, 242. Fanny Kemble was the sister of John Kemble, one of Tennyson's Cambridge contemporaries and close friends—the Kemble he quoted in a letter to Emily Sellwood (Chapter VII, n. 17, above).
4. *Memoir*, I, 44.

warrants his confidence that the seeming injustices within this seg-
ment are a necessary part of a larger, perfect plan:

> It may be that, while we are committed to take our chance in a
> natural system of undeviating operation . . . there is a system of
> Mercy and Grace behind the screen of nature, which is to make
> up for all casualties endured here, and the very largeness of which
> is what makes these casualties a matter of indifference to God.
> . . . To reconcile this [discrepancy between God's loving inten-
> tion and its realization] to the recognized character of the Deity,
> it is necessary to suppose that the present system is but a part of
> the whole, a stage in a Great Progress, and that the Redress is in
> reserve. . . . The mundane economy might be very well as a por-
> tion of some greater phenomenon, the rest of which was yet to be
> evolved. . . . Let us but fully and truly consider what a system is
> here laid open to view, and we cannot well doubt that we are in
> the hands of One who is both able and willing to do us the most
> entire justice. . . . Thinking of all the contingencies of this world
> as to be in time melted into or lost in the greater system, to
> which the present is only subsidiary, let us wait the end with
> patience, and be of good cheer.[5]

And it suggested that even the supplanting of man as he now is by
some more highly developed form of humanity will mean the fulfill-
ment rather than the frustration of his highest aspirations and
hopes. For the prospect of future organic development led the
author to speculate:

> Is our race but the initial of the grand crowning type? Are there
> yet to be species superior to us in organization, purer in feeling,
> more powerful in device and act, and who shall take a rule over
> us! . . . There may then be occasion for a nobler type of human-
> ity, which shall complete the zoological circle on this planet, and
> realize some of the dreams of the purest spirits of the present
> race.[6]

Fanny Kemble justly observed: ". . . the hypothesis . . . that other
and higher destinies, developments, may, and probably do, await
humanity than anything it has yet attained here . . . though most
agreeable to the love of life and desire of perfection of most human
creatures, in no sort hinges logically on to his [Chambers'] *absolute
chain of material progression* and development."[7] But Tennyson
apparently did not share this criticism, for, whatever his debt to the
Vestiges of Creation,[8] section 118 and the Epilogue of *In Memo-*

5. Chambers, *op. cit.*, p. 286.
66. *Ibid.*, pp. 207–8.
7. Kemble, *op. cit.*, III, 245.
8. In a note to the account of Tenny-
son's request for *Vestiges of Creation*
from Moxon, his son stated: "The sec-
tions of 'In Memoriam' about Evolution
had been read by his friends some years
before the publication of the *Vestiges of*

Creation in 1844" (*Memoir*, I, 233, n.
1). This note is ambiguous, however,
since it does not state *which* sections.
And the evidence for the date of the Ep-
ilogue (see Appendix, p. 124) indicates
that it, at least, was not written "some
years before" Tennyson saw Chambers'
book.

riam draw from the evidence of organic development conclusions that were essentiallly Herschel's and Chambers'.

iv

Section 118 is generally regarded as a key statement of the philosophy or "message" of *In Memoriam*, and quite understandably so. For it is Tennyson's most explicit attempt to present some reassuring word on the relation of development to man's beliefs and hopes, probably the most disturbing religious problem of the 1840's to the Victorian public as well as to Tennyson personally.

In the opening stanza Tennyson repudiated the depressing thoughts which he had voiced in section 56—the view "of human love and truth, As dying Nature's earth and lime" (118:3–4). For, as he re-examined the evidence of the past, apparently with the eyes of Chambers rather than of Lyell, he found that it pointed not so much to extinction as to progress. Man must therefore think of himself, not as a prospective fossil—Tennyson's nightmare of section 56—but as "The herald of a higher race" (118:14).

This hopeful prospect for the humanity of the future did not, of course, meet the primary religious demand of the elegies—the demand for personal immortality; nor was it a necessarily reassuring prospect, as Chambers discovered from the reactions to his book. But Tennyson, possibly encouraged by Herschel's optimism in the *Discourse on Natural Philosophy*,[9] also affirmed the progress of the individual to higher spheres and endeavors after death:

> But trust that those we call the dead
> Are breathers of an ampler day
> For every nobler ends. ...   (118:5–7)

There is even less scientific basis for predicting man's onward and upward advance in the after-world than for Chambers' vision of a "nobler type of humanity," despite Isaac Taylor's pretension of presenting a *"physical* theory of another life." There is, furthermore, no natural connection between the two kinds of progression. Tennyson avoided the first difficulty by appealing to faith rather than to reason, urging his readers to "trust" in the expanding life of "those we call the dead." He overcame the other difficulty by asserting that the advance of both the individual and the species is dependent upon a third kind of development: namely, moral; that man is to be

> The herald of a higher race,
> And of himself in higher place.
> *If* so he type this work of time
> Within himself, from more to more.
>   (118:14–17)[1]

Thus Tennyson, in section 118, drew from development not only a religious meaning but also a moral message, giving the elegies a homiletic note worthy of his Apostolic mission:

> . . . Arise and fly
> The reeling Faun, the sensual feast;
> Move upward, working out the beast,
> And let the ape and tiger die.   (118:25–28)

Coleridge had pointed to the moral implications of development in *Aids to Reflection,* when he wrote:

> Thus all lower natures find their highest good in semblances and seekings of that which is higher and better. All things strive to ascend, and ascend in their striving. And shall man alone stoop? . . . No! it must be a higher good to make you happy. . . . Well saith the moral poet—
>
> > Unless above himself he can
> > Erect himself, how mean a thing is man![2]

And Tennyson was no doubt indebted to this interpretation, either directly or via his discussions with the Coleridgians among the Apostles and at the Sterling Club. Section 118 has, therefore, no essential originality; but it reveals Tennyson's penchant for synthesis. Encouraged, no doubt, by the optimistic view of development presented in *Vestiges of Creation,* he was able to combine Chambers' hopes for future humanity with Isaac Taylor's rosy picture of the after-life and Coleridge's moralising, in a seemingly related body of great expectations: namely, that the human race has a great, unlimited future ahead; that the individual, too, will live on in higher, larger spheres; and that the means of achieving both these lines of advance is moral endeavor, which re-enacts in microcosm the long upward struggle of organic life.

v

The Epilogue of *In Memoriam* is even more certainly indebted to *Vestiges of Creation* than is section 118.[3] When Tennyson wrote the Epilogue he apparently already had in mind for the elegies the formal, artificial structure of "a kind of *Divina Commedia,* ending with happiness."[4] For in the Epilogue he wrote of the marriage of his youngest sister, Cecilia, with his friend Edmund

2. *The Complete Works of Samuel Taylor Coleridge* (New York, Harper & Brothers, 1853), I, 181.
3. Since the Epilogue was written late in 1844 or early in 1845, when Tennyson had almost surely obtained *Vestiges of Creation.* For evidence of the Epilogue's date, see Appendix, p. 124.
4. *Memoir,* I, 304.

Lushington, and anticipated the arrival of their child, thus bringing the memorial poems from their early preoccupation with death to the expectation of birth. This promise of birth, in turn, led him to reiterate what is essentially Chambers' optimistic view of the religious meaning of organic development.

As he pictured Cecilia and Edmund Lushington on their wedding journey, Tennyson imagined:

> A soul shall draw from out the vast
> And strike his being into bounds,
>
> And, moved thro' life of lower phase,
> Result in man, be born and think,
> And act and love. . . .   (Epi. 123–127)

He was familiar with the theory of foetal development referred to in lines 125–126 long before he read *Vestiges of Creation,* for a stanza in the 1832 version of "The Palace of Art" specifically refers to this theory.[5] But Chambers' statement that man's "organization gradually passes through conditions generally resembling a fish, a reptile, a bird, and the lower mammalia, before it attains its specific maturity"[6] may have brought the theory to the foreground of his thought. Tennyson was, in any case, surely indebted to Chambers' speculation: "Is our race but the initial of the grand crowning type? Are there yet to be species superior to us in organization, purer in feeling, more powerful in device and act, and who shall take a rule over us!"[7] when he pictured the Lushingtons' child as

> . . . a closer link
> Betwixt us and the crowning race
>
> Of those that, eye to eye, shall look
>   On knowledge; under whose command
>   Is Earth and Earth's, and in their hand
> Is Nature like an open book;
>
> No longer half-akin to brute,
>   For all we thought and loved and did,
>   And hoped, and suffer'd, is but seed
> Of what in them is flower and fruit.   (Epi. 127–136)

And he was almost certainly also indebted to Chambers for the following suggestion that Hallam's rare gifts and virtues had a special relation to the greater man of the future:

5. " 'From change to change four times within the womb/ The brain is moulded,' she began, 'So through all phases of thought I come/ Into the perfect man.' " This stanza was altered in the revised version of "The Palace of Art" included in the *Poems* of 1842, and was replaced by another in the 1853 edition of the *Poems.*
6. Chambers, *op. cit.,* pp. 150–51.
7. *Ibid.,* p. 207.

136 · Eleanor B. Mattes

> Whereof the man, that with me trod
> This planet, was a noble type
> Appearing ere the times were ripe.
>
> (Epi. 137–139)

For Chambers predicted that the "*nobler type* of humanity" he anticipated would "realize some of the dreams of the purest spirits of the present race."[8]

By thus relating Hallam to his interpretation of development Tennyson brought together the original and later concerns of the elegies. And in the closing lines of the Epilogue he brought together the religious reassurances he had offered piecemeal in various earlier sections, by reaffirming the relation of both Hallam and development to God:

> That friend of mine who lives in God,
>
> That God, which ever lives and loves,
> One God, one law, one element,
> And one far-off divine event,
> To which the whole creation moves.
>
> (Epi. 140–144)

This conclusion reflects most of the influences which had gone into the shaping of *In Memoriam*, caught up and combined in what was no doubt in part unanalyzed amalgam and in part deliberate synthesis. It contains verbal echoes of a passage in Revelation 10 which Tennyson greatly admired: "And the angel which I saw stand upon the sea and upon the earth lifted up his hand to heaven, and sware by him that liveth for ever and ever ...";[9] of a question in the "Everlasting Yea" chapter of *Sartor Resartus*: "O Heavens, is it, in very deed, HE, then, that ever speaks through thee; that lives and loves in thee, that lives and loves in me?"[1] and of two lines in one of Hallam's early sonnets:

> Let him gaze here who trusts not in the Love
> Toward which all being solemnly doth move.[2]

The beliefs which it affirms reflect all these influences and also the more recent impressions of *Vestiges of Creation*. The concept of one God, eternally living and loving, is biblical, while the idea of God as law—meaning natural law—is one that scientist-theologians like Whewell emphasized and that Chambers especially stressed throughout *Vestiges of Creation*. The last lines—"And one far-off divine event, To which the whole creation moves"—suggest both the biblical idea of the Kingdom of God and the nineteenth centu-

---

8. *Ibid.*, p. 208. The italics are mine.
9. *Memoir*, I, 279, ñ. 1.
1. Carlyle, *Sartor Resartus*, p. 181.

2. *Writings*, p. 3. Hallam was indebted to Dante for the religious concept underlying these lines.

ry's dearly cherished belief that perfection lay ahead and the whole world was progressing toward it, a belief for which Chambers found scientific evidence in organic development.

vi

Soon after Tennyson had read *Vestiges of Creation* and, presumably, written the Epilogue, he showed the elegies to James Spedding and to Edward Fitzgerald, which led Fitzgerald to write W. B. Donne on January 29, 1845, that "A. T. has near a volume of poems—elegiac—in memory of Arthur Hallam. . . . Spedding praises: and I suppose the elegiacs will see daylight, public daylight, one day."[3] Other friends, notably J. M. Heath and Edmund Lushington, had seen some of the poems before, of course. But their submission as a whole to Fitzgerald and Spedding at this time, with the apparent prospect of publishing, suggests that *Vestiges of Creation* had helped Tennyson to a satisfying solution of the problems he had encountered on his way of the soul, and also to a message. He was at last confident that Hallam lived on in God, where Tennyson could still have communion with him and could anticipate rejoining him. And he could assure both himself and his age that science walked hand in hand with religion after all, bearing witness to a God of eternal process and to the glorious destiny He purposed for humanity, and that the findings of geology, instead of mocking men's aspirations and sufferings, showed them to be indispensable conditions for the progress of mankind.

ELEANOR B. MATTES

Chronology of *In Memoriam*†

There is at present no way to establish an accurate chronology for all the sections of *In Memoriam*. Tennyson passionately resented any critical dissection of this kind and gave only a few, inadvertent clues. Hallam Tennyson shared his father's attitude and added very

3. Fitzgerald, *Letters and Literary Remains*, I, 149.
† The dates of composition assigned by Mattes to the various sections of *In Memoriam* are soundly based on extensive scholarship, and most of them remain unchallenged. Recently, however, scholars have begun to gain access to new manuscript materials which were unavailable in 1951. On the basis of new evidence discovered in them a few of Mattes's dates are now being put in question. See, for example, Christopher Ricks's edition of Tennyson's *Poems* (Longman/Norton, 1969). As new and hitherto unavailable information accumulates we may expect that further revisions in the chronology will be suggested [*Editor*].

little information in his official *Memoir*.[1] The recent biography, *Alfred Tennyson*, by his grandson Charles Tennyson, contributes no new evidence on this point.

There are, however, a few direct statements and indications as to the dates of sections in the *Memoir*,[2] in the notes to the Eversley edition of *Enoch Arden and In Memoriam*, and in the sections themselves. To this nucleus of evidence I have added from various sources: namely, (1) a description of the present Lord Tennyson's manuscript of *In Memoriam* which accompanied an offer to sell the manuscript to the Yale University Library; [3](2) a comparison of the first edition of *In Memoriam* with the "trial issue"[4] that Tennyson had privately printed before the poem was published; (3) clues provided by contemporary books and events; (4) indirect indications and allusions in the elegies.

This body of old and new evidence, together with some admittedly tentative inferences, is the basis for my reconstruction of *In Memoriam's* growth. The internal evidence in the elegies and the relation to contemporary writings have led to the specific dating of individual sections. The description of Lord Tennyson's manuscript has made it possible to visualize the extent of *In Memoriam* somewhere between the end of 1841 and 1845, since this manuscript contains an elegy written in late December of 1841 and does not include the Epilogue, which was written by the summer of 1845. Comparison of the trial issue of the poem with the first edition yielded no important chronological evidence, but revealed Tennyson in the process of final revision.

The table which follows attempts to present concisely all the available evidence concerning the dates of composition of various sections. The chronology is obviously neither complete nor equally well substantiated at all points. It therefore makes no pretension of having independent value, since, if any manuscripts of *In Memoriam* can in the future be examined, they will no doubt nullify some of the likeliest conjectures. But there is enough reliable evidence to indicate the general course of Tennyson's religious thought for the purpose of the present study.

1. There is also considerable ambiguity in the information Hallam Tennyson has provided, which two instances will illustrate. He stated in the *Memoir* (I, 297) that "It was not until May 1850 that 'In Memoriam' was printed and given to a few friends," but an entry in William Rossetti's journal (see Chapter X, n. 1 above) makes it clear that the month was March. Even more confusing are the discrepancies in the lists of "first written sections" in the "trial issue" of the *Memoir*, the published *Memoir*, and the appendix to the Eversley Edition of *Enoch Arden and In Memoriam*. For the trial-issue *Memoir* lists sections 9, 1, 31, 28, 2, 26; the published *Memoir* lists 9, 30, 31, 85, 28; and the Eversley appendix lists 9, 17, 18, 31, 85, 28.

2. There is an occasional statement regarding the date of a section, and Tennyson's correspondence provides a few clues.

3. Professor Richard L. Purdy summarized the important facts in the description, and I have used this summary, through his kindness.

4. Professor Chauncey B. Tinker owns one of the few extant copies of this trial issue, which he generously allowed me to consult.

Date	Section	Evidence
1833	9	Dated October 6, 1833, in J. M. Heath's *Commonplace Book.* (This *Commonplace Book* is in the Fitzwilliam Museum in Cambridge, and there is a microfilm copy in the Yale University Library). According to W. F. Rawnsley (*Tennyson 1809–1909*, p. 17), Tennyson "began his sections of *In Memoriam* within two months of Arthur's death, with 'Fair ship that. . . .' " One of the first-written sections, according to the trial issue of the *Memoir* ([Hallam Tennyson], *Materials for a Life of A. T.* [n.p., n.d.], I, 127–128); the *Memoir* (I, 109); and Hallam Tennyson's statement in the Eversley Edition of *Enoch Arden and In Memoriam* (Eversley, III, 187).
	31	One of the first-written sections, according to the trial issue of the *Memoir* (I, 127–128), the *Memoir* (I, 109), and the Eversley Edition (III, 187). It appears in Heath's *Commonplace Book*, and Charles Tennyson ("J. M. Heath's 'Commonplace Book,' " *The Cornhill Magazine*, CLIII [1936], 438) stated that almost all the material in this *Commonplace Book* is "definitely assignable to a date not later than 1833."
	10	No external evidence. But it is addressed to the ship bringing Arthur Hallam's body to England, which arrived in late December of 1833 (*Memoir*, I, 106).
	11	No external evidence. But it describes an autumn scene and speaks of Hallam's body on "the heaving deep," so it at least seeks to give the impression of being written in the autumn of 1833.
	12 13 14	No external evidence. But, like section 10, they refer to the ship carrying Hallam's remains.
	15	No external evidence. But it describes a later autumn scene than that of 11, while still referring to the journey of Hallam's body.
	30	Dated Christmas Eve, 1833, in Heath's *Commonplace Book.*

Date	Section	Evidence
(1833)	(30)	One of the first-written sections, according to the *Memoir* (I, 109). Rawnsley (*loc. cit.*) stated that "the canto, 'With trembling fingers,' was the work of the following December (1834)," but his is weaker evidence than Heath's or Hallam Tennyson's, since it was reported at second hand and many years after *In Memoriam* was published.
1834	17	One of the first-written sections, according to the Eversley Edition (III, 187). It appears in Heath's *Commonplace Book*. But it could not have been written before 1834, since it hails the arrival of the ship bringing Hallam's body, of which Henry Hallam informed Tennyson in a letter written December 30, 1833 (*Memoir*, I, 106).
	18	One of the first-written sections, according to the Eversley Edition (III, 187). It appears in Heath's *Commonplace Book*. It refers to Hallam's burial as about to take place immediately. The date of the burial was January 3, 1834.
	19	It appears in Heath's *Commonplace Book*. But it refers to Hallam's funeral as having taken place.
	85	One of the first-written sections, according to the *Memoir* (I, 109) and the Eversley Edition (III, 187). Several stanzas appear in Heath's *Commonplace Book*, and it is this shorter form of the section to which the *Memoir* and the Eversley Edition must refer, since the longer, published version is addressed to Edmund Lushington, whom Tennyson did not know well before 1840 at the earliest.
	1 2 26	Among the first-written sections, according to the trial issue of the *Memoir* (I, 127–128). Since they are not included in the list of early sections in the published edition of the *Memoir* (I, 109), the evidence is, however, not very strong.

Date	Section	Evidence

(1834)   22   These sections are closely related, both in
         23   wording and theme, to section 26, but are
         24   nowhere mentioned as among the early-
         25   written elegies, so the evidence for placing
              them in this year is purely internal, and weak
              at that.

         72   According to a note in the *Memoir* (I, 305,
              note 1), "No. LXXII refers to the first anni-
              versary of the death Sept. 15th, 1833." This
              does not necessarily mean that 72 was writ-
              ten at the time of the first anniversary, of
              course; for the note is appended to Tenny-
              son's comment on his three-year structural
              division of *In Memoriam*, which obviously
              does not correspond with the actual chronol-
              ogy of composition. But there is no evidence
              to challenge an 1834 dating.

         28   One of the first-written sections, according
              to the *Memoir* (I, 109), the trial issue of
              it (I, 127–128), and the Eversley Edition
              (III, 187). This evidence by itself might
              suggest 1833 rather than 1834. Line 13, how-
              ever, reads, "This year I slept and woke with
              pain," which indicates the passing of at least
              a year since Hallam's death. An 1834 dating
              is also confirmed by the fact that it was not
              28, but 30, to which J. M. Heath referred
              when he spoke of the "two companions to
              'Fair Ship'" (*Memoir*, I, 142), and quoted
              his sister Julia's comment on "The Xmas"
              (*loc. cit.*); for Heath's *Commonplace Book*
              includes section 30, but not 28, and 30 rather
              than 28 is, therefore, "The Xmas" compan-
              ion piece to the very early "Fair Ship."

1835   29   No certain evidence. But it is not included
              in any of the lists of the first-written sections
              or in Heath's *Commonplace Book*, and sec-
              tions 30 and 28, the two Christmas poems
              so included, date from 1833 and 1834, re-
              spectively, which implies a later date for 29.
              There is also no sequence of thought be-
              tween 28 and 29 or 29 and 30, which suggests
              that each section was written separately, at
              a different Christmas, and that they were

Date	Section	Evidence

(1835) (29) placed together when Tennyson decided to publish the elegies as a single long poem. While the foregoing evidence points to an 1835 or later dating for section 29, it was, on the other hand, definitely written before 1837, since the setting is the Somersby home that was associated with Arthur Hallam, and by the Christmas of 1837 the Tennysons were at High Beech. Either 1835 or 1836 is, therefore, an almost equally likely date; but the emphasis upon grief—"With such compelling cause to grieve" (29:1)—makes the earlier date somewhat more probable.

34
35
36 For this dating there is only the internal, tentative evidence that these sections reflect Wordsworth's views on immortality and on the relation between "natural religion" and the Christian revelation, and that Tennyson was reading "a great deal of Wordsworth" in 1835 (*Memoir*, I, 151).

1836 98 It is addressed to Charles Tennyson and refers to his approaching wedding trip, which followed his marriage on May 24, 1836.

89 There is no evidence for the exact year. But the season described seems to be summer, and the scene is the lawn of Somersby Rectory, which the Tennysons left in 1837; so this section was written by 1837 and probably before, since it is not one of the "removal" poems, which almost certainly date from the spring or summer of 1837. There is, on the other hand, no evidence that it is one of the early sections, so either 1836 or, possibly, 1835 is the most likely date.

99 It celebrates the anniversary of Hallam's death on September 15th and was definitely written at Somersby, since it speaks of "meadows breathing of the past, And woodlands holy to the dead" (99:7–8); so it was written at least by 1836, the September of 1836 being the last the Tennysons spent at Somersby. Since Tennyson placed it after 72, another poem concerned with this anniversary, and 72 was written in 1834 or, pos-

Date	*Section*	*Evidence*
(1836)	(99)	sibly, 1835, 99 must be assigned to either 1835 or 1836. I suggest 1836 because it immediately succeeds 98, which was definitely written in 1836.
	78	Since Tennyson considered this section an introduction to the second of the three major divisions of *In Memoriam* (*Memoir*, I, 305), it was apparently written later than 28, which introduces the first division. The last two stanzas also suggest some years' interval since Hallam's death. It was written while the Tennysons were still at Somersby, on the other hand, so cannot be later than 1836, the last Christmas they were there. 1836 therefore seems the most probable date.
	40 43 46 63 73	No external evidence. But 40:17–20, the general thought of 43, 46:5–8, 63:10–12, and 73:1–4 seem indebted to Isaac Taylor's *Physical Theory of Another Life* (see above, pp. 41–43), which appeared in 1836. This relationship, of course, suggests only the earliest possible date, not the exact year, but the tone and the speculations of these sections seem definitely to predate the kind of questioning that was stimulated by Tennyson's reading of Lyell's *Geology* in 1837 (*Memoir*, I, 162).
1837	107	No external evidence. But it was written on an anniversary of Hallam's birthday, February 1, and from the Somersby setting is to be dated no later than 1837, the last February the Tennysons spent there. Its position in the third, last division of the sections indicates, on the other hand, that it was probably not among the earlier-written poems. So 1837 or, possibly, 1836 seems the most likely date.
	111	No external evidence. But 111:1–4—

The churl in spirit, up or down
  Along the scale of ranks, thro' all,
  To who may grasp a golden ball,
By blood a king, at heart a clown.

Date	Section	Evidence
(1837)	(111)	

(111) seems to refer to William IV, of whom Lytton Strachey wrote: "He was one part blackguard, people said, and three parts buffoon" (*Queen Victoria* [London, Chatto and Windus, 1921], p. 39). William IV died on June 20, 1837, and such a reference would have been more likely before rather than after his death; it would certainly not have been written after Victoria had been reigning any length of time. As with section 107, however, the position of the poem in the last division of *In Memoriam* precludes the likelihood of a very early date. Hence 1837 seems the most probable year.

95 The experience 95 describes took place on the lawn of Somersby Rectory, in the summer (95:4), and therefore no later than 1837. It obviously did not occur during the earliest period of Tennyson's depression and grief, however, so an 1837 or possibly 1836 dating is the most likely. But the date of composition may not coincide with the date of the experience and may, in fact, be as late as 1842, for G. G. Bradley wrote, in his reminiscences of August, 1842 (*Memoir*, I, 205): "I was greatly struck by his describing to us on one singularly still starlit evening, how he and his friends had once sat out far into the night having tea at a table on the lawn beneath the stars, and that the candles had burned with steady upright flame, disturbed from time to time by the inrush of a moth or cockchafer. . . . I do not know whether he had already written, or was perhaps even then shaping, the lines in 'In Memoriam,' which so many years afterwards brought back to me the incident."
There is no way of deciding between an 1837 and an 1842 dating, and for the purpose of the preceding study it is not essential to do so, since the experience described was what made its impact upon Tennyson.

100
101 They were written in anticipation of the Tennysons' removal from Somersby Rectory
102 in the summer of 1837.

Date	Section	Evidence
(1837)	103	It describes a dream of Tennyson on the eve of his departure from Somersby. It may, of course, have been written later, in retrospect, so the evidence is not conclusive.
	55	No evidence as to exact date. But it certainly precedes 56, which I assign to 1837, for 56:1 picks up and challenges 55:7, quoting the exact words.
	56	It was almost certainly prompted by Lyell's *Principles of Geology*, in which Tennyson "during some months of 1837 . . . was deeply immersed" (*Memoir*, I, 162).
	104 105	They describe a Christmas Eve, ostensibly the first Christmas Eve away from Somersby. These sections are such studied parallels to 28 and 30 that they may, however, have been written or revised much later, to mark the third division in Tennyson's final arrangement of the elegies as a single poem. The evidence is therefore inconclusive, although there is no conflicting indication of a later date.
1839	114	No certain evidence. But Tennyson expressed a similar point of view to that of 114 in a letter of 1839 to Emily Sellwood, writing: "John Kemble . . . is striving against what he calls the 'mechanic influence of the age and its tendency to crush and overpower the spiritual in man,' and indeed what matter it how much man knows and does if he keeps not a reverential looking upward?" (*Memoir*, I, 169.) Both Kemble's crusade against the "mechanic influence of the age" and Tennyson's distinction between knowledge and wisdom in 114 seem indebted to Carlyle, whose *Miscellanies* appeared in 1839, so there is additional cause to associate 114 with 1839.
	54	No certain evidence. But Tennyson voiced a similar attitude in a letter of 1839 to Emily Sellwood: "Why has God created souls knowing they would sin and suffer? . . . There is no answer to these questions except

Date	Section	Evidence
		in a great *hope* of universal good. . . ." (*Memoir*, I, 170).
(1839)	86	Hallam Tennyson stated his father "notes . . . in his own hand" that 86 was written at Barmouth (*Memoir*, I, 313, text and note 2). Bradley (*op. cit.*, p. 15) pointed out that Tennyson visited Barmouth in 1839 (after writing the two letters cited as evidence for the possible dates of 114 and 54), during a tour in Wales (*Memoir*, I, 173–74), and at no other time between 1833 and 1850, so far as is known.
1840	6	Edmund Lushington's reminiscences mention Tennyson's recitation of section 6 at Christmas, 1841, and imply that it was written in the months since Lushington had last seen the "memorial poems" (*Memoir*, I, 202), apparently late in 1840. Section 6 may be therefore ascribed either to late 1840 or 1841.
1841	50	No certain evidence for the exact year. But it was written before Christmas, 1841, since 51, which was written at that time, takes up the thought of 50 to give it a new turn. On the other hand, the seeming influence of Lyell's *Geology* would place 50 at least as late as 1837.
	51	Edmund Lushington stated that Tennyson has "just composed" section 51 when he saw it at Christmas, 1841 (*Memoir*, I, 203).
		Other elegies unquestionably belong to this year, for by Christmas, according to Lushington (*Memoir*, I, 202), "the number of the memorial poems had rapidly increased since I had seen the poet, his book containing many that were new to me." But there is at present no means of identifying them.
Almost certainly by 1845	3, 4, 5 16	These sections, together with those already dated, comprise the present Lord Tennyson's manuscript of *In Memoriam*. Since this

Date	Section	Evidence
(by 1845)	20, 21	manuscript does not contain the Epilogue, which was certainly written by the summer of 1845 (see below, p. 124), one may assume that the sections it does contain were all written before that date.
	27	
	32, 33	
	37, 38	
	41, 42	
	44, 45	
	47, 48, 49	
	52, 53 57, 58	
	60, 61, 62	
	64, 65, 66, 67, 68, 69, 70, 71	
	74, 75, 76, 77	
	79, 80, 81, 82, 83, 84 87, 88	
	90, 91, 92, 93, 94	
	106	
(by 1845)	108, 109, 110	

Date	Section	Evidence
	112, 113	
	115, 116,	
	117	
	122	

1845   Epilogue   Although the Epilogue gives the impression that it was written on the wedding day of Cecilia Tennyson and Edmund Lushington, which was October 10, 1842, Lushington first saw it in the summer of 1845 (*Memoir*, I, 203). Since Tennyson had spent August and September of 1844 at the Lushingtons' home, Park House (*Letters and Literary Remains of Edward Fitzgerald*, I, 140), he would hardly have failed to show Lushington the Epilogue, or at least to mention it, if it were already written at that time. So one may date it between October, 1844, and the summer of 1845 on this evidence. The obvious influence of *Vestiges of Creation* (see above, pp. 83–86), which Tennyson requested Moxon to send him, in a letter of November, 1844, confirms this dating and further narrows it to sometime between December, 1844, and the summer of 1845.

1848   The *Memoir* (I, 282) contains an undated letter to Aubrey de Vere, that Hallam Tennyson assigned to 1848 and placed after another letter to de Vere dated "October," in which Tennyson stated: "With respect to the 'Elegies,' I cannot say that I have turned my attention to them lately."

1849   Prologue   So dated by Tennyson in published poem.

121   The year cannot be determined exactly. But, in a chapter of reminiscences, Willingham F. Rawnsley wrote: "My earliest remembrance of him [Tennyson] is of his visiting my parents at Shiplake, before 1850, when I was turned out of my little room in order that he might have a place of his own to smoke in. He was then still working on 'In Memoriam,' and it was in this little room

Date	Section	Evidence

(1849)   (121)   of mine that he wrote the 'Hesper Phosphor' canto" (H. D. Rawnsley, *Memories of the Tennysons*, p. 121). Since Willingham Rawnsley was born in 1845, his memory cannot have gone back very much further than 1850, so the likeliest date for 121 "before 1850" seems to be 1849. The section is also absent from Lord Tennyson's manuscript and from the trial issue of *In Memoriam*, which confirms a very late dating.

Criticism

BASIL WILLEY

In Memoriam†

If 1833 had been Tennyson's black year, 1850 was his *annus mirabilis*. That year, *In Memoriam* was published, and a fortnight later he was married to Emily Sellwood, after a broken engagement which had dragged on for twelve years. And as if this were not enough to atone for all that Tennyson had endured of neglect, disparagement, bereavement and loneliness, Wordsworth died, leaving vacant the Laureateship at the very moment when Tennyson, with the immense success of *In Memoriam*, had become a national institution.

The success and influence of *In Memoriam* illustrate its truly representative quality. The Victorians loved it, and were moved by it, because it dealt seriously and beautifully with the very problems that most concerned them: problems arising from the gradual fading-out of the older spiritual lights in the harsh dawn of a new and more positive age. For *In Memoriam* (it need hardly be said) is far from being a continuous lament over Arthur Hallam. It begins, of course, with the bereavement, with personal grief and lamentation, and with the inevitable questionings about the soul's survival in a future life. Gradually the immediate sorrow recedes, giving place to poignant recollection, and then to more general meditations on man's place in Nature and the impact of science upon religious faith. As in *The Two Voices*, a mood of reconciliation, even hope, is at last reached and the reasons of the heart are vindicated against the reasonings of the intellect. It is needless and beside the mark to look for any greater unity or closer pattern in the poem than this. Tennyson gave a semblance of design to it by rearranging many of the sections and by introducing recurrent Christmases. But it remains a series of elegiac poems strung upon the thread of the poet's own life and following the curve of his development. It is in fact Tennyson's intimate spiritual journal of those years, and it succeeds largely *because* it lacks a more formal structure. Its desultory, informal character ensures its freedom from bardic posturings or routine gestures; the various sections come straight from Tennyson's heart, and were—as he calls them—'brief lays, of sorrow born', or

> 'Short swallow-flights of song, that dip
> Their wings in tears, and skim away.'

† From *More Nineteenth-Century Studies: A Group of Honest Doubters* (London, Chatto and Windus, 1956), pp. 79– 105. The author's footnotes have been omitted.

This meant that Tennyson's lyric power, the greatest of his gifts, was allowed full play, and we get therefore something very unusual: a long poem free from epic pomp, and built up, like a coral-reef, entirely from living organisms. Moreover, in this poem we find all Tennyson's distinctive graces in fragrant blow together. His artistry is at its height, every verse and line being wrought as near perfection as he could make it; yet such is the pressure of emotion, so compelling the need for utterance, that artificiality is avoided. Similarly, *In Memoriam* is the richest of all repositories of the five-word jewels, exquisite landscapes, renderings of the shifting panorama of the seasons; but these are here employed as vehicles and symbols of the poet's changing moods and share in his imaginative life: they never strike us, as often elsewhere (especially in the *Idylls of the King*), as decoration mechanically and coldly applied from without.

The problems confronted in *In Memoriam*, though forced upon Tennyson by personal experience and by the spirit of his age, are neither local nor ephemeral; they are universal, in that they are those which are apt to beset a sensitive and meditative mind in any age. Has man an immortal soul? Is there any meaning in life? any purpose or design in the world-process? any evidence in Nature, in philosophy or in the human heart, for a beneficent Providence? These issues are dealt with by Tennyson, not in the manner of a thinker—whether philosopher, theologian or scientist—but in the manner of a well-informed modern poet: that is, in the manner of one who, though not ignorant of what the specialists are saying, cares for their results only insofar as they are felt in the blood, and felt along the heart, affecting there the inmost quality of living.

There is another significant point about the way in which Tennyson faces experience in this poem: he faces it, virtually, as a soul unprovided with Christian supports. In spite of the Prologue, 'Strong Son of God, immortal Love' (which was in fact composed at the end), *In Memoriam* is not a distinctively Christian poem. The doubts, misgivings, discouragements, probings and conjectures which make it humanly moving could not have existed in a mind equipped with the Christian solutions. It is well to remember, sometimes, how much in literature as a whole presupposes a suspension, not of disbelief, but of belief. Most of literature lives on the level of Nature, not of grace. And thus *In Memoriam* is not concerned with the impact of the Zeitgeist upon Christian doctrine or apologetic, nor does it proffer Christian consolation. It goes behind Christianity, or passes it by, confronting the preliminary question which besets the natural man, the question whether there can be any religious interpretation of life at all. What made the poem acceptable even to the Christian reader in the Victorian age was that having, though with diffidence and humility, vindicated the believing temper, accepted the reasons of the heart, Tennyson had opened a door which gave access to the Christian territory.

Those who mistake Tennyson for an 'escapist' might ponder the following remark of A. C. Bradley:

'... with the partial exception of Shelley, Tennyson is the only one of our great poets whose attitude towards the sciences of Nature was what a modern poet's ought to be; ... the only one to whose habitual way of seeing, imagining, or thinking, it makes any real difference that Laplace, or for that matter Copernicus, ever lived'.

From his earliest manhood Tennyson breathed the atmosphere of scientific theory and discovery, and throughout his life his meditations were governed by the conceptions of law, process, development and evolution—the characteristic and ruling ideas of his century. Of course, the challenge of science to religious orthodoxy was no new manifestation peculiar to the century. Copernicus had challenged it by destroying the geocentric world-picture; the mechanico-materialism of the seventeenth and eighteenth centuries had undermined the miraculous elements of Christianity. Nevertheless the middle decades of the nineteenth century are rightly felt to be the *locus classicus* of the science-and-religion conflict; and that, perhaps, for two main reasons. First because, to the older idea of immutable law operating throughout the physical universe in the inorganic sphere, there was now added the idea of inexorable development proceeding within the organic world, moulding and modifying living species. Secondly, because this great idea, arriving upon the scene in a century of cheap printing and a vastly augmented reading public, soon advanced outside the studies of philosophers and noblemen—to which 'advanced' thought had hitherto been largely confined—and reached the average man, the sort of man who had generally been in possession of a simple conventional faith.

The first aspects of science that interested the young Tennyson seem to have been astronomy (in particular the nebular theory, propounded by Laplace in 1796) and embryology. Wordsworth, in an oft-quoted passage of the Preface to Lyrical Ballads, had predicted that poetry would eventually be able to absorb the results of science and carry them alive into the heart; Tennyson fulfilled that prophecy in Wordsworth's lifetime. Here is his poetic version of the nebular theory (it is the exordium of Professor Psyche's lecture in *The Princess*):

'This world was once a fluid haze of light,
Till toward the centre set the starry tides,
And eddied into suns, that wheeling cast
The planets: then the monster, then the man.'

It will be noticed that he does not stop at the planets, but carries
the development on to man, conceiving the whole process as one.
But years before *The Princess* he had written, and deleted from the
published version, the following stanzas for *The Palace of Art*
(1832):

> 'Hither, when all the deep unsounded skies
>   Shudder'd with silent stars, she clomb,
> And as with optic glasses her keen eyes
>   Pierced thro' the mystic dome,
>
> Regions of lucid matter taking forms,
>   Brushes of fire, hazy gleams,
> Clusters and beds of worlds, and bee-like swarms
>   Of suns, and starry streams.'

Two more of the excised stanzas run thus:

> ' "From shape to shape at first within the womb
>   The brain is moulded", she began.
> "And thro' all phases of all thought I come
>   Unto the perfect man.
>
> All nature widens upward. Evermore
>   The simple essence lower lies,
> More complex is more perfect, owning more
>   Discourse, more widely wise." '

Here we see not only the conception of biological evolution but
supporting evidence for it taken from the new science of embryol-
ogy, which taught that the brain of the foetus passed through all
the previous phases of evolution, recapitulating in brief the whole
history of the species. It is recorded of Tennyson that, right back in
his undergraduate days, he once propounded, at a Trinity discus-
sion, the theory that 'the development of the human body might
possibly be traced from the radiated, vermicular, molluscous and
vertebrate organisms.'

But it was from geology that Tennyson received the most decisive
shock. We know that for some months in 1837 he was 'deeply
immersed" in Charles Lyell's celebrated *Principles of Geology*
(1830–33). What was there in this book to disturb him or any
other reader? Its main thesis was that the present state of the
earth's crust is to be accounted for, not, as in Cuvier's theory, by a
series of catastrophic changes, but by the continuous operation,
through immense tracts of time, of the natural forces still at work
(erosion, gradual earth-movement, sedimentation, etc.). This
sounds innocent enough, but the sting of it was that it presupposed
for the earth a vastly greater age than was allowed for in the
accepted biblical chronology, and thrust far back, if not out of the

picture altogether, the notion of divine creation and superintend-
ence. First cooling gases, then aeons of erosion: what, then, of the
Seven Days' creation, Adam and Eve, and the Flood? Secondly,
Lyell went on to show that in the course of these gradual changes
species after species of living creatures had become extinct through
inability to adapt themselves to changed environments. 'The inhab-
itants of the globe', says he,

> 'like all the other parts of it, are subject to change. It is not only
> the individual that perishes but whole species.'
> 'None of the works of a mortal being can be eternal. ... And
> even when they have been included in rocky strata, ... they must
> nevertheless eventually perish, for every year some portion of the
> earth's crust is shattered by earthquakes or melted by volcanic
> fires, or ground to dust by the moving waters on the surface.'

This teaching, though it might have no direct bearing upon the
doctrine of immortality, seemed to weaken its probability, and cer-
tainly weakened any alleged support derivable by analogy from
Nature. Worse still it seemed hard to reconcile with the belief that
'God is love indeed, and love Creation's final law'. What, according
to Lyell, has become of the Heavenly Father without whose care
and compassion not one sparrow falls to the ground?

Before quitting Lyell's *Geology*, it is worth noting that Lyell him-
self was quite willing to profess belief in the *fact* of divine activity,
provided that science were left free to investigate and demonstrate
the mode of it. This was the formula adopted (quite rightly) by the
nineteenth century reconcilers of science and religion in general.
Lyell was astute enough, moreover, to have thought out a suitably
insinuating manner of approaching the orthodox:

> 'If you don't triumph over them, but compliment the liberality
> and candour of the present age, the bishops and enlightened
> saints will join us in despising both the ancient and modern phys-
> ico-theologians. ... I give you my word that full *half* of my his-
> tory and comments was cut out, and even many facts; because
> ... I ... felt that it was anticipating twenty or thirty years of the
> march of honest feeling to declare it undisguisedly.'

It was, of course, all very well to take this line, and to say: "Science
the enemy of religion? Not a bit of it, my dear sir! We're not deny-
ing that God does all this, we're merely showing you how he does
it." I say, 'All very well', because there were many who felt that a
God who moved in such a very mysterious way was not the God of
their fathers. Some found it more comforting to ascribe to him the
attribute of non-existence. Others, of whom Tennyson was
one, felt (or came to feel) that the whole spectacle of Nature
was somehow irrelevant to faith. Even in the early days, at one of

the Apostles' debates at Cambridge, he had voted 'No' on the question 'Is an Intelligible First Cause deducible from the Phenomena of the Universe?' And later, he is reported to have said, of the wonders disclosed by the microscope, 'Strange that these wonders should draw some men to God and repel others. No more reason in one than in the other.' This attitude distinguishes Tennyson, and others of this period, not only from Wordsworth but from that line of thinkers who, from the seventeenth century onwards, had been demonstrating the Wisdom of God from the Creation. I suspect that it was also at variance with his own subconscious feeling.

However, Tennyson read other books in which a scientific attitude was combined with more explicit reassurances. Mrs Mattes has shown that in October 1843 he possessed a copy of Herschel's *Preliminary Discourse on the Study of Natural Philosophy* (first published 1830). She quotes these typical extracts, illustrating the optimistic gloss which Herschel put upon the grim story of geology.

> 'Is it wonderful that a being so constituted [i.e. man] should first encourage a hope, and by degrees acknowledge an assurance, that his intellectual existence will not terminate with the dissolution of his corporeal frame but rather that, in a future state of being ... endowed with acute senses, and higher faculties, he shall drink deep at that fountain of beneficent wisdom for which the slight taste obtained on earth has given him so keen a relish?'
>
> '... we cannot fail to be struck with the rapid state of dilatation which every degree upward of the scale, so to speak, exhibits, and which, in an estimation of averages, gives an immense preponderance to the present over every former condition of mankind, and, for aught we can see to the contrary, will place succeeding generations in the same degree of superior relation to the present that this holds to those passed away.'

In short (if we can pick our way through the verbiage), man is rapidly getting bigger and better, and after all a future life seems quite probable—anyway, let's believe it!

About a year later (November 1844) Tennyson wrote to his publisher Edward Moxon:

> 'I want you to get me a book which I see advertised in the *Examiner*: it seems to contain many speculations with which I have been familiar for years, and on which I have written more than one poem. The book is called *Vestiges of the Natural History of Creation....*'

This book (as was pointed out by Mr W. R. Rutland in a very instructive essay called "Tennyson and the Theory of Evolution", over fifteen years ago) contains so many passages which seem to be paraphrased in *In Memoriam* that we cannot doubt its consonance with Tennyson's own thought, and in some particulars its direct influence. Hallam Tennyson has a footnote in his *Memoir*: 'The sections of "In Memoriam" about Evolution had been read by his friends [i.e. in MS.] some years before the publication of *The Vestiges of Creation* in 1844.' But as Mrs Mattes points out, this note does not say which sections, and her evidence indicates that the Epilogue, at least, was not written before 1844. However, only those (if there are still any) who think that Darwin invented Evolution in 1859 will be surprised to find that it is anticipated by Robert Chambers in *Vestiges*, or that Tennyson had anticipated them both. Romanes said that 'In "In Memoriam" Tennyson noted the fact [of Natural Selection], and a few years later Darwin supplied the explanation'. The truth is that the idea of continuous unfolding, development or 'evolution' had been in the air since the latter part of the eighteenth century, being foreshadowed for example by Kant, Goethe and Lamarck. What Darwin did was to collect evidence, not for the fact of evolution, but for the mode of its operation.

Many readers found *Vestiges* disturbing; not so Tennyson. Its harsher implications were already familiar to him, and its consolations were to him truly reassuring. We can form an idea of both these aspects from the following passages (both quoted by Mr Rutland in the above-mentioned essay):

'We have seen powerful evidence that the construction of this globe and its associates, and inferentially of all the other globes of space, was the result, not of any immediate or personal exertion on the part of the Deity, but of natural laws which are the expressions of His will. What is to hinder our supposing that the organic creation is also a result of natural laws, which are in like manner an expression of His will?'

'The Great Ruler of Nature has established laws for the operation of inanimate matter, which are quite unswerving, so that when we know them we have only to act in a certain way with respect to them in order to obtain all the benefits and avoid all the evils connected with them. He has likewise established moral laws in our nature, which are equally unswerving, and from obedience to which unfailing good is to be derived. But the two sets of laws are independent of each other. ... It is clear, moreover, from the whole scope of the natural laws, that the individual, as far as the present sphere of being is concerned, is to the Author of Nature a consideration of inferior moment. Everywhere we see the arrangements for the species perfect; the individual is left, as it were, to take his chance amidst the mêlée of the various laws affecting him.'

Man is thus part of the animal or organic creation, and subject to its laws. Yet Chambers has this reflection to add:

'It may be, that, while we are committed to take our chance in a natural system of undeviating operation, and are left with apparent ruthlessness to endure the consequences of every collision into which we knowingly or unknowingly come with each law of the system, there is a system of Mercy and Grace behind the screen of nature, which is to make up for all the casualties endured there, and the very largeness of which is what makes these casualties a matter of indifference to God. For the existence of such a system, the actual constitution of nature is itself an argument. . . . Thinking of all the contingencies of this world as to be in time melted into or lost in the greater system, to which the present is only subsidiary, let us wait the end with patience, and be of good cheer.'

And lastly, this, which parallels the conclusion of *In Memoriam:*

'It is startling to find an appearance of imperfection in the circle to which man belongs, and the ideas which rise in consequence are no less startling. Is our race but the initial of the grand crowning type? Are there yet to be species superior to us in organization, purer in feeling, more powerful in device and act, and who shall take a rule over us? . . . There may be then occasion for a nobler type of humanity, which shall complete the zoological circle on this planet, and realize some of the dreams of the purest spirits of the present race.'

It was, then, in the context of such ideas as these that *In Memoriam* was composed. But, needless to say (I hope it is needless), we have not 'accounted for' the poem by mentioning some of the books that Tennyson was reading at the time. If *In Memoriam* were merely a versification of such trite reflexions as I have been quoting, it would be of little more account than they. This consideration applies in general to all philosophical poetry, poetry with a 'message'. Readers (and Victorian readers were especially prone to this) often discuss such poetry as if its doctrine were something detachable, something which could be expressed in prose and presented as its essence or inmost meaning. True, it *can* be so presented, but in that case the 'message' of *In Memoriam* (for instance) could as well be learnt direct from Lyell, Herschel or Chambers. It is not that the 'thought' is unimportant in this or other reflective poetry; the point is that it is important in a different way. If its importance were equivalent to that of its prose counterpart, I should not be devoting this attention to Tennyson now. Instead, I should only be entitled to say something like this: 'Lyell, Herschel, Chambers and Tennyson all considered that, while there was no direct evidence for a life after death, the evidence against its probability was not sufficient to proclude any reasonable man from believing in it if he found it comforting.' But, in fact, Tennyson's statement of this great thought has generally been felt to be worth more than that of the other three authors. Why? not because he 'means' anything different, but because he means it from a far greater depth and in a far richer context. Meaning in poetry, as we all know, is far more complex than meaning in logical statement; it operates through image, symbol, rhythm, suggestion and association, and therefore calls forth from us a far more complete response—'complete' in that the emotions, imagination and sensibility are involved as well as the intelligence. A poem, like a piece of ritual, *enacts* what a credal statement merely *propounds*; "this", says the poem in effect, "is a tract of experience lived through in the light of such-and-such a thought or belief; this is what it feels like to accept it". As Professor I. A. Richards has said, a poet is usually more valuable to us when he is feeling something than when he is 'feeling that' something. I think it likely that what, for Tennyson, chiefly kept alive the heart in the head was the influence of Carlyle, working upon a soul prepared by a Christian upbringing and not unacquainted with flashes of mystical insight.

Perhaps the reader may find it convenient to have before him here a few of the stanzas (familiar though they be) which show most clearly how Messrs Lyell, Herschel and Chambers appear when felt along the heart:

LV

'Are God and Nature then at strife,
    That Nature lends such evil dreams?
    So careful of the type she seems,
So carleless of the single life;

That I, considering everywhere
    Her secret meaning in her deeds,
    And finding that of fifty seeds
She often brings but one to bear,

I falter where I firmly trod,
    And falling with my weight of cares
    Upon the great world's altar-stairs
That slope thro' darkness up to God,

I stretch lame hands of faith, and grope,
    And gather dust and chaff, and call
    To what I feel is Lord of all,
And faintly trust the larger hope.

LVI

"So careful of the type?" but no.
    From scarped cliff and quarried stone
    She cries, "A thousand types are gone:
I care for nothing, all shall go.

"Thou makest thine appeal to me:
    I bring to life, I bring to death:
    The spirit does but mean the breath:
I know no more." And he, shall he,

Man, her last work, who seem'd so fair,
    Such splendid purpose in his eyes,
    Who roll'd the psalm to wintry skies,
Who built him fanes of fruitless prayer,

Who trusted God was love indeed
    And love Creation's final law—
    Tho' Nature, red in tooth and claw
With ravine, shriek'd against his creed—

Who loved, who suffer'd countless ills,
    Who battled for the True, the Just,
    Be blown about the desert dust,
Or seal'd within the iron hills?

No more? A monster, then, a dream,
    A discord. Dragons of the prime,
    That tare each other in their slime,
Were mellow music match'd with him.

O life as futile, then, as frail!
    O for thy voice to soothe and bless!
    What hope of answer, or redress?
Behind the veil, behind the veil.'

In these two Sections (LV and LVI) we have Tennyson feeling the
first shock of Lyell and Chambers (or of the interpretations they
stand for). Nature seems to deny the law of love, and man is (in
Mrs Mattes's phrase) 'a prospective fossil'. After faintly trusting the
larger hope, Tennyson sinks to even dimmer depths of perplexity;
hope seems to vanish, truth is for ever hidden behind the veil, and
he vainly longs for Hallam's reassuring voice. However, in a later
Section (CXVIII) he makes a new synthesis of his former thoughts:
above all, he unites in one comprehensive view what Chambers sep-
arates: physical and moral law:

CXVIII
'Contemplate all this work of Time,
    The giant labouring in his youth;
    Nor dream of human love and truth,
As dying Nature's earth and lime;

But trust that those we call the dead
    Are breathers of an ampler day

> For ever nobler ends. They say,
>   The solid earth whereon we tread
>
> In tracts of fluent heat began,
>   And grew to seeming-random forms,
>
>   The seeming prey of cyclic storms,
> Till at the last arose the man;
>
> Who throve and branch'd from clime to clime
>   The herald of a higher race,
>   And of himself in higher place,
> If so he type this work of time
>
> Within himself, from more to more;
>   Or crown'd with attributes of woe
>   Like glories, move his course, and show
> That life is not as idle ore,
>
> But iron dug from central gloom,
>   And heated hot with burning fears,
>   And dipt in baths of hissing tears,
> And batter'd with the shocks of doom
>
> To shape and use. Arise and fly
>   The reeling Faun, the sensual feast;
>   Move upward, working out the beast,
> And let the ape and tiger die.'

Man is the product of the natural law, but he must now take conscious part in the evolutionary process, transferring it from the physical to the moral level. Moreover, this very obligation strengthens the probability that the process does not end with physical death, but that the dead are breathers of an ampler day.

Since I am concerned here not exclusively with Tennyson's thoughts and honest doubts, but also with certain aspects of his poetry as such, I will refer to a few more passages of *In Memoriam* which seem relevant. The first illustrates not only the quality of Tennyson's musings on the tragic ironies of circumstance, but also the difference between a prosaic and a poetic statement of the same 'thought'. What, in Chambers, reads: 'the individual is left, as it were, to take his chance amidst the mêlée of the various laws affecting him', becomes in Tennyson's poetry:

> 'O father, wheresoe'er thou be,
>   Who pledgest now thy gallant son;
>   A shot, ere half thy draught be done,
> Hath still'd the life that beat from thee.

> O mother, praying God will save
> Thy sailor,—while thy head is bow'd,
> His heavy-shotted hammock-shroud
> Drops in his vast and wandering grave.' [vi.]

The next Section is an example of something I have mentioned:
Tennyson's use of his descriptive power, not to decorate, but to
enact, realize or symbolize a mood. The mood is that of loss and
dereliction, and this is communicated through a picture of London
at its dreariest:

> 'Dark house, by which once more I stand
> Here in the long unlovely street,
> Doors, where my heart was used to beat
> So quickly, waiting for a hand,
>
> A hand that can be clasp'd no more—
> Behold me, for I cannot sleep,
> And like a guilty thing I creep
> At earliest morning to the door.
>
> He is not here; but far away
> The noise of life begins again,
> And ghastly thro' the drizzling rain
> On the bald street breaks the blank day.' [vii.]

The series dealing with the return of Arthur Hallam's remains by
ship to England contains several signal examples of the same power.
The moods vary from the 'calm despair' of xi, which is rendered
through an autumn landscape seen from a Lincolnshire hilltop, to
the feverish agitation of xv:

> 'To-night the winds begin to rise
> And roar from yonder dropping day:
> The last red leaf is whirl'd away,
> The rooks are blown about the skies;
>
> The forest crack'd, the waters curl'd,
> The cattle huddled on the lea;
> And wildly dash'd on tower and tree
> The sunbeam strikes along the world:'

Note here the deftness with which Tennyson secures his effect with
the minimum of significant details; a windy autumn sunset is real-
ized with the utmost economy and compression. The winds 'roar
from yonder dropping day': that tells us that the wind is westerly,
and prepares us for the appearance, from beneath the cloud-rim, of
the angry ray from the setting sun, which 'strikes along the world',
apparently 'dashed' there by the wind itself. The rooks, whose

return to their rookery at dusk is normally a slow procession, are 'blown about the skies', hence we feel the wind that buffets them. And all this *is* Tennyson's mood: it is not there simply as an exhibition of virtuosity. A little further on he speaks of

> '. . . yonder cloud
>
> That rises upward always higher,
>   And onward drags a labouring breast,
>   And topples round the dreary west,
> A looming bastion fringed with fire.'

The last line of this, especially, is a fairly obvious jewel from the Nature-notes, yet it escapes frigidity by becoming a powerful symbol of Tennyson's smouldering unrest and sense of impending sorrow.

From about the second Christmas, the 'low beginnings of content' begin to sound faintly; joy in Nature reappears, and a mood of wistful recollection becomes habitual. This sense of rebirth is conveyed with magnificent power in Section LXXXVI (composed at Barmouth, perhaps in 1839), in which the coalescence of subject and object, Nature and feeling, is complete:

> 'Sweet after showers, ambrosial air,
>   That rollest from the gorgeous gloom
>   Of evening over brake and bloom
> And meadow, slowly breathing bare
>
> The round of space, and rapt below
>   Thro' all the dewy-tassell'd wood,
>   And shadowing down the horned flood
> In ripples, fan my brows and blow
>
> The fever from my cheek, and sigh
>   The full new life that feeds thy breath
>   Throughout my frame, till Doubt and Death,
> Ill brethren, let the fancy fly
>
> From belt to belt of crimson seas
>   On leagues of odour streaming far,
>   To where in yonder orient star
> A hundred spirits whisper "Peace".'

Romantic? Sentimental? Perhaps, but not if 'sentimental' means full of unmastered or ill-ordered feeling. Romantic certainly, if by that we mean overflowing with powerful emotion expressed in natural imagery. It is none the worse for that. Indeed, I think we have here a poetic structure as subtly articulated as any of Donne's, though it is made up of sense-impressions and feelings rather than of thought or impassioned wit. To begin with, Tennyson shows true

imagination, in the Coleridgean sense, in detecting the correspond-
ence between his subjective state—recovery, renewal after sorrow—
and a particular manifestation of weather experienced on the Welsh
coast: the relenting of the elements at the close of day after rain.
The clearance of the sky and the liberation of his soul are made one
and the same; absolution and remission are shed abroad simultane-
ously throughout the visible scene and within his own heart. The
process actually goes on within these four verses, which move stead-
ily onwards, with the majestic march of the retreating clouds,
unbroken by any pause between the quatrains. To achieve such a
sweep in a series of four-lined stanzas is itself a *tour de force*, but
the triumph consists mainly in the linking of the various elements
of observation and feeling, the fusing of outer and inner. Tenny-
son's virtuosity, his victory over his own stanza-form, appears strik-
ingly in the continuity of the flow, and above all in

> '. . . slowly breathing bare
> The round of space, . . .'

where the passage across what is normally a break gives precisely the
required sense of steady clearance, the word 'bare' acquiring double
force from its own exposed position. Nature breathes again after
storm, and the clearing breeze which sweeps through sky and wood
is also the new life which penetrates his frame, releasing and tran-
quillizing his imagination. The deftness with which the symbols of
peace are assembled together in a composite structure at the end,
producing at once a completed picture of that particular scene, and
also a sense of calm of mind, all passion spent, is worthy of admira-
tion. If there are any criteria which would not allow this to be great
poetry, so much the worse for the criteria.

I referred above to the quasi-mystical intuitions which from time
to time visited Tennyson. One of these is described in Section xcv,
which commemorates a summer night at Somersby. The passage
thus relates to an occasion before 1837 (when the family left the
Rectory), but it may well have been composed later. Evidently the
experience sank deep, for G. G. Bradley, alluding to August 1842,
wrote:

> 'I was greatly struck by his describing to us on one singularly
> still starlit evening, how he and his friends had once sat out far
> into the night having tea at a table on the lawn beneath the
> stars, and that the candles had burned with steady upright flame,
> disturbed from time to time by the inrush of a moth or cock-
> chafer. . . . I do not know whether he had already written, or was
> perhaps even then shaping, the lines in "In Memoriam" which so
> many years afterwards brought back to me the incident.'

The Section is worth quoting, not only for its climax, but for its setting:

> 'By night we linger'd on the lawn,
>   For underfoot the herb was dry;
>   And genial warmth; and o'er the sky
> The silvery haze of summer drawn;
>
> And calm that let the tapers burn
>   Unwavering: not a cricket chirr'd:
>   The brook alone far-off was heard,
> And on the board the fluttering urn:
>
> And bats went round in fragrant skies,
>   And wheel'd or lit the filmy shapes
>   That haunt the dusk, with ermine capes
> And woolly breasts and beaded eyes;
>
> While now we sang old songs that peal'd
>   From knoll to knoll, where, couch'd at ease,
>   The white kine glimmer'd, and the trees
> Laid their dark arms about the field.'

The others departed one by one, leaving him alone with the night and with his own thoughts. A hunger seized his heart for Hallam, and he took out and read some of his dead friend's letters:

> 'And all at once it seem'd at last
> The living soul was flash'd on mine,
>
> And mine in this was wound, and whirl'd
>   About empyreal heights of thought,
>   And came on that which is, and caught
> The deep pulsations of the world.'

And came on that which is: Wordsworth had said 'And I have felt A presence', or 'Rapt into still communion that transcends The imperfect offices of prayer and praise'; so poets from time to time try to communicate the incommunicable. But no one who has ever felt this oneness with the real, this contact with 'that which is', can ever after remain long in unbelief or half-belief, or fail to see life steadily and whole.

The following Section (xcvi) is interesting, if only because it contains the oftenest-quoted phrase in Tennyson:

> 'There lives more faith in honest doubt,
> Believe me, than in half the creeds.'

This is his reply to someone (blue-eyed and sweet-hearted, so pre-

sumably Emily Sellwood?) who had told him doubt was 'Devil-
born'. No; Hallam's example proves the contrary:

> 'He fought his doubts and gather'd strength,
> He would not make his judgment blind,
> He faced the spectres of the mind
> And laid them: ...'

The object of Faith is a Power that dwells in darkness and cloud as
well as in light, and a man who has never doubted cannot possess
that tensest kind of faith which consists, not in doubt's non-exist-
ence, nor even in its annihilation, but in believing in despite of it,
and dwelling in 'tracts of calm from tempest made'.

Section cxiv deals with the Carlylean (pre- and post-Carlylean as
well) theme of the superiority of 'Wisdom' over mere 'Knowledge';
knowledge may advance, but without reverence and charity it will
be sterile. Akin to this in thought is cxx, where he rejects the kind
of 'science' which is content with reducing man to the level of
Nature:

> 'I think we are not wholly brain,
> Magnetic mockeries; ...
>
> .   .   .   .
>
> Not only cunning casts in clay:
>   Let Science prove we are, and then
>   What matters Science unto men,
> At least to me? ...'

Tennyson held that we are more than the matter of our bodies and
brains, thus he was not worried by explanations of our animal
origin; the value of an end-product was not, for him, affected by
knowledge about its beginnings.

We come at length to Section cxxiv, where, at the climax of the
poem, Tennyson states the faith he has attained. For a man of his
upbringing, a man so awake to spiritual reality and so mystically
inclined, a believing attitude was inevitable and necessary. But, as
we have seen, it was not achieved without conflict, or by putting
out the eyes of the mind. What especially gives Tennyson his repre-
sentative quality, and also earns him our respect, is that to the best
of his ability he kept pace with all new truths, and, much as he
longed for religious assurance, would accept none unless it was com-
patible with them. It was thus that he came to base his faith on
what seemed the only invulnerable foundation: the needs and
affirmatives of the heart.

> 'That which we dare invoke to bless;
>   Our dearest faith; our ghastliest doubt;
>   He, They, One, All; within, without;
> The Power in darkness whom we guess;

I found Him not in world or sun,
    Or eagle's wing, or insect's eye;
    Nor thro' the questions men may try,
The petty cobwebs we have spun:

If e'er when faith had fall'n asleep,
    I heard a voice "believe no more"
    And heard an ever-breaking shore
That tumbled in the Godless deep;

A warmth within the breast would melt
    The freezing reason's colder part,
    And like a man in wrath the heart
Stood up and answer'd "I have felt".'

'I found Him not in world or sun': in spite of his impassioned and lifelong attention to Nature, and his incomparable success in rendering her, it was not there, not in the classic evidences of wisdom and design in the universe, that he found God. I mentioned his remark about the miscroscopic world—how strange it seemed to him that its wonders should either strengthen or weaken faith: he found Him not in 'insect's eye'. We recall that even at Cambridge he had voted 'No' at a College discussion on the question 'Is an Intelligible First Cause deducible from the Phenomena of the Universe?' And if not in Nature, certainly not in metaphysical cobweb-spinning. Because, rejecting these former props of orthodoxy, Tennyson fell back upon the inward evidence, the reasons of the heart, he has been accused, like other believers of his and other times, of wishful thinking. This is perhaps not the place to discuss such a question; I would only remark that in taking up this position Tennyson was in accord with some of the profoundest insights of the ages, and of his own age in particular. From the time of David, through St Anselm with his *crede ut intelligas*, Pascal with his 'this then is faith, God known in the heart, not proved by the reason', down to Coleridge and Carlyle and Kierkegaard, there had been a recognition that faith is not a matter of rational demonstration; that were it so, it would cease to be faith—i.e. a matter of religious duty, a vital commitment—and become compulsory knowledge; and that its acceptance means an act of the will: a plunge, a venture, or what is now sometimes called 'an existential choice'. If we remember all this, we may be less ready to despise Tennyson—as some of his critics have done—for coming to rest in a similar affirmation. If a man persisted in believing that the earth was flat, or that it rested in space upon the horns of a bull, and the bull upon the shell of a tortoise—if he obstinately clung to these views simply because he felt them in his heart to be true, we should rightly consider him eccentric, and possibly mad. But the shape and

position of the earth are matters of empirical observation and math-
ematical calculation, whereas religious belief is not. In this sphere,
the writ of the rational understanding does not run, and we are per-
mitted—no, enjoined—by our experience as responsible moral
agents to commit ourselves to those hypotheses without which the
good life becomes difficult and, as some find, impossible. Whether
or no the reader agrees with this, I hope he will at least allow that
Tennyson's position commands respect.

Very characteristically, he added a qualifying stanza to those
above quoted, feeling, no doubt, that he might seem to have
triumphed too easily over the voice which said "believe no more":

> 'No, like a child in doubt and fear:
> But that blind clamour made me wise;
> Then was I as a child that cries,
> But, crying, knows his father near.'

And here let me draw attention to what seems to me the most
remarkable of Victorian comments on Tennyson. It is by Henry
Sidgwick, who, having resigned his Trinity Fellowship on account
of 'honest doubt', and spent the rest of his life fluctuating between
faith and agnosticism, was peculiarly well qualified to offer an opin-
ion. There are two comments recorded in the *Memoir of Henry
Sidgwick* (1906); the first, written in his Journal for February 10,
1887, is this:

> 'Perhaps a certain balancedness is the most distinctive charac-
> teristic of Tennyson among poets. . . . Perhaps this specially
> makes him the representative poet of an age whose most charac-
> teristic merit is to see both sides of a question. Thus in *In
> Memoriam* the points where I am most affected are where a cer-
> tain *retour sur soi-même* occurs. Almost any poet might have writ-
> ten,

> > And like a man in wrath the heart
> > Stood up and answered, I have felt.

> But only Tennyson would have immediately added:

> > No, like a child in doubt and fear.'

The second is a much longer passage; it was written nearly ten years
later, after Tennyson's death, for the use of Hallam Tennyson in
his *Memoir* of his father. Here are some relevant extracts from his
letter to Hallam:

> 'To begin, then: our views on religious matters [i.e. Sidgwick's
> own and those of his like-minded contemporaries] were not, at
> any rate after a year or two of the discussions started in 1860 by
> *Essays and Reviews*, really in harmony with those which we

found suggested by *In Memoriam*. They were more sceptical and less Christian. . . . And this sceptical attitude has remained mine through life; while at the same time I feel that the beliefs in God and in immortality are vital to human well-being.

'Hence the most important influence of *In Memoriam* on my thought, apart from its poetic charm as an expression of personal emotion, . . . lay in the unparalleled combination of intensity of feeling with comprehensiveness of view and balance of judgment, shown in presenting the *deepest* needs and perplexities of humanity. And this influence, I find, has increased rather than diminished as years have gone on, and as the great issues between Agnostic Science and Faith have become continually more prominent. In the sixties I should say that these deeper issues were somewhat obscured by the discussions on Christian dogma, inspiration of Scripture, etc. . . .

'During these years we were absorbed in struggling for freedom of thought in the trammels of a historical religion: and perhaps what we sympathized with most in *In Memoriam* at that time, apart from the personal feeling, was the defence of "honest doubt", . . . and generally the *forward* movement of the thought.

'Well, the years pass, the struggle with what Carlyle used to call "Hebrew old clothes" is over, Freedom is won, and what does Freedom bring us to? It brings us face to face with atheistic science: the faith in God and Immortality, which we had been struggling to clear from superstition, suddenly seems to be *in the air*: and in seeking for a firm basis for this faith we find ourselves in the midst of the "fight with death" which *In Memoriam* so powerfully presents.

'What *In Memoriam* did for us, for me at least, in this struggle was to impress on us the ineffaceable and ineradicable conviction that *humanity* will not and cannot acquiesce in a godless world.

'The force with which it impressed this conviction was not due to the *mere intensity* of its expression of the feelings which Atheism outrages and Agnosticism ignores: but rather to its expression of them along with a reverent docility to the lessons of science which also belongs to the essence of the thought of our age.

'I remember being struck with a note in *Nature*, at the time of your father's death, which . . . regarded him as pre-eminently the Poet of Science. I have always felt this characteristic important in estimating his effect on his generation. Wordsworth's attitude towards Nature was one that, so to say, left Science unregarded. . . . But for your father the physical world is always the world as known to us through physical science: the scientific view of it dominates his thoughts about it; and his general acceptance of this view is real and sincere, even when he utters the intensest feeling of its inadequacy to satisfy our deepest needs. Had it been otherwise, had he met the atheistic tendencies of modern Science with more confident defiance, more confident assertion of an

Intuitive Faculty of theological knowledge, overriding the results
laboriously reached by empirical science, I think his antagonism
to those tendencies would have been far less impressive.
'I always feel this strongly in reading the memorable lines . . .
[here he quotes the two stanzas ending

> ' . . . the heart
> Stood up and answered "I have felt".'

'At this point, if the stanzas had stopped here, we should have
shaken our heads and said, "Feeling must not usurp the function
of Reason. Feeling is not knowing. It is the duty of a rational
being to follow truth wherever it leads."
'But the poet's instinct knows this; he knows that this usurpa-
tion by Feeling of the function of Reason is too bold and confi-
dent; accordingly, in the next stanza he gives the turn to humility
in the protest of Feeling which is required (I think) to win the
assent of the "man in men" at this stage of human thought:

> No, like a child . . . etc.
> . . . .
> And what I am beheld again
>   What is, and no man understands;
>   And out of darkness came the hands
> That reach through nature, moulding man.

'These lines I can never read without tears. I feel in them the
indestructible and inalienable minimum of faith which humanity
cannot give up because it is necessary for life; and which I know
that I, at least so far as the man in me is deeper than the method-
ical thinker, cannot give up.'

No better illustration could be found, I think, of that poised
uncertainty of the devoutly inclined agnostic mind, to which *In
Memoriam* made so strong an appeal. At the same time Tennyson's
deeply religious nature, and the intensity of his longing for assur-
ance, could not but reach the hearts of his Christian readers also,
even though with them a touch of pity would mix itself with their
sympathetic response. For when all was said, Tennyson had *not*
found that degree and kind of certainty which revealed religion,
through dogma and Church, claimed to give. The Churchman R.
H. Hutton (editor of *The Spectator*) wrote in 1892:

> 'There was an agnostic element in Tennyson, as perhaps in all
> the greatest minds, though in him it may have been in excess,
> which kept re-iterating: "We have but faith, we cannot know",
> and which, I should say, was never completely satisfied even of
> the adequacy of dogmatic definitions which his Church recog-
> nized . . . He finds no authoritative last word as many Chris-

tians find in ecclesiastical authority. . . . The generally faltering voice with which Tennyson expresses the ardour of his own hope, touches the heart of this doubting and questioning age, as no more confident expression of belief could have touched it. The lines of his theology were in harmony with the great central lines of Christian thought; but in coming down to detail it soon passed into a region where all was wistful, and dogma disappeared in a haze of radiant twilight.'

The Prologue to *In Memoriam* was the last Section to be written (1849). It was written to show the Christian world (and Emily Sellwood in particular) how far Tennyson could, with perfect sincerity, go in the direction of Christianity. Some of its phrases (I have italicized them) show the truth of R. H. Hutton's comment:

> 'Strong Son of God, immortal Love,
>   Whom we, that have not seen thy face,
>   By faith, and faith alone, embrace,
> *Believing where we cannot prove;*
> . . . .
>
> Thou *seemest* human and divine,
>   The highest, holiest manhood, thou:
> . . . .
>
> Our *little systems* have their day;
>   They have their day and cease to be:
>   They are but broken lights of thee,
> And thou, O Lord, art more than they.
>
> *We have but faith: we cannot know;*'

Yet even this dissatisfied the fastidious Henry Sidgwick: 'I have always felt that . . . the effect of the introduction does not quite represent the effect of the poem. Faith, in the introduction, is too completely triumphant.'

The Two Voices had ended, as we saw, with Sabbath calm and domestic bliss; *In Memoriam* ends with a marriage-song, addressed to Edmund Lushington and Tennyson's sister Cecilia. It was, for more reasons than one, an appropriate conclusion. Hallam had been engaged to another of his sisters, and the approaching wedding of Cecilia enabled Tennyson to end on the desired note of hope and rebirth, all thoughts turned towards the future. By a happy stroke of synthesis, too, he was able to link the marriage, and its hoped-for offspring, not only with Hallam but also with the main evolutionary drift of the whole poem—even with that old thought of embryonic development which had interested him long before he had read *Vestiges*; and, finally, with the Victorian dream of progress and a loftier race:

'A soul shall draw from out the vast
And strike his being into bounds,

And, *moved thro' life of lower phase* [my italics]
Result in man, be born and think,
And act and love, a closer link
Betwixt us and the crowning race

Of those that, eye to eye, shall look
On knowledge....

.   .   .   .

No longer half-akin to brute,
For all we thought and loved and did,
And hoped, and suffer'd, is but seed
Of what in them is flower and fruit;

Whereof the man, that with me trod
This planet, was a noble type
Appearing ere the times were ripe,
That friend of mine who lives in God,

That God, which ever lives and loves,
One God, one law, one element,
And one far-off divine event,
To which the whole creation moves.'

T. S. ELIOT

In Memoriam†

Tennyson is a great poet, for reasons that are perfectly clear. He has three qualities which are seldom found together except in the greatest poets: abundance, variety, and complete competence. We therefore cannot appreciate his work unless we read a good deal of it. We may not admire his aims: but whatever he sets out to do, he succeeds in doing, with a mastery which gives us the sense of confidence that is one of the major pleasures of poetry. * * *

* * *

It is, in my opinion, in *In Memoriam*, that Tennyson finds full expression. Its technical merit alone is enough to ensure its perpetuity. While Tennyson's technical competence is everywhere masterly

† From *Essays Ancient and Modern*   186–203.
(London, Faber and Faber, 1936), pp.

and satisfying, *In Memoriam* is the most unapproachable of all his poems. Here are one hundred and thirty-two passages, each of several quatrains in the same form, and never monotony or repetition. And the poem has to be comprehended as a whole. We may not memorize a few passages, we cannot find a "fair sample"; we have to comprehend the whole of a poem which is essentially the length that it is. We may choose to remember:

> Dark house, by which once more I stand
> Here in the long unlovely street,
> Doors, where my heart was used to beat
> So quickly, waiting for a hand,
>
> A hand that can be clasp'd no more—
> Behold me, for I cannot sleep,
> And like a guilty thing I creep
> At earliest morning to the door.
>
> He is not here; but far away
> The noise of life begins again,
> And ghastly thro' the drizzling rain
> On the bald street breaks the blank day.

This is great poetry, economical of words, a universal emotion related to a particular place; and it gives me the shudder that I fail to get from anything in *Maud*. But such a passage, by itself, is not *In Memoriam*: *In Memoriam* is the whole poem. It is unique: it is a long poem made by putting together lyrics, which have only the unity and continuity of a diary, the concentrated diary of a man confessing himself. It is a diary of which we have to read every word.

Apparently Tennyson's contemporaries, once they had accepted *In Memoriam*, regarded it as a message of hope and reassurance to their rather fading Christian faith. It happens now and then that a poet by some strange accident expresses the mood of his generation, at the same time that he is expressing a mood of his own which is quite remote from that of his generation. This is not a question of insincerity: there is an amalgam of yielding and opposition below the level of consciousness. Tennyson himself, on the conscious level of the man who talks to reporters and poses for photographers, to judge from remarks made in conversation and recorded in his son's Memoir, consistently asserted a convinced, if somewhat sketchy, Christian belief. And he was a friend of Frederick Denison Maurice —nothing seems odder about that age than the respect which its eminent people felt for each other. Nevertheless, I get a very different impression from *In Memoriam* from that which Tennyson's

contemporaries seem to have got. It is of a very much more interest-
ing and tragic Tennyson. His biographers have not failed to remark
that he had a good deal of the temperament of the mystic—cer-
tainly not at all the mind of the theologian. He was desperately
anxious to hold the faith of the believer, without being very clear
about what he wanted to believe: he was capable of illumination
which he was incapable of understanding. The "Strong Son of God,
immortal Love," with an invocation of whom the poem opens, has
only a hazy connexion with the Logos, or the Incarnate God. Ten-
nyson is distressed by the idea of a mechanical universe; he is natu-
rally, in lamenting his friend, teased by the hope of immortality and
reunion beyond death. Yet the renewal craved for seems at best but
a continuance, or a substitute for the joys of friendship upon earth.
His desire for immortality never is quite the desire for Eternal Life;
his concern is for the loss of man rather than for the gain of God.

> shall he,
> Man, her last work, who seem'd so fair,
> Such splendid purpose in his eyes,
> Who roll'd the psalm to wintry skies,
> Who built him fanes of fruitless prayer,
>
> Who trusted God was love indeed,
> And love Creation's final law—
> Tho' Nature, red in tooth and claw
> With ravine, shriek'd against his creed—
>
> Who loved, who suffer'd countless ills.
> Who battled for the True, the Just,
> Be blown about the desert dust,
> Or seal'd within the iron hills?

That strange abstraction, "Nature," becomes a real god or goddess,
perhaps more real, at moments, to Tennyson than God ("*Are God
and nature then at strife?*"). The hope of immortality is confused
(typically of the period) with the hope of the gradual and steady
improvement of this world. Much has been said of Tennyson's
interest in contemporary science, and of the impression of Darwin.
In Memoriam, in any case, antedates *The Origin of Species* by sev-
eral years, and the belief in social progress by democracy antedates
it by many more; and I suspect that the faith of Tennyson's age in
human progress would have been quite as strong even had the dis-
coveries of Darwin been postponed by fifty years. And after all,
there is no logical connexion: the belief in progress being current
already, the discoveries of Darwin were harnessed to it:

No longer half-akin to brute,
    For all we thought, and loved and did
    And hoped, and suffer'd, is but seed
Of what in them is flower and fruit;
Whereof the man, that with me trod
    This planet, was a noble type
    Appearing ere the times were ripe,
That friend of mine who lives in God,

That God, which ever lives and loves,
    One God, one law, one element,
    And one far-off divine event,
To which the whole creation moves.

These lines show an interesting compromise between the religious attitude and, what is quite a different thing, the belief in human perfectibility; but the contrast was not so apparent to Tennyson's contemporaries. They may have been taken in by it, but I don't think that Tennyson himself was, quite: his feelings were more honest than his mind. There is evidence elsewhere—even in an early poem, *Locksley Hall*, for example—that Tennyson by no means regarded with complacency all the changes that were going on about him in the progress of industrialism and the rise of the mercantile and manufacturing and banking classes; and he may have contemplated the future of England, as his years drew out, with increasing gloom. Temperamentally, he was opposed to the doctrine that he was moved to accept and to praise.

Tennyson's feelings, I have said, were honest; but they were usually a good way below the surface. *In Memoriam* can, I think, justly be called a religious poem, but for another reason than that which made it seem religious to his contemporaries. It is not religious because of the quality of its faith, but because of the quality of its doubt. Its faith is a poor thing, but its doubt is a very intense experience. *In Memoriam* is a poem of despair, but of despair of a religious kind. And to qualify its despair with the adjective "religious" is to elevate it above most of its derivatives. For *The City of Dreadful Night*, and *A Shropshire Lad*, and the poems of Thomas Hardy, are small work in comparison with *In Memoriam*: It is greater than they and comprehends them.[1]

1. There are other kinds of despair. Davidson's great poem, *Thirty Bob a Week*, is not derivative from Tennyson. On the other hand, there are other things derivative from Tennyson besides *Atalanta in Calydron*. Compare the poems of William Morris with *The Voyage of Maeldune*, and *Barrack Room Ballads* with several of Tennyson's later poems.

In ending we must go back to the beginning and remember that *In Memoriam* would not be a great poem, or Tennyson a great poet, without the technical accomplishment. Tennyson is the great master of metric as well as of melancholia; I do not think any poet in English has ever had a finer ear for vowel sound, as well as a subtler feeling for some moods of anguish:

> Dear as remember'd kisses after death,
> And sweet as those by hopeless fancy feign'd
> On lips that are for others; deep as love,
> Deep as first love, and wild with all regret.

And this technical gift of Tennyson's is no slight thing. Tennyson lived in a time which was already acutely time-conscious: a great many things seemed to be happening, railways were being built, discoveries were being made, the face of the world was changing. That was a time busy in keeping up to date. It had, for the most part, no hold on permanent things, on permanent truths about man and God and life and death. The surface of Tennyson stirred about with his time; and he had nothing to which to hold fast except his unique and unerring feeling for the sounds of words. But in this he had something that no one else had. Tennyson's surface, his technical accomplishment, is intimate with his depths: what we most quickly see about Tennyson is that which moves between the surface and the depths, that which is of slight importance. By looking innocently at the surface we are most likely to come to the depths, to the abyss of sorrow. Tennyson is not only a minor Virgil, he is also with Virgil as Dante saw him, a Virgil among the Shades, the saddest of all English poets, among the Great in Limbo, the most instinctive rebel against the society in which he was the most perfect conformist.

Tennyson seems to have reached the end of his spiritual development with *In Memoriam*; there followed no reconciliation, no resolution.

> And now no sacred staff shall break in blossom,
> No choral salutation lure to light
> A spirit sick with perfume and sweet night,

or rather with twilight, for Tennyson faced neither the darkness nor the light in his later years. The genius, the technical power, persisted to the end, but the spirit had surrendered. A gloomier end than that of Baudelaire: Tennyson had no *singulier avertissement*. And having turned aside from the journey through the dark night, to become the surface flatterer of his own time, he has been rewarded with the despite of an age that succeeds his own in shallowness.

CARLISLE MOORE

Faith, Doubt, and Mystical Experience in "In Memoriam"†

We are still wont to think that Tennyson must abide our question because he confused personal confession and public prophecy. *In Memoriam* especially, with its wavering progression from a deeply-felt religious doubt to the proclamation of a universal faith, has been dismissed as a typical instance of Victorian rationalization which no longer speaks to us. Yet with all the commentaries, analyses, and keys which have appeared since 1850 the poem still eludes consensus. In its own time readers generally accepted it as a poem of faith and rejoiced with Kingsley to find "in the science and history of the nineteenth century new and living fulfilments of the words which we learnt at our mothers' knee."[1] But the praise was not unanimous. Some critics thought the doubt which they saw there made the faith less than "honest," and objected to Tennyson's admitting it even into the concluding sections.[2] Nevertheless, for half a century *In Memoriam* brought solace to worried and struggling believers, many of whom did not perceive and were therefore not troubled by its ambiguities, while those readers who did perceive them were comforted by the commentaries which, like A. C. Bradley's, charted the triumphal journey from doubt to faith.[3]

The critical reaction came when religion began to lose its hold on the individual conscience. Carlyle's loss of the traditional faith in which he had been reared produced what William James called "the sick shudder of the frustrated religious demand."[4] Leslie Stephen, writing about his own similar loss a generation later, confessed, "I did not feel that the solid ground was giving way beneath

† *Victorian Studies*, 7 (1963), 155–69.

1. Edgar F. Shannon, *Tennyson and the Reviewers* (Cambridge, Mass., 1952), p. 149.
2. Strongest objections to Tennyson's theological doubts came from the High Church *English Review* which scolded him for having no faith at all, and from the Thunderer's *Times* which denounced "the enormous exaggeration of the grief," and the tone of "amatory tenderness"; further recognition of the serious doubt in the poem can be seen where it is recommended as spiritual therapy for the bereaved, e.g., by Lewes writing in the *Leader*: "All who have sorrowed will listen with delight to the chastened strains here poured forth in *In Memoriam*" (Shannon, pp. 142, 149–157).
3. A *Commentary on Tennyson's In Memoriam*, 3rd ed. (London, 1936), pp. 36–43. Among the many which preceded Bradley's (originally published in 1901) were F. W. Robertson, *Analysis of Mr. Tennyson's "In Memoriam"* (London, 1862); Alfred Gatty, *A Key to Tennyson's "In Memoriam"* (London, 1881); John F. Genung, *Tennyson's "In Memoriam": Its Purpose and Structure* (London 1881); and Elizabeth R. Chapman, *A Companion to "In Memoriam"* (London, 1888). For a recent analytical and structural study of the poem see Eleanor B. Mattes, *In Memoriam: The Way of a Soul* (New York, 1951).
4. *Will to Believe and Other Essays* (New York, 1927), p. 42.

my feet, but rather that I was being relieved of a cumbrous burden. I was not discovering that my creed was false, but that I had never really believed it."[5] As the need for spiritual support diminished, or was satisfied by other supports, religion as an institution began to lose its social value. Separated from ethics it did not have to be regarded as the indispensable basis of all moral conduct. One could be both happy and good, apparently, without benefit of faith. In *Memoriam*, therefore, with its intense spiritual struggles seemed to an agnostic to be a somewhat foolish and misguided poem, the faith attained therein meaningless or insincere. It is not without irony that Tennyson was rescued from the neglect in which most Victorians languished during the early decades of this century when it was discovered that those struggles had produced some of his best poetry. It mattered little that in the hands of Sir Harold Nicolson the rescue involved splitting Tennyson in two and throwing away the worser half: the "prosperous Isle-of-Wight Victorian" wrote pontifical verse lacking both inspiration and sincerity, but elsewhere, in the lines of the "lonely, frightened spirit crouched broodingly over thoughts of death . . . the mystical genius of Tennyson comes upon one in a flash, and there can be no question of the reality of his emotion and his impulse."[6] Later T. S. Eliot's critical authority made it more than ever impossible to read *In Memoriam* as a poem of faith, though he did defend it against the charge of insincerity.[7] All that remained to be said in behalf of Tennyson's long struggle for faith was that he had fought a good fight and remained a good doubter.

The critical wheel had thus turned full circle. From being hailed as a noble poem of faith despite its admixture of doubt, *In Memoriam* came to be defended as a moving poem of doubt despite its unconvincing faith. In both cases large portions of the whole were ignored or ruled out of consideration. Each judgment reflected special views of its age: post-Darwinian and post-Freudian. But it may be asked whether such partial readings of the poem can be said to do it justice. Having discovered the genuineness of the doubt, perhaps we should re-examine the faith, should ask whether in the light of that "mystical genius" of Tennyson's which Nicolson recognized both are not admissable and, indeed, wholly reconcilable,

5. *Some Early Impressions* (London, 1924), p. 70.
6. *Tennyson* (London, 1923), pp. 14, 27.
7. Eliot, in *Essays Ancient and Modern* (London, 1936), favored discarding the faith which "is a poor thing" and keeping the doubt which "is a very intense experience"; but he insisted that to be adequately understood the poem must be read entire (pp. 182–188). Following Eliot, Samuel C. Burchell, in "Tennyson's Dark Night," *South Atlantic Quarterly*, LIV (1955), thinks the twentieth century first to appreciate *In Memoriam* as an expression of anguish and doubt: "There is a concreteness in the pessimism and despair of Tennyson and *In Memoriam*, and it is something for which we can have great sympathy . . . after a period of being a schoolboy's medicine and a clergyman's platitude, *In Memoriam* now finally merits the serious attention of modern critics" (p. 81).

when the poem is seen in relation to the phenomenon of religious conversion.

In its external, formal aspect *In Memoriam* is a public utterance, a conspicuous attempt to reconcile opposing tendencies which seemed to Tennyson and his contemporaries to be threatening the foundations of English society. Viewed thus it is fundamentally an effort to save religion from science by adducing a Coleridgean philosophy of religious experience against the demonstration of God from nature, or by reconciling the nineteenth-century belief in the progress of the species with the Christian concept of salvation.[8] Beneath this great argument lies Tennyson's intimate response to Hallam's death cast into language which expresses his shifting thoughts and moods over a period of seventeen years. Though he employed many of the familiar terms and concepts of his time he also, in a remarkable way, conveyed the mystical quality of his own vision and experience. T. S. Eliot remarks that Tennyson's "surface" (by which he means technical skill) "is intimate with his depths." But for Eliot, Tennyson's depths are depths of sorrow; Tennyson is "the saddest of all English poets" (p. 203). It is strange that the poet of "the moment in the rose-garden" should have taken no notice of Tennyson's similar moment in the garden at Somersby. The trance-like experience of Section XCV marks the climax of the poet's efforts to commune with the spirit of Hallam; it provides a nexus between the disparate elements of doubt and faith; and it tends to draw the poem away from the tradition of the pastoral elegy, in which the turning point, "He is not dead, he lives!," is so often merely a rhetorical device, and associates the poem with another kind of tradition altogether, that of religious conversion. Jerome H. Buckley pointed out in 1951 that "Though loosely organised as an aesthetic whole, *In Memoriam* closely followed the general pattern of nineteenth-century conversion" in the way it "traced the soul's growth from unshadowed hope through the denial of life itself towards the final conquest of doubt and despair."[9] But he did not explore the work from this point of view except to demonstrate that in it and similar works the pattern of conversion often found expression in certain recurring images of fire and water, of which Teufelsdroeckh's "Baphometic Fire-Baptism" in *Sartor Resartus* is probably the clearest example.

As the stock-in-trade of Methodism, conversion became immensely popular in the late eighteenth and early nineteenth centuries. Against a background of philosophic skepticism on the one

8. See Graham Hough, "The Natural Theology of *In Memoriam*," *Review of English Studies*, XXIII (1948), 244–256; and John D. Rosenberg, "The Two Kingdoms of *In Memoriam*," *Journal of English and German Philology*, LVIII (1959), 228–240.

9. *The Victorian Temper* (Cambridge, Mass., 1951), p. 87.

hand and of the hard Calvinist creed of damnation on the other, there developed a widespread feeling that a saving faith was attainable by everyone, whatever his status, through a sudden electrifying emotional and spiritual crisis, and thousands were "reborn" in a quick and easy way that sensitive minds distrusted. Herr Teufelsdroeckh observed sardonically that such conversions represented "a new-attained progress in the Moral Development of man; hereby has the Highest come home to the bosoms of the most Limited; what to Plato was but a hallucination, and to Socrates a Chimera, is now clear and certain to your Zinzendorfs, your Wesleys, and the poorest of their Pietists and Methodists."[1] Teufelsdroeckh's own conversion belongs to a different order, for it was not primarily an acceptance of Christ nor was it induced by a heavy burden of sin, but rather by a fear that God did not love the world. With some romantic dramatization, Teufelsdroeckh repeats in its main outlines Carlyle's own spiritual crisis experienced on Leith Walk in 1821.[2] Not a doctrinal conversion, like Newman's adoption of a creed and submission to authority, this was rather, like Mill's reading of Marmontel, a spontaneous awakening, an intellectual and emotional discovery of new truths which though not self-induced answered a personal need and, in Carlyle's case, was strongly mystical. Moreover, it was attended by the two conditions which seem to characterize the intellectual species of conversion. The first of these conditions is a state of mind which for reasons known or unknown has become unbearable and is rationally irremediable. The occasion may be a fear for one's own security, or virtue, or a broader concern for the spiritual welfare of society or the cosmos. The second is the occurrence of a climatic experience during which a power greater than oneself is felt to be taking control and directing one towards a solution.[3] Often this does not complete the conversion but only begins it. Sometimes it is followed by a prolonged period of doubt which delays and modifies the faith ultimately attained. Sometimes there are repetitions of the original experience. Even John Wesley's

1. *Sartor Resartus*, ed. C. F. Harrold (New York, 1937), p. 198.
2. See my *"Sartor Resartus* and the Problem of Carlyle's Conversion," *PMLA*, LXX (1955), 662–681.
3. For more detailed analysis of conversion see William James, *Varieties of Religious Experience* (London, 1902), pp. 189–258; A. D. Nock, *Conversion* (Oxford, 1933), pp. 1–16, 254–271; and Robert H. Thouless, *The Psychology of Religion* (Cambridge, 1923), pp. 187–224. Among the class of spontaneous, or involuntary, conversions, James distinguishes the moral conversion, involving little or no intellectual readjustment, from the fuller, spiritual one which involves far-reaching intellectual and emotional changes. These vary in three main respects: the state of consciousness out of which they arise, the nature of the crisis itself, and the effects of the crisis. The inductors may be a feeling of personal sinfulness, weariness of self (accidie), or the fear of a godless world. (For Carlyle, Mill, and Tennyson, the crux was not a burden of sin, or even the loss of belief in God, but the lack of moral, rational meaning in the universe and human life.) Though sometimes gradual the crisis is more often instantaneous, attended by trance or vision: and the effects are a feeling of peace and harmony, a perception of truths not known before, and an enhanced view of the objective world (pp. 248 ff.). There is an interesting discussion of "The Metaphysics of Conversion" by R. H. Hutton in his *Contemporary Thought and Thinking* (London, 1894), I, 369–376.

conversion, which he dated precisely at a quarter of nine, 24 May 1738, was followed by fears and agonizing doubts.

Both of these conditions are to be found in *In Memoriam*. The grief and "wild despair" which are now so much admired cannot be endured indefinitely. Hallam's death, the "soul-shaking event" in his otherwise undramatic life, had exacerbated Tennyson's already brooding and hypersensitive temperament to a state of depression which no mere passage of time can remedy. Domestic and personal troubles before 1833 had prepared the way: the death of his father in 1831, the mental breakdown of his younger brother Edward and the opium-addiction of Charles in 1832, and Croker's harsh treatment of his 1832 *Poems* in the *Quarterly Review*. After 1833 the burden of family business fell on his shoulders when Frederick left on a pleasure trip to Italy. He was concerned for his mother, for his sister Emily who had been engaged to Hallam, and for Septimus who was also, for a time, threatened with a mental breakdown. The unfriendly reception of his poems continued to worry him, and kept him from venturing to publish another volume. There was little money to support the large family, and when his grandfather died in 1835 the Somersby Tennysons were, as always, slighted.[4] Upon these depressing circumstances the loss of Hallam came like the jolt which turns already sub-freezing water to ice: "Break, thou deep vase of chilling tears, /That grief hath shaken into frost!"[5] Preoccupied already with the bearing of science on religion, he could not fail to find in this personal loss a demonstration of the finality of death and the remoteness of God.

It is significant that there is no sense of sin, or sinfulness, in Tennyson's unhappiness. He fears divine neglect, not divine punishment (LII), and grieves because he has been left desolate, "widowed," and alone, with no sure prospect of reunion with the one in whom he had found not only affection but support in a world growing increasingly harsh and alien. With Hallam gone even Christ seemed distant. During that first Christmas of 1833 he thought of Christ only in connection with the miracle of Lazarus which occurred long ago (XXXI), and the second Christmas did not banish his sense of loss.[6] There is some tendency to identify Hallam and Christ in spirit, to think longingly of Christ as a

4. Charles Tennyson, *Alfred Tennyson* (New York, 1949), pp. 105–154. See also R. W. Rader's "Tennyson in the Year of Hallam's Death," *PMLA*, LXXVII (1962), 419–424, for a study, using fresh materials, of Tennyson's inner grief and outer behavior in 1834.
5. Sec. IV; see Thomas Bayne, "Carlyle and Tennyson," *N & Q*, 7th ser., XI (1891), 204.
6. Sec. LXXVIII. Though few readers doubt the depth of his grief, some have wondered whether it was quite healthy for a man to grieve so long for another man, as if there were a decent maximum as well as a decent minimum for mourning. Paull F. Baum's view, in *Tennyson Sixty Years After* (Chapel Hill, 1948), is that "the composition of these elegies [became] a kind of habit and the death of Hallam a kind of convenience to the muse" (p. 116), but this deliberately ignores the early and lasting association in Tennyson's mind of Hallam's death with the distressing problem of man's ultimate destiny.

human savior (XXXII, XXXVI) who, as he saved Lazarus and inspired Mary's perfect faith, may with "mortal sympathy" and love save Hallam in the other world; but this develops slowly. Meanwhile, God is remoter still. Although His existence seems sure, His goodness and love cannot be seen in His creation of nature "red in tooth and claw" (XXXIV, LV, LVI). However self-centered his despair, Tennyson's concern for the immortality of all souls is real: "Else earth is darkness at the core,/And dust and ashes all that is" (XXXIV). The threat of current evolutionary ideas to the doctrine of immortality was equally real, and the more disturbing because it did not help, as Lionel Stevenson remarks, to read into these ideas a spiritual principle of successively higher incarnations of the soul. For he had still to persuade himself (and others) in a more than purely rational and logical way that man's "inward sense of immortality is stronger and truer than the inconsistent physical forms of the universe."[7] Even after the intellect was satisfied the heart still felt the loneliness and grief of personal loss: "We cannot hear each other speak" (LXXXII). It remained for an intuitive conviction of immortality to be achieved through an actual, possibly a mystical, contact with the spirit of the lost one.

This brings us to the second necessary condition of conversion. "Tennyson was at heart a mystic," wrote Sir Charles Tennyson, "with a capacity for true mystical experience."[8] Many evidences of this may be found in his poems, from among the earliest ("Armageddon," 1823–24) to the latest ("The Ring," 1889). In Memoriam contains many signs of it, and in an important group of sections, from XC through XCIV, there is a plea for a vision of Hallam which is answered with the trance-like experience which ultimately gives him the assurance he has sought.

Everything had led up to this episode. The opening sections, with their mood of enforced calm expressing the poet's loss and initial shock, the subsequent despair and confusion, nevertheless con-

7. Lionel Stevenson, Darwin Among the Poets (Chicago, 1932), p. 89.
8. Six Tennyson Essays (London, 1954), p. 96. See also James Knowles, "Aspects of Tennyson," Nineteenth Century, XXXIII (1893), 169, 186. According to Sir Charles, Tennyson was not a complete mystic but "possessed in some degree the power mystics have claimed through the centuries, to establish immediate communication ... between the spirit of man, entangled among material things, and ... God" (p. 71). Tennyson believed that he possessed this power and told both Tyndall and Knowles how he could induce trance-states by concentrating on his own name (Alfred Lord Tennyson, A Memoir, by His Son [London, 1897], II, 473–474). He described it also in "The Ancient Sage." This has led some critics, e.g., Robert Preyer, "Tennyson as an Oracular Poet," Modern Philology, LV (1958), 250, to dismiss his mystical experience as self-hypnosis. That it is larger than this, and unforced, seems evident from its presence throughout his poetry. The experience described in In Memoriam, as we shall see, is spontaneous. He distrusted the current cult of spiritualism, and was self-conscious about his own modest capacity, protesting to Tyndall: "By God Almighty, there is no delusion in the matter! It is no nebulous ecstasy, but a state of transcendent wonder, associated with absolute clearness of mind" (A Memoir, II, 473–474).

stitute a developing (if not orderly) series of lucid pictures of the past (the yew tree, the house on Wimpole Street) and the imagined present (the ship returning, anticipations of its arrival, the burial) which are threaded with his increasing anguish. As efforts to control it, or divert it, or reason it away, fail, the larger significance of Hallam's death becomes clearer, creating fresh fears, and Tennyson comes to feel the need of some sort of contact with Hallam's spirit to revive his belief in man's immortal spirit and in love as the universal law (XLII).

In response to this need, but also as a direct expression of Tennyson's sensibility, there are mystical intimations throughout the poem, from the earliest sections, in which he hopes that he may "reach a hand thro' time to catch/The far-off interest of tears"; and in the presence of the old yew tree he feels himself disembodied: "I seem to fail from out my blood/And grow incorporate into thee." In Section XII he again describes himself as leaving his own body, "I leave this mortal ark behind,/A weight of nerves without a mind," and hasting over seas to the ship which brings the dead Hallam home he can only "circle moaning in the air" and return "to where the body sits, and learn/That I have been an hour away." This half-dream, half-trance leads to the fear, in Section XVI, that his grief has unbalanced his mind, "made me that delirious man/Whose fancy fuses old and new,/And flashes into false and true." When with the oscillating movement of the poem calm returns, and the first Christmas brings a degree of resignation (" 'Tis better to have loved and lost . . ."), he begins to search for convincing evidence of immortality in man's life ("My own dim life should teach me this,/That life shall live for evermore" [XXXIV], or in the "tale" of the life and resurrection of Christ (XXXVI), or, hopefully, within his own consciousness. Truths lie "Deep-seated in our mystic frame," but "darkly-joined." Perhaps in the same way that there united the Wordsworthian possibility of receiving intimations of our life before our birth, in "A little flash, a mystic hint," so there is the possibility of communication between souls in the afterlife and here.

> If such a dreamy touch should fall,
>   O turn thee round, resolve the doubt;
>   My guardian angel will speak out,
> In that high place and tell thee all.   (XLIV)

This seems to anticipate, though as yet without much hope, a communion with the spirit of Hallam in some sort of trance or vision, and it is clear that Tennyson attaches immense importance to such experiential evidence in the resolution of his doubts. Soon he gives more direct expression to his desire to be made aware of Hallam's actual presence: "Be near me when my light is low ... Be near me when the sensuous frame/Is rack'd with pangs that conquer trust ... when my faith is dry ... when I fade away" (L); then more generally:

> Be near us when we climb or fall:
> Ye watch, like God, the rolling hours
> With larger other eyes than ours,
> To make allowance for us all.   (LI)

If Hallam remains distant it is not, Tennyson believes, because of his own human shortcomings, the despair, the sensuous nature, the spiritual dryness, of which he is humbly aware, for he is confident his love for Hallam will redeem him (LII).

Meanwhile rational consolation ("Oh yet we trust that somehow good/Will be the final goal of ill" [LIV]) yields inevitably to rational depression: "O for thy voice to soothe and bless!/What hope of answer, or redress?/Behind the veil, behind the veil" (LVI). The next large group of sections (LVII-LXXXIX) dwells on wavering moods of resignation and despair, while the anniversary of Hallam's death (LXXII), the second Christmas (LXXVIII), and the New Year (LXXXIII), pass him by without much helping or hurting. He did dream of a "mystic glory" shining on Hallam's grave (LXVII), but in this dream ("kinsman thou to death and trance") his efforts to see Hallam's features are frustrated and confused,

> Till all at once beyond the will
> I hear a wizard music roll,
> And thro' a lattice on the soul
> Looks thy fair face and makes it still.   (LXX)

Still, there is no communion or sign of recognition in such dreams or fancies, and the poet reaches a state of emotional equilibrium (LXXXII, LXXXIII) in which, blaming no person or thing ("I wage not any feud with Death"), he seems resigned to his "low beginnings of content" (LXXXIV), and grateful at least for the memory and friendship of Hallam. It is in such a state of resignation that, according to James,[9] religious conversions are likely to occur. It is the turning point both of the poem and of the poet's hopes. At the very bottom of his fortunes he realizes that there is "in my grief a strength reserved." There are "mighty hopes that make us men." And though "in dear words of human speech/We

9. James cites the apathy and exhaustion of Teufelsdroeckh on the Rue de l'Enfer. Tennyson's mood of resignation and acceptance, bringing a certain relief, invites the mystical contact: "So long as the egoistic worry of the sick soul guards the door, the expansive confidence of the soul of faith gains no presence. But let the former faint away, even but for a moment, and the latter can profit by the opportunity" (p. 212).

two communicate no more," he has a premonition that "I shall prove/A meeting somewhere, love with love" (LXXXV). Still sad, he now thinks less about himself, more about Hallam's days at Cambridge (LXXXVII) and at Somersby (LXXXIX), and this leads directly into a group of sections (XC-CVI) in which Tennyson invokes the spirit of Hallam: "Come, beauteous in thine after form,/And like a finer light in light" (XCI), culminating in the unmistakable awareness of his spirit in Section XCV.

The trance occurs in a large group of sections in which Tennyson describes the circumstances leading up to his mystical experience and records its immediate consequences. In Section XC he begins to think about what he desires so much, namely the return of Hallam. But the subject is, at this stage, general and hypothetical. If men could return from death they might not be welcomed back either by their wives, now "in other hands," or by their sons, jealous of their inheritance; but these wives and sons have not felt love. Tennyson, who has, can only cry to Hallam, "Come thou back to me!," and in the next section (XCI) he asks Hallam to appear either in body or in visible spirit. Ever prone to doubt, Tennyson now fears that he might distrust such a vision (XCII) as a "canker of the brain," and might discredit the phantom's spoken prophecies as mere presentiments. "I shall not see thee," he writes in the next section (XCIII). Therefore, he begs Hallam to "Descend, and touch, and enter" so that he may feel his presence. Yet, this may be impossible, since (XCIV) one needs a peaceful and serene spirit to hold communion with the dead.

It is clear that up to this point Tennyson has been preparing both himself and us for the climactic experience which is told in Section XCV. Providing an effective change of pace and tone, this section is the richly descriptive narrative of one summer evening at Somersby (1835), spent singing old songs with the members of his family and watching the approach of night, when, after the others had gone to bed and he was alone, he reread Hallam's letters, and suddenly felt a presence.

> So word by word, and line by line,
>   The dead man touched me from the past,
>   And all at once it seem'd at last
> The living soul was flashed on mine.

> And mine in this was wound, and whirl'd
>   About empyreal heights of thought,
>   And came on that which is, and caught
> The deep pulsations of the world.   (XCV)

It is well known that until 1878 the phrases "The living soul" and "mine in this" read "His living soul" and "mine in his." For twenty-eight years this section of the poem described a personal contact with Hallam's spirit, a contact which by itself could indeed resolve all doubts and restore one's faith in immortality. It was a record of genuine mystical experience, a clear sign from a beloved spirit in the next world which, because it effected, or seemed to effect, the dispelling of all religious doubts, had all the earmarks of a conversion comparable in its way with St. Paul's.

Among critics Section XCV has occasioned both perplexity and indignation. Why, if he wanted to record a conversion, did Tennyson make emendations which removed the personal element, and throw the whole thing into doubt? And why did he wait so long to make them? John D. Rosenberg writes, "If 'The living soul' is not Hallam's, the lines are without meaning"; for Paull F. Baum they cause the whole section and with it the whole poem to fail as a clear and honest work of art.[1] It is certainly true that the earlier version is the clearer. We may well ask why it did not satisfy Tennyson. Certainly the bereaved poet desired an intimate, even a physical contact. But we have seen that he has already rejected this possibility (XCII, XCIII) in favor of a vaguer if no less real spiritual one. We have no way of knowing whether the contact described in the earlier version is what he thought he had felt, or what he wanted to think he had felt. In time he was convinced that it suggested a more personal contact than the trance justified. There is, indeed, ample meaning in the amended version if it is understood that Hallam's spirit is not in a state of isolation but exists as an all but indistinguishable part of the universal spirit of the Deity. The poet, reading Hallam's letters, feels in his trance the touch of this spirit, which conveys a comforting sense of the closeness of his friend and convinces him for the moment that they have touched. It is this necessary ambiguity that the final version seems meant to convey: the contact suggested both Hallam and the Deity. The poem cannot be called dishonest unless its maker is here compromising his belief or distorting his actual experience. Tennyson seems to have tried, rather, to correct the record. To James Knowles he said later that what he felt was "perchance the Deity ... my conscience was troubled by 'his'. I've often had a strange feeling of being bound and wrapped in the Great Soul" (Knowles, p. 186). Nor does it seem just to commit the poem to clarity, if it deals with

1. Rosenberg, p. 234n; Baum, pp. 307–308. While granting beauty in many of the lyrics Baum accuses Tennyson of "perverting" his poem; he should not have attempted to "arrange" them at all. Further, his glossing of "The living soul" as "The Deity, maybe" betrays a "weakness inherent in Tennyson's character ... we have a right to expect some sort of clear statement: either it *was* the Deity—for the purposes of the poem, of course—or it was not" (p. 307).

an experience that by its very nature is beyond clarity, and if its parts are consistent with the whole. The idea of Hallam merged in the Deity is no afterthought but finds grateful expression in many of the later sections (e.g., XCVII, CXXII, CXXIV, CXXX):

> To feel thee some diffusive power,
> I do not therefore love thee less . . .

> Tho mix'd with God and Nature thou,
> I seem to love thee more and more.   (CXXX)

Though at the expense of clarity, the emendations enlarge and universalize the whole experience of the trance. They also introduce an admixture of doubt into the very middle of the newly-awakened faith which, religiously and psychologically, is not unprecedented. The faith of the saints was made arduous by doubt. Quite apart from the emendations, however, Tennyson's trance was followed immediately by doubt: "At length my trance/Was cancell'd, stricken through with doubt."[2] It is not surprising that its end should have been sudden, the return to reality a shock. "Sometimes," he told Knowles, "I get carried away out of sense and body, and rapt into mere existence, till the accidental touch or movement of one of my own fingers is like a great shock and blow and brings the body back with a terrible start" (Knowles, p. 169). It is the nature, not the actual occurrence of the experience that the poet doubts. Tennyson is not, in fact, so worried as his critics are by the uncertainty of his trance-contact, but seems content not to know whether it was Hallam or "some higher name" he has touched, or both. The last four stanzas of this section, which Bradley calls "one of the most wonderful descriptive passages in all poetry" (p. 192), express a mood of exalted calm.

That the experience belonged to the phenomenon of conversion is clear from what follows. Through it his doubts have been scotched, his faith has become stronger. He thinks now of another, perhaps Hallam, who fought against doubt to a stronger faith (XCVI); he reflects that honest faith in these times does not exclude doubt, that even the strongest faith "Dwells not in the light alone/But in the darkness and the cloud,/As over Sinai's peaks." His own faith was intuitive, based not only on "the unreality of the material and the reality of the spiritual world but on the

---

2. Sec. XCV. I take it that "cancell'd" does not mean repudiated but, rather, brought so suddenly to an end that Tennyson could not be sure of either the nature or the identity of the spirit whose presence he had felt. Bradley concludes: "Probably at the moment of the experience he did think his friend's soul was present, but thereafter never felt any certainty on the subject" (p. 191n). But this uncertainty did not "cancel" the growing certainty, stemming from this experience, that his plea for contact with Hallam had somehow been granted.

mystic's power of spiritual communion and the capacity of the human mind to transcend the material and in some sense apprehend infinity" (*Six Tennyson Essays*, pp. 110–111). Rational argument had failed as the basis for religious evidence, but there was the appeal to experience, the same appeal which is found in Coleridge, Carlyle, and Maurice, and earlier in Kant and Schleiermacher: "the heart/Stood up and answer'd 'I have felt'" (CXXIV). The "Ring out wild bells" passage (CVI) celebrates his victory, and he resolves to cease his introspective grief and, after Goethe and Carlyle, accept sorrow as a strengthener of the soul. In Section CXX he compares his struggles with St. Paul's; he recalls the climactic trance of Section XCV, repeating his uncertainty about its precise nature ("Oh, wast thou with me, dearest, then,/Whilst I rose up against my doom"), and asks Hallam to return ("be with me now,/And enter in at breast and brow") in another mystical experience

> As in the former flash of joy,
> I slip the thoughts of life and death;
>
> And all the breeze of fancy blows,
> And every dewdrop paints a bow,
> The wizard lightnings deeply glow,
> And every thought breaks out a rose.   (CXXII)

No second trance occurs, but Tennyson is not despondent on this occasion either, for his memory of the first has enabled him to accept the ordinary state of human ignorance. Having transcended this state once, in a "flash of joy," he is strong enough to withstand all rational doubts and natural terrors:

> And all is well, tho' faith and form
> Be sunder'd in the night of fear;
> Well roars the storm to those that hear
> A deeper voice across the storm.   (CXXVII)

Natural terrors will remain, though deprived of their old effect because of the "deeper voice" which came to him from a divine source "across" (not in, or through) the storm.

Yet the repeated "all is well" of Sections CXXVI and CXXVII, mentioned along with war, social injustices, and dying aeons, conveys a profound sense of sadness that so much evil should be prerequisite to eventual good. The triumph is muted. Such faith as he has won leaves great questions unanswered: Why so much evil? Why is our vision so limited? Like religious skeptics of all ages, he "would see a sign." He had felt one, and he was grateful for the evidence which despite "The freezing reason's colder part" enabled him to believe that "all is well." The attitude is not very different from T. S. Eliot's in "Little Gidding": "Sin is Behovely, but/All shall be well, and/All manner of thing shall be well." Beginning with doubt and fear, Tennyson ends with doubt and hope. It should not be giving him too much the benefit of his doubts to say that this attitude is not dated, but will have relevance for as long as man separates faith and reason.[3]

It is at this point that we can see why *In Memoriam* is neither a poem wholly of faith nor one wholly of doubt. Its faith admits an ignorance of the whole truth and leaves room for doubt; its doubt, having made room for itself after Hallam's death, had to make room for faith after the trance of Section XCV. Love and hope are the bonds. For if religious faith is necessarily incomplete, so is science. A faith which is at once intuitive and intellectual will not be attainable until faith and knowledge meet. Tennyson hoped that with evolutionary progress man would ultimately find that religion and science reveal one and the same truth.[4] Meanwhile, one of the strengths of the Christian religion, as Sir Thomas Browne had observed, is its absence of logical proof. If miraculous visions occurred daily we should depreciate or ignore them, like the Israelites who "made their gods of gold,/Altho' the trumpet blew so loud" (XCVI). Not that doubt is to be nurtured: it is to be endured, like a hairshirt, as a chastener of one's faith. Far from falling back on the standard affirmations of his day,[5] Tennyson chose a limited faith which required courage to sustain. The position taken in the concluding sections and the Prologue was his final position. That he never went beyond it has been lamented and deplored, but considering its dependence on the progress of the species, it is a position which hardly admits of much advancement in a lifetime.

3. In his *Tennyson, the Growth of a Poet* (Cambridge, Mass., 1960), Jerome H. Buckley also sees the trance as effecting Tennyson's recovery of faith: "his experience has given him the certitude that 'science' could not establish and therefore could not destroy. Though unable to sustain his vision, the 'I' of the poem finds his mystical insight the surest warrant for spiritual recovery." After comparing Tennyson's faith with Pascal's ("who likewise trusted the reasons of the heart which reason could not know") and with Kierkegaard's existentialism ("which similarly balances the demands of the inner life against the claims of nineteenth-century 'knowledge' "), he concludes that it had genuine relevance and importance in a Victorian England which was finding all dogmatic positions increasingly vulnerable. Jonathan Bishop, in "The Unity of 'In Memoriam' " (*Victorian Newsletter*, No. 21 [Spring 1962], p. 13, n. 7) agrees.
4. Sec. CXXVIII, and the Prologue; also *A Memoir*, I, 323.
5. This indictment still persists. See Jacob Korg, "The Pattern of Fatality in Tennyson's Poetry," *VNL*, No. 14, (Fall 1958), pp. 8–11.

When all is said, *In Memoriam* remains one of the most egoistic of elegies. The selfless sorrow felt for Hallam's premature death is soon obscured by Tennyson's tragic bereavement, by his anguished desire for sensible contact with Hallam, and by his prolonged efforts to establish the idea of a loving deity. The poem would be more autobiography than elegy if Tennyson had not contrived so well to work his experience into the traditional elegiac form. It was, I think, the trance that enabled him to use the elegiac turning-point, "He is not dead, he lives!," with conviction, to combine the pattern of elegy with the pattern of conversion. Yet he departs more from that of elegy. As Bradley observed, the turning point is not so clearly marked as in *Lycidas* and *Adonais*. Indeed it is hard to locate at all (p. 30). But this is because Tennyson is following his own experience rather than poetic tradition. The announcement that "he lives!," accordingly, had to be delayed until after the period of uncertainty and doubt that succeeded the trance, and as with Carlyle, whose "Everlasting Yea" had to follow the long "Centre of Indifference," his faith evolved slowly.

But if *In Memoriam* is not pure elegy, neither is it a straight record of experience. Tennyson arranged the elegies to lead from the moment of mystical contact through a slow recovery to a faith that stopped short of completion, at least in the Wesleyan sense. Brought up in the evangelical tradition, he came naturally by his knowledge of conversion and its various stages. For his final construction of the whole it was his own much less dramatic conversion that supplied the pattern, but even this was modified to admit discourses and arguments that had little to do with that experience. The result is a form which, like the envelope-quatrain, he made uniquely his own. His success, considering the difficulties he encountered, is almost without precedent. Few long poems achieve such a synthesis of disparate parts. During the long period of its composition Tennyson gained not only artistic development[6] but religious and emotional maturity. We have seen that along with the many strands of thought and feeling that run through it—reflections on science, on nature, on society, on the relationships between this life and the next, on the Christmases and the anniversaries, and on his concern for his relatives and friends—there is the clear strand of mystical experience leading up to and beyond the gentle but significant trance in the garden at Somersby which enabled him to recover his faith, determined the peculiar leaven of doubt in that faith, and, finally, enriched the inner character of the poem itself.

6. For an excellent study of the maturing of Tennyson's conception and mastery of his poetic art during these years, see E. D. H. Johnson, "*In Memoriam*: The Way of the Poet," *VS*, II (1958), 139–148.

A. C. BRADLEY

The Structure of *In Memoriam*†

I. The most obvious sign of definite structure in *In Memoriam* consists in the internal chronology, and it will be well to begin by making this clear.

Tennyson[1] himself tells us (*Memoir*, I. 305) that the divisions of the poem are made by the Christmas-tide sections (xxvIII., LxxvIII., cIv.). That the first of these refers to the first Christmas after the death of the friend in autumn is evident from xxx., 14–16:

> We sung, tho' every eye was dim,
> A merry song we sang with him
> *Last year:*[2]

and we certainly receive the impression from the other Christmas poems that the second refers to the Christmas of the next year, and the third to that of the next again. Thus, when we have reached section cIv., we are distant from the death of the friend about two years and a quarter; and there is nothing in the sections after cIv. to make us think that they are supposed to cover any length of time. Accordingly, the time imagined to elapse in the poem may be set down as rather less than three years.

These results are confirmed by other facts. Between the Christmas poems there come occasional sections indicating the progress of time by reference to the seasons and to the anniversaries of the death of the friend; and between two Christmas poems we never find a hint that more than one spring or one summer has passed, or that more than one anniversary has come round. After the third Christmas we have a spring poem (cxv.), but after this no sign of summer or of the return of the anniversary of the friend's death.

The unmistakable indications of the internal chronology are shown in the following table:

Section XI.	Early Autumn.
xv.	Later.
xxvIII.-xxx.	Christmastide.
xxxvIII.-IX.	Spring.
LxxII.	Anniversary.

† From *A Commentary on Tennyson's "In Memoriam,"* 3rd rev. ed. (London, Macmillan, 1910), pp. 20–35.

1. It will be understood that generally, both in this Introduction and in the Notes, when I speak of 'the poet' I mean the poet who speaks *in* the poem. I refer to the author who composed the poem as 'Tennyson' or 'the author.'

2. These lines are decisive, and their evidence is not weakened by the fact that some poems referring to the burial precede this first Christmas section, whereas the burial of Arthur Hallam did not really take place until after Christmas, 1833. The author did not choose to make the internal chronology coincide with the actual order of events.

LXXVIII.	Christmastide.
LXXXIII.	Delaying Spring.[3]
LXXXVI., LXXXVIII.	Spring.
LXXXIX., XCV., XCVIII.	Summer.
XCIX.	Anniversary.
CIV., CV.	Christmastide.
CVI.	New Year's Day.
CVII.	Winter.
CXV., CXVI.	Spring.

Against all these indications there seems nothing to be set except the few passages already noted, where a phrase or the tone of a section appears to be not quite in harmony with this internal chronology. That these passages are so few is a proof of the care taken by the author to preserve the clearness and consistency of the scheme. And it is undoubtedly of use in giving the outlines of a structure to the poem, and of still greater use in providing beautiful contrasts between the sections which deal with the recurring seasons and anniversaries; though it is somewhat unfortunate that the contents of some of the final sections imply a greater distance of time from the opening of the series than is suggested by the chronological scheme.

II. If we describe in the most general terms the movement of thought and feeling in *In Memoriam*, the description will be found to apply also to *Lycidas* or *Adonais*. In each case the grief of the opening has passed at the close into triumph: at first the singer thinks only of loss and death, and at last his eyes are fixed upon the vision of a new and greater life. But in *Lycidas* and *Adonais* this change is expressed in one continuous strain, and is therefore felt by the reader to occupy but a few hours of concentrated experience; and in *Adonais* especially the impression of passionate rapidity in the transition from gloom to glory is essential to the effect. In *In Memoriam* a similar change is supposed to fill a period of some years, and the impression of a very gradual and difficult advance is no less essential. It is conveyed, of course, not only by the indications of time which have just been considered, but by the mere fact that each of the 131 sections is, in a sense, a poem complete in itself and accordingly felt to be the expression of the thought of one particular time.

In many cases, however, we soon observe that a single section is not really thus independent of its predecessor and successor. On the contrary, some are scarcely intelligible if taken in isolation; and again and again we discover groups which have one subject, and in which the single sections are devoted to various aspects of this one subject. The poet in his progress has come upon a certain thought, which occupies him for a time and is developed through a series of stages or contrasted with a number of other thoughts. And even in

---

3. That this is not a New Year's Day poem is shown in the Notes.

cases where we cannot trace such a close connection in thought we often find that several consecutive sections are bound together, and separated from the poems that surround them, by a common tone of feeling. These groups or clusters correspond with single paragraphs of *Lycidas*, or with single stanzas or groups of stanzas in *Adonais*; and their presence forms a second means by which a certain amount of structure is given to the poem.

There are many readers of *In Memoriam* who have never read the poem through, but probably everyone who has done so has recognised to some extent the existence of groups. Everyone remarks, for instance, that near the beginning there are a number of sections referring to the coming of the ship, and that there are other consecutive poems which deal with Christmastide. But perhaps few readers are aware of the large part played by these groups. The fact is that, taken together, they account for considerably more than one-half of the poem; and in this estimate no notice has been taken of mere pairs of connected sections, such as XIX., XX.; XLVIII., XLIX.; LVII., LVIII.; CXV., CXVI.; or of parts of the poem where the sections, though not so closely connected as to form a distinct group, are yet manifestly united in a looser way. If these additions are made to our estimate, it will be found to include nearly 100 poems out of the total of 131.

Of the remaining sections (*a*) a small number may properly be called occasional poems, though the positions which they occupy in the whole are always more or less significant. Such are LXXXVII., which describes the visit to Cambridge; XCVIII., on the brother's tour to Vienna; the long retrospective poem, LXXXV.; or the poem on Hallam's birthday, CVI. (*b*) Others at once remind us of preceding sections suggested by a like occasion, and in this way bring home to us the change which has taken place in the poet's mind during the interval. The Christmas poems are the most prominent instance; the later spring poems recall the earlier; the second 'Risest thou thus' brings back the first; the two sections beginning, 'Dark house,' and the two poems on the Yew-tree, form similar pairs. (*c*) Lastly, we find that the sections which immediately follow connected groups are often of one and the same kind. The subject which has occupied the poet's thoughts being dismissed, there follows a kind of reaction. He looks inward, and becomes more keenly conscious of the feeling from which his attention had been for the time diverted (*e.g.* XXXVIII.), or of the feeling in which his thoughts have culminated (*e.g.* LVII.). Not seldom this feeling suggests to him some reflection on his own songs: his singing comforts him on his dreary way, or he feels that it is of no avail, or that it expresses nothing of his deepest grief. And not only thus at the close of groups, but at various other points throughout *In Memoriam* there occur sections in which the poet's songs form the subject, pointing backwards and forwards to one another, and showing the change which passes over his mind as time goes on (*e.g.* v., xxi., lviii., cxxv.). In these various ways, as well as by the presence of definite groups, some kind of connection is established between section and section, almost throughout the whole of the poem.

III. We are now in a position to observe the structure of this whole, reserving for the Commentary the fuller characterisation of particular parts.

The 'Way of the Soul' we find to be a journey from the first stupor and confusion of grief, through a growing acquiescence often disturbed by the recurrence of pain, to an almost unclouded peace and joy. The anguish of wounded love passes into the triumph of love over sorrow, time and death. The soul, at first almost sunk in the feeling of loss, finds itself at last freed from regret and yet strengthened in affection. It pines no longer for the vanished hand and silent voice; it is filled with the consciousness of union with the spirit. The world, which once seemed to it a mere echo of its sorrow, has become the abode of that immortal Love, at once divine and human, which includes the living and the dead.

Is it possible to find in this 'Way' any turning-point where grief begins to yield to joy,—such a turning-point as occurs in *Adonais* when indignation rouses the poet from his sorrow, and the strain suddenly rises into the solemn affirmation,

'Peace, peace! he is not dead, he doth not sleep.'

If so, *In Memoriam* may be considered to fall into two fairly distinct parts, though the dividing-line would not necessarily come, any more than in *Adonais*, at the centre of the poem.

It might seem natural to take the long section lxxxv. as marking such a line of division, for here the poet himself looks back over the way he has traversed, and when he renews his journey the bitterness of grief seems to have left him. But the passing away of this bitterness has been already clearly observable before section lxxxv. is reached, and the change of tone after that section does not seem sufficiently decided to justify us in regarding it as a central point in the whole.

More tempting would be a proposal to consider section lvii. as marking the centre of *In Memoriam*. In these verses the most troubled and passionate part of the poem reaches the acme of a climax, while after them there is, on the whole, a steady advance towards acquiescence. But in reality the distress which culminates in section lvii. is characteristic only of the group which closes with that section; it is not a distress which has deepened from the outset of the poem; indeed, many tokens of advance have been visible before that group is reached, and the main direction of the movement towards it is definitely upward.[4]

If a turning-point in the general feeling of *In Memoriam* is to be sought at all, it must certainly be found not in section LVII., nor in section LXXXV., but in the second Christmas poem, LXXVIII. It seems true that, in spite of gradual change, the tone of the poem so far is, on the whole, melancholy, while after LXXVIII. the predominant tone can scarcely be called even sad; it is rather the feeling of spring emerging slowly and with difficulty from the gloom of winter. And it is probable that Tennyson himself intended this change to be associated with the second coming of Christmas, since the first and the third coming also announce a definite change, and since he says that the divisions of *In Memoriam* are made by the Christmas sections. At the same time it is questionable whether the transition at section LXXVIII. is so marked as to strike a reader who was not looking for signs of transition; and, this being so, it would seem to be a mistake to regard *In Memoriam* as a poem which, like *Adonais*, shows a dividing line clearly separating one part of the whole from the other. Its main movement is really one of advance almost from the first, though the advance is for a long time very slow.

Falling back, then, on the divisions pointed out by the author, we may attempt to characterise the four parts into which the poem will fall, to show the groups contained in each, and to indicate the principal changes in the course of ideas through which the mind of the poet moves.

Part I. To the First Christmas.
Sections i–xxvii.

The general tone of this part, which is supposed to cover a space of about three months, is that of absorption in grief; but the poet gradually rises from mere suffering to a clearer conviction that

> 'Tis better to have loved and lost
> Than never to have loved at all,

---

4. I am not converted, therefore, by Mr. Beeching's words, which have appeared since the above was written: 'Here the poem, as at first designed, seems to have ended. The 57th elegy [58th in the copyright text] represents the Muse as urging the poet to a new beginning; and the 58th [59th] was added in the fourth edition, as though to account for the difference in tone between the earlier and later elegies' (Introduction, p. x). Apart from the objection urged above, the first sentence here seems to be scarcely consistent with Tennyson's own account of the composition of *In Memoriam*, nor can I believe that he ever thought of ending his poem in tones of despair. But it is certainly true that there is a more marked *break* at Section LVII. than at LXXVIII. or LXXXV. (The suggestion that the poem was originally intended to cease with LVII, was made in 1892 by Mr. Jacobs (p. 92), whose book was not known to Mr. Beeching.)

and that love may, and ought to, survive the loss of the beloved.
There is throughout scarcely any reference to the continued exist-
ence of the lost friend.

This part contains two distinct groups:

(1) Sections IX.–XVII. (*or* XX.),[5] referring to the coming of the
ship (or to this and to the burial).

(2) Sections XXII.–XXV., a retrospect of the years of friendship.

Part II. To the Second Christmas.
Sections xxviii.–lxxvii.

This part of the poem has some marked characteristics. (a) From
beginning to end the idea of the continued life of the dead is prom-
inent, far more prominent than in any of the other three parts. (b)
It is through reflection on this idea and on the problems suggested
by it that the poet wins his way forward; so that this is the part of
In Memoriam which contains most semi-philosophic speculation.
(c) Hence this part consists almost wholly of distinct groups with
intervening sections, and there are but few 'occasional' poems.

The following brief analysis of the groups will indicate the course
of the poet's thoughts:

(1) Sections XXVIII.–XXX. Christmastide. The thought of the contin-
ued life of the dead emerges in an hour of exaltation.

(2) Sections XXXI.–XXXVI. This continued life is at once a 'truth
revealed,' and a fact implied in the constitution of human
nature. The group accordingly is concerned in part with the
difference between two forms of faith in immortality.

(3) Sections XL.–XLVII. Immortality being assumed, the question of
future reunion is raised. This involves the question (which is
the main subject of the group) whether the earthly life is
remembered beyond death. Only an affirmative answer would
satisfy the demand of love.

(4) Sections L.–LVI. The poet's desire that the dead friend should
remember him and be near him *now* (as well as in a future
life) is followed by fears and doubts raised by the thought,
first, of his own unworthiness, and then of all the pain, waste,
and evil in the world. These doubts cannot be silenced by
reason; and the poet's hope that good is the end of evil, and
love the law of creation, is sustained only by blind trust.

(5) Sections LX.–LXV. The poet returns to his desire that his friend
should think of him *now*. His hopes and fears on this subject
are free from the distress of the preceding group, and issue in

5. Here, as in a few other cases, it is a matter of doubt, and even of indiffer-ence, at which of two sections the group is best taken to close.

the acceptance of ignorance, and in faith that love cannot be lost. Here, and in the remainder of Part II., there is a gradual advance towards quiet regret, sympathy with others, and a peaceful recognition of the beauty of the past and the influence of the lost frriend.

(6) Sections LXVII.-LXXI. On Night, Sleep, and Dreams.

(7) Sections LXXIII.-LXXVII. On Fame. The poet writes of his friend's loss of fame on earth and gain of fame in another world, and of the brevity of any fame which his own songs could win for his friend.

Part III. To the Third Christmas
Sections xxviii.–lxxvii.

Of the four parts this contains the greatest number of sections which may be called 'occasional.' The idea of the future life retires again into the background.

(1) The prevailing tone of sections LXXIX.–LXXXIX. (not to be considered a group) is that of quiet and not unhappy retrospection, and a sense of new and joyful life begins to appear.

(2) Sections XC.-XCV. form a closely connected group on the possible contact of the living and the dead. The idea is considered from various sides, and appears to be realised in the trance recorded in XCV.

(3) Sections C.-CIII. form a group which has for its subject the poet's farewell to the home of childhood. He begins to turn his eyes from the past.

Part IV. From the Third Christmas.
Sections civ.–cxxxi.

Throughout this part, even when the poet is thinking of the past, he is looking forward into the future. Regret is passing away, but love is growing and widening. The dead friend is regarded not only as a friend, but as a type of the nobler humanity to come, and as mingled with that Love which is the soul of the universe.

(1) Sections CIV.-CVI. form a group dealing with Christmas and New Year in the new home.

(2) Section CVII., CVIII. express the poet's resolve to turn from the grief of the past.

(3) Section CIX.-CXIV. describe the character of the dead friend, and incidentally the dangers of the progress of mankind.

(4) Sections CXVII.-CXXXI. are not so closely connected as to form a group, but they are united by their expression of faith in the

200 · *Paull F. Baum*

future both of the individual and of humanity. In form many of them are retrospective, the poet looking back to the struggles through which he has won his way to entire faith in the omnipotence of love.[6]

6. In conversation with Mr. James Knowles, Tennyson gave a division of *In Memoriam* into nine parts, as follows: (1) I.–VIII,; (2) IX.–XX.; (3) XXI.–XXVII.; (4) XXVIII.–XLIX.; (5) L.–LVIII.; (6) LIX–LXXI.; (7) LXXII.–XCVIII.; (8) XCIX.–CIII.; (9) CIV.–CXXXI. As nothing is said of this arrangement in his notes on *In Memoriam* printed in the *Memoir*, it is to be supposed that he was not satisfied with it. It ignores the Second Christmas poem.

PAULL F. BAUM

[Some Deficiencies of *In Memoriam*] †

'In Memoriam' is not only a monument to Arthur Hallam and a record of Tennyson's personal suffering at Hallam's early death, it is also the "way of the soul"—a somewhat pretentious phrase, but Tennyson's own—his representation of everyman's pain when confronted with death, the struggle with doubt, and the triumphant assertion of God's love. The poet is at first overcome with his own loss, questions the ways of God to man, seeks consolation for himself, and in fighting his own fight, reveals the grounds of consolation and hope for all mankind.

What, now, is Tennyson's answer? Put in the briefest form, Tennyson's answer to the problem of human existence is the belief in personal immortality. "His belief in personal immortality," said Knowles, "was passionate—I think almost the strongest passion he had"; and outside of 'In Memoriam,' in the *Memoir* and in other records of conversations with the poet, there is abundant substantiation of this statement.[1] "The chief consideration which induced Tennyson to cling to faith in immortality," says Masterman, "and the argument which he asserts almost defiantly throughout the remainder of his poetical career, is the impossibility of the deliberate acceptance of the negative belief." For to Tennyson as to many others "life, regarded simply as life terminating in death, yields no meaning whatever." As a corollary to this, he clings to a belief in the possibility of communion with the dead. Thence he proceeds,

† From *Tennyson Sixty Years After* (Chapel Hill, N.C., University of North Carolina Press, 1948), pp. 121–32.
1. Tennyson is reported once as saying: "I'll shake my fist in God Almighty's face and say it isn't fair, if I find there is no immortality" (D. A. Wilson, *Carlyle on Cromwell and Others*, p. 325). The vehemence betrays a want of confidence. Said Tennyson to Carlyle: "Your traveller comes to an inn and lies down in his bed almost with the certainty that he will go on his journey rejoicing the next morning." Carlyle only grunted in reply. Afterwards FitzGerald remarked to Tennyson: "You had him there"; but Tennyson admitted later to Miss Thackeray (Lady Ritchie) that it only proved "how dangerous an illustration is."

relying on the then undeveloped theories of evolution, to a belief in the gradual improvement of the human race. Accepting the doctrine of development from the inanimate to animate life, or at least of the development of brute into man and man into superior man, he found it repugnant to think that this development should stop abruptly with death. And further, in order that this view should yield its fullest meaning and satisfaction, there must be the concomitant development of the spiritual element, already latent in man, into the highest and ultimate realization, its absorption into the divine—though in consistency with his belief that "individuality endures" he was obliged sometimes (as in XLVII) to deny absolute absorption or to speak with oracular ambiguity.

* * *

The real charge * * * against 'In Memoriam' is of course not that it is Victorian in theology and social ideas or that its answers to the doubts which spring from intense sorrow are not the answers which we of another generation desire—not, in a word, in the *thought* of the poem at all (though largely in the *thinking*), but rather that it does not satisfy what Arnold called "the laws of poetic truth and poetic beauty." Arnold never quite explained what these laws are, nor has anyone else, but we have a general idea. 'In Memoriam' is certainly a criticism of life and it has plenty of high seriousness—though many of the sections are seriously deficient in this quality—but it lacks form and coherence (what Arnold called, after Goethe, architectonics) and it lacks that clearness and sureness of treatment which its subject emphatically demands.

The form, a series of short lyrics, is not suited to a sustained philosophical poem. The plan, a discontinuous record of incidents, moods, and meditations, is fatally improper to a serious presentation of one of the most difficult and profound subjects which interest the human mind and spirit; and Tennyson's own confession (or boast) of the casual way in which the poem grew would be sufficient, if internal evidence were not abundant, to condemn his method. For such a subject only a carefully plotted and clearly articulated plan could hope to succeed; yet Tennyson's plan was, having let his little memorial poems accumulate until they were numerous enough to publish, to give them the appearance of order by indicating a few dates and grouping them as best he could on a theoretical thread of grief, doubt, hope, and faith.

* * *

'In Memoriam' has moreover too much variety, both of style and of content. In style it ranges from the plainest possible language to passages which are exceedingly obscure, not only because the subject matter is difficult but because the expression is over-elaborate, even to loose grammar and faulty syntax. In style it ranges also from a fine simplicity to false rhetoric and pseudo-poetic diction; from pure lyric strains to displays of over-strained virtuosity. It shifts without warning from the communication of high thoughts and powerful emotions to the cheap and easy sentimental appeals of the domestic idyll.

And this excess of variety is not only in style, but likewise in content. The poem includes more kinds of subject than can be successfully moulded into a real unity. There are splendid descriptions of nature, in which Tennyson almost always excels; lyric cries of the suffering heart; moving analyses of both doubt and despair; confused and almost inarticulate outpourings of grief; expositions, both straightforward and indirect, of reasoned questioning;—and all these blend together into one great elegiac tone. But there are also many *excursus*, digressions, footnotes, irrelevancies—for example, about his brothers and sisters and their personal affairs, details about Arthur Hallam which he fails to make interesting to us though they interest him closely, details about the family's moving from Somersby and the Christmas celebrations—all of which he has reported faithfully but has not transmuted into poetry. Besides these foreign elements which he has not integrated with his elegy there are the uncomfortably frank personal apologies about his own indulgence in grief, the sad mechanic exercise of composition, and the futility of fame; and still less amenable to incorporation with his main theme, the little indigent observations about contemporary conditions. But the poem's greatest handicap of disunity springs from Tennyson's deliberate extension of his professed subject, the consolation which came to him from his hardwon belief in personal immortality, to include an assured prophecy of a golden age upon earth. Not only do we mortals pass (under conditions never even examined) to a state of both human and spiritual perfection in a life beyond this life, but the race itself is promised a similar perfection in a future life terrestrial. This, if it is an argument at all, is an argument by analogy merely, and a very imperfect analogy, but it is an argument extraneous to his chief concern which was the reconciliation to death. It suggests a confusion between two kinds of immortality which is patent in the Epilogue.

* * *

From Tennyson's statement that the sections were composed somewhat at haphazard, together with the fact that he did not succeed in arranging them, either by mere transposition or by filling out with fresh sections the wanting parts, into a formal unity and orderly coherence, we are warranted in reading them as a notebook or journal of mourning and of the loss and recovery of faith. The logical steps by which Tennyson's mind and heart ascended from despair to consolation, from doubt to an assertion (even if not a conviction) of faith are not all present in the poem: they do not need to be, since it is a poem. We have only the steps which the poet chose to record and publish. We do however witness his suffering in many intimate details; he confides to us the shadows and gleams of light as they came to him, the moments which to him seemed important then though to us they may appear inconsequent because they are not ours and because he has not fused them into a true whole. We are thus permitted to observe Tennyson's mind through many of the stages of his experience, even when his thoughts are unworthy and the tone confessional; we are premitted to hear him talking to himself, now about Arthur in the other world, now about his brothers in this; we are permitted to see him now yearning for comfort, now distracted by trivial incidents, now seeking ecstatic communion with the dead, now agreeably at home with the living. Read in this sense 'In Memoriam' is a remarkably frank and disarming revelation. If we find some of Tennyson's meditations uninteresting, some of his observations commonplace, some of his experiences without salt or liveliness for us, this is (to put it paradoxically) a judgment on the poet not on the poem, on the material, not on the treatment—though such a distinction may be critically improper—for he has put before us a narrative of his experience, realistic at the risk, which all realism runs, of being dull, but impressive in its honest unreserve, even if unimpressive at all points in what it portrays. In so far as our minds are in sympathy with the kind of experience Tennyson has to display we shall be moved by his sincerity, touched by his sorrow, and gratified by the comfort which he finally wrings from his suffering. Read in this sense 'In Memoriam' becomes a long lyrical domestic idyll, autobiographical in the first instance, with the immediate appeal of all autobiography, but also a story-situation like that of 'The May Queen' or 'Enoch Arden' and the other Idylls of the Hearth, though different in technical presentation just as 'Maud' is different, and like 'Maud' somewhat rambling and unfocussed in outline but brightened by fine passages of varying tone and color. This, I submit, is a sympathetic way of reading 'In Memoriam' and was that of many of the poet's contemporaries; but it is uncritical.

For if, on the other hand, our minds are not naturally sympathetic to a story of this sort, if we do not readily share the kind of personal suffering which was Tennyson's, if the kind of religious doubt which he felt is foreign to us, if our hearts do not passionately yearn for direct communion with those who are separated from us by death, and if our minds can be satisfied without a belief in the everlasting survival of the individual self; then, in spite of the biographic interest in 'In Memoriam' the poem will not awaken a quick response in us (as it did at first), and we will look for that lit-

erary art, that dramatic power by which all great poetry enlists our
affections and stirs our emotions and creates a sense of our common
human experience even when the immediate grounds for it are not
there. We will demand in the poem that dramatic art by which we
are made to share those emotions and experiences which are not
naturally within our range, that intense illusion of reality which
makes the characters and incidents of great drama and fiction, and
the emotions of great lyric poetry, more real than our own little
lives. And this quality we shall not always find, for 'In Memoriam'
as a whole does not possess it. Tennyson * * * has left us a poem
which as a whole is of considerable biographic and documentary
interest, but without permanent attractiveness.

"It must be remembered," however, said Tennyson, "that this is
a poem, *not* an actual biography. ... 'I' is not always the author
speaking of himself, but the voice of the human race speaking thro'
him." *Not always*; but how is the reader to know when Tennyson is
speaking in his own voice and when through the mask? The "way
of the soul" seems very like an afterthought and "not always" an
evasion. Yet this would not greatly matter if the poem would sup-
port the interpretation which Tennyson has asked us to read into it.
One could not only forgive, one could even justify, the poet in
claiming a deeper significance than he was at first aware of, if that
meaning can be fairly found in it. If it can, we shall abandon the
position which regarded 'In Memoriam' as a large-scale domestic
idyll and reread the poem as—though not always—the way of the
soul. That is, we shall project the incidents of the poem beyond
Tennyson's own personal experience and regard them as typical of
the experience of the race. Tennyson is to be identified with man-
kind and the domestic details of his story are to be understood as
but illustrations of what we all have suffered and learned—not all
of them, to be sure, but we are to use our tact and discretion in
deciding which to generalize and which to accept literally. Such is
Tennyson's claim. It means that we, all men, share not only his pas-
sionate sense of bereavement (as at times we all have done), but
also his anxiety to know and see after death the friend he has lost in
his life; not only his questionings of divine justice, but also his
acceptance of honest doubt as the ground of religious faith; not
only his gradual acknowledgement of faith without the necessity of
proof, but his special reasons, never made entirely perspicuous, for
intuitive faith; not only his belief in the evolution of man from the
brute animals (now a commonplace), but also his hopes of a mil-
lenial perfection of the race as a source of comfort in our daily dis-
comfitures. Again Tennyson seems to have mistaken some of the
ideas prevalent in his time and cogent for many of his generation
(but not questions of importance at all times) for the simple uni-
versal beliefs which in one language or another all civilized mankind

accept. Just as the intimate details about Arthur Hallam and Tennyson's family were too specific to be acceptable for the purposes of poetic truth, so the religious and social tenets, vague as some of them are, are too specifically local and topical for the appeals of universal truth. This does not mean that they are all wrong; only that they are Victorian and cannot be acknowledged without the discount to which all local and temporary versions of truth are subject. Some of the emotions, some of the experiences, some of the findings of 'In Memoriam' *are* of universal application, and by them parts of the poem will live; but as a single poem it has had its day and ceased to be.—To most of us this was already obvious, but the reasons for its failure had to be examined.

The facts, moreover, of the poem's irregular origin, its growth by accumulation rather than by design, must be held to militate against its success as a philosophical delineation of the soul's education by love and sorrow. In this sense, Tennyson's soul was self-educated. Without a carefully conceived plan no poet could hope to execute such a grandiose design,—the chief theme fully thought through and its many implications and contributory elements plotted and placed. Instead, Tennyson seems to have improvised, to have felt his way along—the poem itself is evidence of this, without his own statement—and the most he could expect or claim is that we should recognize with sympathy the drawbacks of such a method. Nor is it to be denied that there is a certain piquancy or immediacy in this friendly appeal. But it was a small gain for a great loss.

Indeed, the subject, if firmly grasped and clearly developed, has immense advantages. To record the suffering of a personal loss and make that the basis of a declaration of faith fought for against the heavy odds of philosophic and religious doubt was a new opportunity, apparently never seized by any poet before him. It was an opportunity for a great original modern work, the great Christian poem of the nineteenth century (as Kingsley actually called it); but Tennyson was unfitted for it by his youth, his training, and his theology. His mind had not been disciplined with a severe application to logical thought and speculation. He was not deeply read in the best that philosophy and religion had discovered on his special subject, though he read widely. He was not really a Christian, though Stopford Brooke tried valiantly to prove that he was. (Emily Sellwood knew better, and this was one of the reasons which postponed their marriage.) He felt no profound faith which was wrested from him by Hallam's death—at least I find no evidence of it either in the biography or in the poem. He was still searching for the grounds of faith when Hallam died; he had not reached the stage which genuinely religious minds achieve early or never at all, though they may lose it again and again, the recognition that faith is either a gift or an act of will, and not a matter for argument and logical demonstration. In spite of going through the motions, or rather, going through the emotions, Tennyson never quite reached that stage. He tried logic and it failed him (as of course it must); or if not logic, the method and appearance of logic. And he fell back upon assertion in lieu of conviction, upon trust and hope because he found nothing else. What he really sought, like so many of his contemporaries, was not faith, religious faith, but confidence and assurance of his own religious inclinations. His culminating achievement is the great hymn to Divine Love which is the Prologue to 'In Memoriam.' It is a humble confession of human weakness and his own impotence, and clutching after comfort—"believing where we cannot prove"—with full admission of its elusiveness. There is all the sadness of defeat and none of the triumph of victory in the crucial stanza—

> We have but faith: we cannot know; . . .
> And yet we trust it comes from thee,
> A beam in darkness: let it grow.

This is still the language of doubt, for beneath its humility is uncertainty. True faith is acceptance, whole and unqualified. Read for example, Gerard Manly Hopkins, Tennyson's later contemporary. Yet against this stand the assertions of triumph in the latter part of the poem (cxxiv-cxxxi), a fine poetic climax (barring the overfeminine language of cxxix); and this contrast, together with Tennyson's remark to Knowles that it was all too hopeful, makes the question of insincerity difficult to escape, or what is equally damaging, mental confusion. To have staked his whole theological position on the survival of personality after death marks a limitation in Tennyson's grasp of religion; and the brave summing up by his son in the *Memoir* (1,311) shows that while Tennyson regarded himself in his later life as thoroughly religious the terms of his thinking were vague, indecisive, and not a little confused.

JOHN D. ROSENBERG

The Two Kingdoms of *In Memoriam*†

I

The praise of Tennyson's ear is sometimes a prelude to the damning of his mind. Thus when Auden, who conceives of Tennyson as a kind of disembodied ear, mindless and melancholy, tells us that he had "the finest ear, perhaps, of any English poet," he at once adds that "he was also undoubtedly the stupidest."[1] But can we so simply dissociate the use of language from the use of reason? Surely the stupid poet is a bad poet. Perhaps if Tennyson's contemporaries had less eagerly encumbered their laureate with the mantles of the philosopher and prophet, we might not now be so sceptical of his intelligence.

Yet it is more than the image of the unsmiling, bearded, public bard which inhibits our response to Tennyson. We react to Victorian poetry with an incapacitating sense that too much of it is, in Morris' phrase, the idle singing of an empty day. Thus in a perceptive analysis Cleanth Brooks expresses surprise on finding ambiguities in "Tears, Idle Tears." The tears are not idle, he points out, but limpid with the virtues we associate with seventeenth-century verse. He concludes that Tennyson has unwittingly *blundered* into ambiguity.

Our notion of Tennyson's perfect but mindless craftsmanship blinds us to his remarkably poised handling (especially evident in *In Memoriam*) of symbols and their associated movements of passion and idea. Perhaps symbol seems too sophisticated, passion too violent, a term for Tennyson. But do we deny the terms to, say, Emily Dickinson because, like Tennyson in one of his many styles, she also clothes energy of idea and emotion in the sparsest of diction? Are we instantly certain which of the two wrote:

> For this alone on Death I wreak
> The wrath that garners in my heart:
> He put our lives so far apart
> We cannot hear each other speak.[2]

II

In Memoriam was composed over a seventeen-year period, from 1833, when Arthur Hallam died, to 1849, the year before Tennyson published the elegy dedicated to his friend. The poem was widely read as an orthodox testament of Victorian faith, and as such it has been reread and misread in our own century.[3] Yet the opening lines (among the last to be composed), in which the tone of affirmation is struck after years of the doubter's agony, betray an astonishing uncertainty. The Prologue is clogged with qualifications working antiphonally against the statement of faith, which is most vigor-

1. *A Selection from the Poems of Alfred Lord Tennyson*, ed. W. H. Auden (Garden City, 1944), p. x.
2. *In Memoriam*, LXXXII, stanza 4.
3. In Hugh I'Anson Fausset's *Tennyson: A Modern Portrait* (London, 1923), p. 154, the poem is characterized as a rehash of the "old belief in a Divine Providence, blindly held by the simple."

ously offered in the first line but then retracted, celebrated, denied, and asserted through not only the Prologue but the entire poem. Admittedly only a poet with a great ear is capable of such counterpoint, but the mindless poet would be equally incapable of handling the subtler modulations of Tennyson's theme. The ear itself is here an intellectual instrument used not to rouse our admiration for a variation in vowel but to initiate the reader to the contrasting tones and rhythms by which Tennyson is later to reveal his agonized or exultant soul.

Thus, although the first line of the Prologue invokes the "Strong Son of God, immortal Love," the poet admits that "We have but faith: we cannot know" (1.21): he can only *"trust"* (1.39) that Hallam lives eternally with the Strong Son of God. This final admission is extraordinary, for it climaxes seventeen years of obsessive meditation on the death and after-life of the poet's friend. It epitomizes the energetic conflict between doubt and the will to believe which makes *In Memoriam* the most dramatic as well as the most religious of English elegies. This is the point of T. S. Eliot's important comment on the poem: "It is not religious because of the quality of its faith, but because of the quality of its doubt."[4]

In the early sections of *In Memoriam,* when the sudden pain of loss is at its keenest, images of darkness and death are forced upon us. The Strong Son of God, embraced by faith in the Prologue, gives way to Tennyson's clasping of Death in the raven blackness and *danse macabre* of Section I. Death's predominance is further symbolized in Section II by the old yew tree, whose roots grasp at the headstones of the dead and whose branches are without bloom. Sorrow, Priestess of Death in Section III, tells the poet that the sun is dying and that nature herself is a lifeless phantom. With Section VI we come upon a series of domestic idylls, "little pictures" of Victorian life which are, unhappily, interspersed throughout the poem. Each of the idylls depicts a miniature of humanity suffering under the weight of mortality. The last, with its overtones of romantic love, prepares us for the great seventh section:

> Dark house, by which once more I stand
> Here in the long unlovely street,
> Doors, where my heart was used to beat
> So quickly, waiting for a hand,
>
> A hand that can be clasp'd no more—[5]
> Behold me, for I cannot sleep,

4. *Selected Essays,* 3rd. ed. (London, 1951), p. 336.
5. Compare the companion poem, CXIX, 1. 12: "I take the pressure of thine hand." I am indebted to Professor Jerome H. Buckley for having suggested to me the importance of the image of the hand throughout *In Memoriam.*

> And like a guilty thing I creep
> At earliest morning to the door.

> He is not here; but far away
> The noise of life begins again,
> And ghastly thro' the drizzling rain
> On the bald street breaks the blank day.

In making this pained visitation, the poet has become a nocturnal creature ("I cannot sleep"), the darkness shrouding him "like a guilty thing" and severing him from the normal waking world. With the self-evident opening of the third stanza—"He is not here"—Tennyson is forced to recognize anew his first shocked astonishment at Hallam's death. That shock is heightened by a probable allusion to the Gospels, in all of which, save that of St. John, the angel announces before the empty sepulcher, "He is not here" but has risen in immortal glory. Yet Tennyson, standing before the darkened, empty house—itself an image of the tomb—is nowhere more conscious of Hallam's *mortality*, a consciousness painfully intensified by the contrast between the dead friend and the risen God.

We feel ourselves closer to Hallam's death in the opening sections of *In Memoriam* than at any other point. That event clouds all of nature and grates against the harmony of life itself. Before the dark house, as the "blank day" breaks, Tennyson hears the waking sounds of the city as a "*noise* of life," a distant cacophony from which, in the hostility of his isolation, he is utterly apart. The dawn, symbol of rebirth, is without light—merely a lesser darkness looming through the rain. The poem has reached a point analogous to the heavy close of the eighth stanza of Wordsworth's Immortality Ode:

> Full soon thy Soul shall have her earthly freight,
> And custom lie upon thee with a weight,
> Heavy as frost, and deep almost as life!

The note must change or Tennyson will lapse into inaudibility, chilled into silence by those tears of Section III which grief "hath shaken into frost."

III

The poem now moves to a series of lyrics (Sections IX through XVII) about the "fair ship" which bears the "lost Arthur's loved remains" home to England. Hallam, who died on land, dies once more as Tennyson pictures him engulfed "fathom-deep in brine," the "hands so often clasp'd" in his, now tossing "with tangle and with shells" (X, ll. 17–19). The clasping of hands is weighted, as it was in Section VII, with the sense of impossibility; it has yet to become Tennyson's symbol of reunion in the shared immortal life. Still, there has been a change. The tears once shaken to frost have thawed, as the poet tells us in Secton XIII that his eyes now "have leisure for their tears."

On the first joyless Christmas after Hallam's death (XXX) Tennyson prays that "The light that shone when Hope was born"—the hope of immortal life—be lit again. Without that hope he is convinced that "earth is darkness at the core" (XXXIV), a vast dark house from which the human race is doomed never to arise. He asserts the immortality of the soul not as a religious dogma but as a personal necessity. The argument recalls Arnold's claim in the preface to *God and the Bible* that one of the two evident facts about Christianity is "that men cannot do without it." *In Memoriam* is Tennyson's assertion that *he* could not do without its promise of personal immortality. "The cardinal point of Christianity," his son quotes him as saying, "is the Life after Death."[6]

Tennyson's obsession with that life makes much of *In Memoriam* inaccessible to the modern reader. Our own obsessions have become secularized and we are at a loss to follow a poet who through some thirty-seven stanzas (XL-XLVII) pursues such questions as, Do the dead remain inactive until some general awakening (XLIII), or do they at once begin a new life, forgetting us entirely (XLIV)? It would seem that the problem of a poet's beliefs embarrasses us in direct proportion as they approach us in time. We know all about the ghost in *Hamlet*, scrupulously suspending our disbelief in him so that we may believe in the exigencies of Hamlet's dilemma. But the "ghost" of *In Memoriam* eludes us completely. Because he eludes us, we conclude in our secret hearts that Tennyson, if not the stupidest, is certainly the most naïve of poets. Yet to overlook Tennyson's passionate quest for Hallam's "ghost" is to fail to see that *In Memoriam* is one of the great love poems in English.

For Hallam when alive was very nearly the center of Tennyson's life, and Hallam dead was the focal point of his life during the poem's composition. Despite its overlay of conventional pastoral elegy,[7] *In Memoriam* is deeply, in places almost obnoxiously, per-

6. Hallam Tennyson, *Alfred Lord Tennyson: A Memoir by His Son* (New York, 1897), I, 314.

7. This element of *In Memoriam* is generally overlooked, largely because it occurs in "quiet" passages deliberately spaced as moments of rest between the climactic sections. But despite Tennyson's personalization of the traditional elegy, he was too resourceful a poet not to use its conventions to mute the louder notes of his anguish. Thus we find references to "The murmur of a happy Pan," to singing on 'Argive heights," and "To many a flute of Arcady." One quatrain is given to the conceit of the poet as a shepherd making "pipes" of the grass on Hallam's grave; another depicts the "bitter notes" he sings upon his "harp"; and a third presents the familiar floral catalogue of the pastoral elegy. References might be multiplied, but see especially XXI, i; XXIII. iii and vi; LXXXIII, iii; CXXV, i.

sonal. Herein lies its uniqueness and distressing modernity among the major English elegies. Edward King is irrelevant to *Lycidas*; Keats is only the occasion for *Adonais*; but Arthur Hallam—above all Tennyson's love for Hallam—is the overriding subject of *In Memoriam*. Indeed, Tennyson's unending speculation on immortality is rooted in his inexhaustible impulse to visualize and to *touch* Hallam. Hence the ubiquitous image of the hand.

After the victorious affirmation concluding the immortality group —"And I shall know him when we meet" (XLVII)—Tennyson plunges into the panic despair of Section L:

> Be near me when my light is low,
>> When the blood creeps, and the nerves prick
>> And tingle; and the heart is sick,
> And all the wheels of being slow. . . .

The regressive movement culminates in Sections LIV-LVI. The poet compares himself to

>> An infant crying in the night;
>> An infant crying for the light,
> And with no language but a cry.
> (LIV, ll. 18–20)

The primitive fear of "Be near me . . ." here becomes a plea for release from the animal terror of extinction. Without assurance of that release, Nature herself is a hostile goddess, a shrieking Fury "red in tooth and claw" (LVI,l.15). "I bring to life, I bring to death" (LVI,l.6), she cries, usurping the work of the Prologue's Strong Son of God who "madest Life" and "madest Death" (ll.6–7). Shall man, Nature's final creation, who "trusted God was love indeed,"

> Who loved, who suffer'd countless ills,
>> Who battled for the True, the Just,
>> Be blown about the desert dust,
> Or seal'd within the iron hills?   (LVI, ll. 17–20)

We are at the opposite pole from the confident assertion of Section XLVII—"And I shall know him when we meet." Hallam's death, first felt by Tennyson alone, has here been generalized to include the whole of living nature in one arid, iron negation.

Nature retains her hostility in the great lyric marking the first anniversary of Hallam's death (LXXII), a day which rises howling, blasts the poplar and the rose, and is "mark'd as with some hideous crime"—the slaying of Hallam. Only with the second Christmas after his death is there a clear release from the paralyzing preoccupation with loss. "O last regret," Tennyson exclaims, "regret can die!" (LXXVIII). He can now grace his theme with paradox, marking that detachment from the past necessary for the full growth of his faith in Hallam's immortality.

Death, the dark-handed criminal of the anniversary poem, becomes "holy Death" in LXXX, sanctified by contact with Hallam. In LXXXIV Tennyson feels "The low beginnings of content." In LXXXVII, lingering outside Hallam's former rooms at Cambridge, he is for the first time capable of recollection in tranquility (st. 6–10), a tranquility which becomes absolute in LXXXIX as he recalls his friend's idyllic visits to the Tennyson home at Somersby. But after these calm retrospects Tennyson's desire for the sight and touch of Hallam returns with increased intensity. In XCIII he cries to Hallam, "Descend, and touch, and enter," a desire gratified in XCV, one of the four or five climactic lyrics of *In Memoriam.*

It opens in the calm of evening with the poet and his family together on the lawn. The trees lay their "dark arms" about the fields, and as night falls the family departs, symbolizing the larger society from which Tennyson's grief has isolated him. He reads Hallam's letters written during the period of friendship (the "glad year" of l.22) and finds that the dead leaves still retain their life. Then the dead man himself becomes a living spirit which "touches" Tennyson's own, their souls now intertwined as were once their hands:

> So word by word, and line by line,
>   The dead man touch'd me from the past,
>   And all at once it seem'd at last
> The living soul was flash'd on mine,[8]
>   And mine in this was wound, and whirl'd
>   About empyreal heights of thought . . .

The two souls "come on that which is" and feel "the deep pulsations of the world." But Tennyson's "trance" is at length "stricken thro' with doubt" (l. 44), and the blinding flash of his vision fades into the less revealing light of the visible world:

> And suck'd from out the distant gloom
>   A breeze began to tremble o'er
>   The large leaves of the sycamore,
> And fluctuate all the still perfume,
>
> And gathering freshlier overhead,
>   Rock'd the full-foliaged elms, and swung

8. A. C. Bradley (*A Commentary on Tennyson's "In Memoriam"* [London, 1929], p. 90) observes that until *ca.* 1878 "*The* living soul" read "*His* living soul" and "mine in *this*" read "mine in *his*." If "The living soul" is not Hallam's, the lines are without meaning. For the remarkable impression Hallam left with his contemporaries, see Gladstone's eulogy quoted in the *Memoir*, I, 299.

The heavy-folded rose, and flung
The lilies to and fro, and said,

"The dawn, the dawn," and died away;
And East and West, without a breath,
Mixt their dim lights, like life and death,
To broaden into boundless day.

The breeze speaks only four words, which Tennyson translates into a parable interpreting much of *In Memoriam*. Light and dark, day and night—*"like life and death"*—are dual aspects of that single reality to which the poet aspires, the eternal life-after-death in which Hallam will not appear in a moment's flash but abide with Tennyson in the lasting light of "boundless day."

IV

Section XCV reveals the symbolic structure of *In Memoriam* with unusual clarity. That structure at times parallels and at times is independent of the poem's formal division into seasons. Within this section Tennyson achieves the transition from images of darkness and death to light and the promise of reunion with Hallam. The parallel movement in the formal organization of the poem is marked by Section CVI ("Ring out, wild bells, to the wild sky"), which celebrates the third Christmas after Hallam's death. Although it contains irrelevancies and its manner is forced, the dramatic success of this set-piece is unquestionable. The *tone* is right, for the wild ringing of the bells to the wild sky counterbalances the earlier hysteria of grief and the high-pitched shrieking of nature red in tooth and claw. Tennyson now rings out his "mournful rhymes" and rings in "the Christ that is to be" (l. 32). When in quieter voice, he simply tells us that his regret has blossomed into an April violet (CXV, l. 19).

Yet *In Memoriam* demands a more articulate response to the angry questions of Sections LV and LVI than the mere ringing of bells. How can we be certain that God and Nature are not at strife, that immortal Love does in fact govern all creation? Tennyson never attains absolute assurance; instead he attempts something perhaps braver and certainly more difficult—the synthesis of a nightmare with a vision of felicity. For that synthesis he draws on two great myths, the myth of Progress and the Christian vision of the Kingdom of Heaven on Earth. With these he slays the dragon of doubt first shocked into formidable being with Hallam's death in 1833 and later grown to monstrous proportions with Tennyson's reading of Lyell's *Principles of Geology* in 1837. From geological evidence Lyell argued that "species cannot be immortal, but must perish one after the other, like the individuals which compose them."[9] Thus man, the creation of immortal Love in the Prologue, appears in Sections LV and LVI neither to share his maker's immortality nor to inhabit an earth guided by any conceivable laws of love: "A thousand types are gone," Nature cries, "I care for nothing, all shall go" (LVI, ll. 3–4).

This, then, is the nightmare. Whence the vision of felicity, of faith rather than extinction? Tennyson points to the answer in Section CXVIII, in which man, "Who throve and branch'd from clime to clime," becomes at last "The herald of a higher race" (ll. 13–14). Geology had revealed life as an "idle ore" (l. 20), a desert dust sealed within the iron hills of an earth darkened to the core. But evolution speaks to us of the living forms which may perpetuate the dead.

With increased confidence Tennyson asserts in Section CXXIV that if doubt had ever shaken faith, his heart had stood firm and answered "I have felt." He had once been like "a child in doubt and fear . . . a child that cries" (ll. 17, 19), a conscious echo of the infant of Section LIV, "An infant crying in the night . . . And with no language but a cry." He had then extended lame hands of faith to God but gathered only dust and chaff (LV, ll. 17–18). Now, as when Hallam's soul had flashed on his in Section XCV, he again beholds "What is,"

> And out of darkness came the hands
> That reach thro' nature, moulding men.

Yet these hands, which Tennyson has sought throughout the poem, are not Hallam's but those of the immortal Love of the Prologue which "madest Life" and "madest man" and here shape and animate mankind.

The metamorphosis of Hallam's hands into those of the divinity would be more startling, were it not that in the latter part of *In Memoriam* Tennyson annihilates the distinction between the human and the divine. And with that annihilation Tennyson achieves the synthesis earlier alluded to, drawing at once on the assumptions of nineteenth-century science and orthodox Christianity. The evolutionary argument of Section CXVIII (man thriving from clime to clime) answered adequately to Tennyson's fears of racial extinction in Sections LV and LVI. Yet it failed to guarantee the personal immortality of Hallam. God, reaching hands through

9. Quoted from Eleanor Bustin Mattes, *In Memoriam: The Way of a Soul* (New York, 1951), p. 59. See Chapters VI and VIII for an extremely useful discussion of the wide reading which influenced Tennyson's composition of Sections LV, LVI and CXVIII. The book shows Tennyson in a vital relation to the main intellectual concerns of his time.

nature, might be Love indeed; but for Tennyson it was a feeble love which could not preside over the placing of his own immortal hand in Hallam's. Evolution offered no such union; Christianity did. Thus in the closing lyrics Tennyson joins the promise of the one—Progress—to the promise of the other—Immortality. Evolution's proffered "higher race" becomes interchangeable with Christianity's promised Kingdom of Heaven on Earth. Hallam himself is a citizen of both realms, of the heavenly city which is to be manifested on earth and of the early city which is to evolve into the divine.[1]

It is not surprising, then, that as the poem draws to its close we find Tennyson simultaneously employing the language of religion and of Victorian science. Section CXXVII is especially pertinent, for it contains linguistic strata of Geology and the Apocalypse. Mountains tremble, sheets of ice topple from their peaks

> And molten up, and roar in flood;
> The fortress crashes from on high,
> The brute earth lightens to the sky,
> And the great Aeon sinks in blood.

Earlier (XXXV) Tennyson had described, with geological accuracy, streams which slowly "Draw down Aeonian hills, and sow / The dust of continents to be." Now he deliberately abandons Lyell's hypothesis that the present configuration of the earth is the product of wholly natural forces such as erosion. He reverts to the discredited concept of cataclysmic upheavals and in place of "continents to be" we read of the great Aeon sinking in blood, "compass'd by the *fires of hell*" (l. 17). The language, no longer scientific, recalls that of the destruction of the Great Babylon, of "fire come down from heaven ... and thunders, and lightnings; and ... a great earthquake, such as was not since men were upon the earth."[2]

Hallam, witness to this incandescent holocaust, "*smil[eth]*", knowing all is well" (l.20). The line is very nearly incredible. The smile is diabolic or divine, expressing either pyromaniacal joy or sublime content in the knowledge that the flaming of the earth is prelude to a finer order and a higher race. From the vantage point of the gods Hallam now sees what Tennyson (at the conclusion of CXXVIII) sees only in part:

> That all, as in some piece of art,
> Is toil coöperant to an end.

1. Tennyson suggests that the race will be reborn by evolution or divine grace through some sixty-five sections before man becomes the "herald of a higher race" in CXVIII. In LV, for example, he "faintly trusts" in the "larger hope" of man's salvation. The *Memoir* (I, 321) justifies this reading: "He means by 'the larger hope' that the whole human race would through, perhaps, ages of suffering, be at length purified and saved." In CIII he writes of "that great race which is to be," a clear anticipation of the higher race of CXVIII; and in CVI he rings in "the Christ that is to be."

2. Revelation xiii. 13; xvi. 18.

The cataclysm is subsumed in the cosmic work of art.

Throughout the later poems Hallam has been progressively depersonalized, assuming many of the attributes of the Prologue's Strong Son of God. As human he anticipates evolutionary progress; as divine he fulfills the Gospel's promise of everlasting life. Thus the paradoxical address to Hallam in Section CXXIX: he is "Known and unknown, *human, divine.*" Uncertain of Hallam's identity in Section CXXX—"What art thou then? I cannot guess"—he can nonetheless assert, "I shall not lose thee tho' I die." With the promise of that final possession Tennyson concludes the poem proper:

> O living with that shalt endure
> When all that seems shall suffer shock,
> Rise in the spiritual rock,
> Flow thro' our deeds and make them pure. . . .
>
> Until we close with all we loved,
> And all we flow from, soul in soul.

Tennyson himself glossed "living will" as "Free will in man."[3] Yet in the Prologue he writes "Our wills are ours, to make them thine." This transfer of will enables us to accept the cataclysm of CXXVII as that which only "seems [to] suffer shock," a flaming instant of destruction in the eternity of rebirth, just as the loss of Hallam was a long moment's darkness preceding boundless day. The progression from death to life is again implicit in the reference to the "spiritual rock"[4] from which Moses struck water in the desert and which Paul called the rock that "was Christ"—the same rock from which man partakes of the baptismal waters of rebirth and on which Tennyson bases his faith that we shall "*close* with all we loved . . . soul in soul." The image, appropriately, is of an embrace; the clasping of hands has led to the union of souls.

v

Had Tennyson concluded *In Memoriam* without appending the Epilogue, he would have spared us the longest and most damaging of the poem's domestic idylls. There is much bad verse in another great long poem of the nineteenth century, *The Prelude.* But Wordsworth's ineptitudes are rarely offensive; they are merely unfortunate lapses into prose. Tennyson never deviates into prose but occasionally postures himself into verse. That posture in much of the closing epithalamium is mannered and false, although it is

3. " 'O living will that shalt endure' he explained as that which we know as Free-will, the higher and enduring part of Man" (*Memoir*, I, 319).

4. See I Corinthians x. 4: "for they drank of that spiritual Rock that followed them: and that Rock was Christ."

true that the marriage Tennyson celebrates has its symbolic relation to the whole poem: "It begins," he said, "with a funeral and ends with a marriage—begins with death and ends in promise of a new life—a sort of Divine Comedy, cheerful at the close."[5]

Precisely as "cheerful" is grossly inadequate to the tone of the *Paradiso*, so it is disastrously inadequate to the conclusion of *In Memoriam*. Wrapped in the spell of wedding cheer, Tennyson can refer to the preceding lyrics as "echoes" of a weaker past, as "half but idle brawling rhymes" (ll. 22–23). He here rejects the larger grief and the larger joy of *In Memoriam* in favor of the lesser pleasantries of Cecilia Tennyson's marriage, on a bright Victorian forenoon, to Edmund Lushington. A greater poet, or one less responsive to the demands of his contemporaries, would have embraced both experiences, felt no compulsion to disparage the earlier part of the poem in order to exalt the "cheer" of its conclusion.

Fortunately, however, Tennyson is the master of many styles. Nowhere are they called upon to accomplish more than in the closing verses of the Epilogue. The wedded pair depart; the feast draws to an end and the poet retires in darkness, withdrawing into that isolation from the family group which preceded the flashing of Hallam's soul on his in Section XCV. From the language of polite conversation he moves to that of resolution and prophecy. The twenty-seventh stanza clearly marks the transition:

> Again the feast, the speech, the glee,
>   The shade of passing thought, the wealth
>   Of words and wit, the double health,
> The crowning cup, the three-times-three,   (26)

> And last the dance;—till I retire.
>   Dumb is that tower which spake so loud,
>   And high in heaven the streaming cloud,
> And on the downs a rising fire: (27)

> And rise, O moon, from yonder down,
>   Till over down and over dale
>   All night the shining vapor sail
> And pass the silent-lighted town,   (28)

> The white-faced halls, the glancing rills,
>   And catch at every mountain head. . . .

I have begun to quote a sentence—one of the longest in English poetry—which extends through ten stanzas and thirty-nine lines. Yet it is a compact unity which gathers into its imagery and state-

---

5. A remark made by Tennyson when reading the poem to Knowles. See *The Poetic and Dramatic Works of Alfred* *Lord Tennyson*, ed. W. J. Rolfe (Cambridge, 1898), p. 832.

ment the longer statement of the entire poem. It transports us from
the lesser "noise of life" in society to the enfolding quiet of nature.
We move from microcosm to macrocosm, the moonlight serving
Tennyson's lyric and symbolic intention precisely as the snow, fall-
ing faintly through the universe upon all the living and the nonliv-
ing, serves Joyce's intention at the close of *The Dead*.

The moonlight, playing on mountain and star, touches the
"bridal doors" behind which "A soul shall . . . strike his being into
bounds,"

> And, moved thro' life of lower phase,
> > Results in man, be born and think,
> > And act and love, a closer link
> Betwixt us and the crowning race
>
> Of those that, eye to eye, shall look
> > On knowledge; under whose command
> > Is Earth and Earth's, and in their hand
> Is Nature like an open book.

The foetus, recapitulating the "lower phases" of evolution, will
develop, as had Hallam, into a closer link with the crowning race of
perfected mankind, whose advent had been "heralded" in Section
CXVIII. That race will look on knowledge not as "A beam in dark-
ness" (Prologue, 1. 24) but "eye to eye," just as Hallam in the
penultimate stanza "lives in God," seeing Him not through a glass
darkly but "face to face":

> Whereof the man that with me trod
> > This planet was a noble type
> > Appearing ere the times were ripe,
> That friend of mine who lives in God,
>
> That God, which ever lives and loves,
> > One God, one law, one element,
> > And one far-off divine event,
> To which the whole creation moves.

Hallam is at once the noble type of evolution's crowning race and
forerunner of "the Christ that is to be." The Strong Son of God of
the Prologue again emerges, long after Nature's discordant shriek, as
immortal Love—the God which "ever lives and loves." His crea-
tion, one element, resolves under one law the antitheses of life and
death, darkness and light, destruction and rebirth.

With the "one far-off divine event" we confront Tennyson's final
effort at uniting evolutionary science and Christian faith. For that
event holds out the promise both of the Kingdom of Heaven, when
all shall "live in God," and the Kingdom of Earth, when all shall

have evolved into gods. The nineteenth century's conviction of man's perfectibility and Christianity's conviction of man's redemption become interchangeable. The synthesis is not without its inconsistencies, perhaps its absurdities; but it is the more remarkable in that the hundred years which followed the publication of *In Memoriam* have produced no like attempt more daring, persuasive, or eloquent.

E. D. H. JOHNSON

In Memoriam: The Way of the Poet†

The tendency to regard *In Memoriam* exclusively as spiritual autobiography has obscured the importance of this work as a record of Tennyson's artistic development during the formative years between 1833 and 1850. Yet among the components of the ordeal through which the poet passed in his journey to faith was the search for an aesthetic creed answerable alike to his creative needs and to the literary demands of the age. Of the lyrics making up *In Memoriam*, approximately one quarter[1] relates to this concern; and when taken together, they constitute an index to Victorian poetic theory and practice as suggestive in its way as the testimony of *The Prelude* with reference to the poetry of the Romantic generation.

In tracing the stages through which Tennyson came to an awareness of his mission as a poet, there is no need to get involved in the perplexing problem of dating the sections of *In Memoriam*[2] A. C. Bradley's *Commentary* has demonstrated the organic unity of the elegy in its published form. With three Christmas seasons as chronological points of division, it falls into four parts, the dominant mood progressing from an initial reaction of despair over Hallam's death (1–27), through a period of philosophic doubt (28–77), to nascent hope (78–103), and finally, to a confident assertion of faith (104–131). This paper will undertake to show, first, that Bradley's schematization lends itself equally well to a formal analysis of the evolution of the Tennysonian poetic, and secondly, that the processes of philosophic and aesthetic growth exhibited in the poem are so interrelated in their successive phases as ultimately to be inseparable.

† *Victorian Studies*, 2 (1958), 139–48.
1. The elegy consists of 133 separate poems, of which the following bear on the present discussion: Prologue, 5, 8, 16, 19, 20, 21, 23, 34, 36, 37, 38, 48, 49, 52, 57, 58, 59, 65, 75, 76, 77, 83, 85, 88, 96, 103, 106, 108, 120, 122, 123, 125, 128, Epilogue.
2. For the fullest attempt yet offered to establish a chronological order for the composition of the lyrics, see E. B. Mattes, *In Memoriam: The Way of a Soul* (New York, 1951).

Shattered by grief during the early months of his bereavement, Tennyson found in poetry an anodyne bringing temporary release from obsessive introspection:

> But, for the unquiet heart and brain,
> A use in measured language lies;
> The sad mechanic exercise,
> Like dull narcotics, numbing pain.   (5)

At this time he makes of art a private ceremony, a votive offering to the friend on whose sympathetic encouragement he had been accustomed to rely (8). Vacillating between "calm despair" and "wild unrest," he senses the want of emotional perspective necessary to sustained and disciplined creativity. So crippled seems the shaping power of the imagination that the poet is even provoked to surmise whether the shock of sorrow has not alienated "all knowledge of myself":

> And made me that delirious man
> Whose fancy fuses old and new,
> And flashes into false and true,
> And mingles all without a plan?   (16)

Yet this very impulse toward self-scrutiny had begun to knit "the firmer mind" which Tennyson attributes in the eighteenth lyric to the purgative effect of suffering. The important grouping which follows (19–21) shows the poet at a provisional resting-place affording respite to assess the essentially lyric quality of his response to the experience which he is undergoing. His poetic faculties, incapable of dealing with the full impact of this experience, are commensurate only with the "lighter moods . . .,/That out of words a comfort win." Nevertheless, as though perfection of manner might serve to compensate for superficiality of content, the elaborately wrought metaphors of the nineteenth and twentieth poems point in their deliberate artifice to a notable increase in artistic detachment. Despite the fact that he continues to describe his method of compensation as "breaking into song by fits" (23), Tennyson must by now have begun to entertain thoughts of future publication; for the twenty-first lyric introduces a new element of anxiety over the poet's responsibility to his audience. The slighting comments of a chorus of imaginary interlocutors anticipate the kind of criticism which may be expected to greet a work so subjective in mode. The first speaker condemns the unabashed display of feeling as a eulogy of weakness, while to the second it seems that the poet's inclination "to make parade of pain" originates from an egoistic motive. The third speaker, in drawing attention to the encroachments of democracy on established institutions and to the challenge to received opinions made by science, asks more weightily: "Is this an hour /

For private sorrow's barren song?" To which objections Tennyson, unable as yet to surmount his sense of personal deprivation, can only reply by again pleading that he writes solely in order to give vent to emotions that spontaneously well up: "I do but sing because I must, / And pipe but as the linnets sing."

The passing of the first Christmastide left Tennyson in a more stable frame of mind and disposed, in consequence, to try to come to intellectual terms with the fact of Hallam's death. As the second part of *In Memoriam* shows, however, the search for a meaning in the experience, at least in its initial stages, had no other effect than to involve the mind in the heart's distress. The lyrics relating to poetic theory in this part of the elegy occur in clusters, as follows: 36–38, 48–49 (with which 52 belongs), 57–59, and 75–77. It is significant that each of these groups follows on a section of philosophic inquiry in which speculations precipitated by the irresolvable problems of death and change culminate in a paroxysm of doubt. Whereas the poet had previously looked to art to provide a release from emotional despair, he now discovers its further efficacy in allaying the tormenting "dialogue of the mind with itself."

Tennyson's increasing uneasiness over the limited scope of his work is implied in the derogatory reference of the thirty-fourth lyric to "some wild poet, when he works / Without a conscience or an aim." Yet, what message can be derived from the bleakly materialistic findings of modern historical and scientific knowledge hopeful enough to set beside the homely truths embodied in Christ's parables? In an age of unfaith art perforce abdicates its ethical function in favor of the kinds of teaching that issue in action, "In loveliness of perfect deeds, / More strong than all poetic thought" (36). Guiltily aware of the shaky foundations of his own belief in the Christian revelation, the poet cries: "I am not worthy ev'n to speak / Of thy prevailing mysteries" (37). By so much as daring to trespass on such matters he stands convinced of having "loiter'd in the master's field, / And darken'd sanctities with song." In dismay at the presumption of this first venture beyond the confines of immediate sensation, he falls back on the consolation offered by his "earthly Muse" with her

> little art
> To lull with song an aching heart,
> And render human love his dues . . .

For all the continuing modesty of his pretensions, Tennyson could take additional gratification from the sense that each poem of *In Memoriam* had the truth of fidelity to the mood which had inspired it. Thus, in the sequence preceding the forty-eighth poem, the author's inconclusive brooding, this time over the related enigmas of individual identity and personal immortality, again results in a disavowal of any higher significance for his lyrics than as "Short swallow-flights of song, that dip / Their wings in tears, and skim away." In this very diffidence, however, he recognizes subservience to "a wholesome law," not unlike the Keatsian Negative Capability. And, if his songs leave unplumbed the deeps of human experience, it can at least be asserted in their defense that by giving voice to whatever fancy is uppermost at the moment they register the full range of the poet's sensibility: "From art, from nature, from the schools, / Let random influences glance" (49).

The note of pessimism sounded in the thirty-fifth lyric recurs in the famous fifty-fourth, -fifth, and -sixth poems, formidably reinforced by Tennyson's reading in evolutionary doctrine. Before the blank futility of the view of life here revealed he recoils in horror, conscious of the indignity to Hallam's memory in further pursuing so wild a train of thought (57). At the same time, by forcing him out of purely subjective involvement in his grief, this crisis of doubt leaves in its wake newly won reliance on the capacity of the mind under trial not just to endure, but to grow in dignity. "Wherefore grieve / Thy brethren with a fruitless tear?" the spirit of poetry inquires: "Abide a little longer here, / And thou shalt take a nobler leave" (58). In a still more confident mood the ensuing lyric, which first appeared in the fourth edition of *In Memoriam* (1851), testifies to Tennyson's satisfaction in the discovery that he has gained the power to sublimate private feelings, and as a result to display his sorrow

> With so much hope for years to come,
> That, howsoe'er I know thee, some
> Could hardly tell what name were thine.

Furthermore, just as he has experienced the humanizing effect of suffering (66), so the poet is brought to realize that his constant endeavor to give artistic expression to his ordeal has been a cathartic exercise:

> And in that solace can I sing,
> Till out of painful phases wrought
> There flutters up a happy thought,
> Self-balanced on a lightsome wing ...   (65)

His philosophic misgivings momentarily dormant, Tennyson undertakes in the lyrics immediately preceding the seventy-fifth to memorialize Hallam's brilliant promise and the loss to the age resulting from his untimely death. This subject is deemed too taxing for "verse that brings myself relief"; but there has occurred a significant shift in the reasons which the poet gives for his reluctance to tackle themes of high seriousness. The burden of the blame is now laid on the unpoetic temper of the time, rather than on the writer's own lack of endowment: "I care not in these fading days / To raise a cry that lasts not long." And although, admittedly, no work of art can withstand the erosion of time (76), Tennyson, like Arnold, feels that the hope for modern poetry is nullified from the outset by a hostile *Zeitgeist*. Counteracting this pessimism, however, is the creative self-fulfillment which he increasingly derives from the writing of his elegy; and the tone on which the second part ends is anything but apologetic in the earlier manner:

> My darken'd ways
> Shall ring with music all the same;
> To breathe my loss is more than fame,
> To utter love more sweet than praise.   (77)

The attitude of stoic resignation with which Tennyson greets the second Christmas season is prelude to the recovery of hope in the third part of the poem. Concurrently, art ceases to be valued so much as a distraction from the central conflict in which the writer's deeper thoughts and emotions are involved. The process of spiritual regeneration thus has its aesthetic analogue in the closer identification of artistic considerations with the main themes of the elegy. For example, the coming of spring in the eighty-third lyric is made an image not only for the healing principle of growth, but also for the reawakening of the creative impulse which, too long sorrow-bound, now "longs to burst a frozen bud / And flood a fresher throat with song."

That Tennyson remained distrustful of the promptings of the poetic imagination is evident from the long retrospective eighty-fifth lyric in which he considers whether his pretended communion with Hallam's spirit is not willful self-deception: "so shall grief with symbols play / And pining life be fancy-fed." Yet, there is no disposition to discount the importance of artistic endeavor as a means of assimilating experience:

> Likewise the imaginative woe,
> That loved to handle spiritual strife,
> Diffused the shock thro' all my life,
> But in the present broke the blow.

As if poetry were, indeed, the spontaneous voice of hope reborn, Tennyson is more and more inclined to trust its directive power. Significant in this respect is his changing response to nature. In the first part of *In Memoriam* the phenomenal world had been invoked more often than not to mirror and hence to intensify subjective moods. In the second part the natural order had been questioned in more impersonal terms in a vain attempt to establish some sanction for human values. The eighty-eighth lyric, however, takes the form

of a transcendental paean in praise of the beauty and vitality inher-
ent in nature:

> And I—my harp would prelude woe—
> I cannot all command the strings;
> The glory of the sum of things
> Will flash along the chords and go.

The series of poems beginning with ninety is climaxed by the
mystical revelation of the ninety-fifth, in which Tennyson fleetingly
achieves union in the spirit with Hallam. Although his friend's own
search for faith is ostensibly the subject of the following lyric, the
moral that "There lives more faith in honest doubt, / Believe me,
than in half the creeds" is unmistakably derived from the writer's
own experience. And by the same token, it is his own poetic prog-
ress that Tennyson has in mind when he equates the struggle for
intellectual certitude with artistic growth:

> one indeed I knew
> In many a subtle question versed,
> Who touch'd a jarring lyre at first,
> But ever strove to make it true:
>
> Perplext in faith, but pure in deeds,
> At last he beat his music out.

The departure from Somersby, now first announced, is symbolic
in more senses than one; and the allegorical one hundred and third
poem fittingly brings the third part of *In Memoriam* to a conclu-
sion with Tennyson's resolve to rededicate his poetry to more ambi-
tious goals. The interpretation of this lyric offers no special difficul-
ties, but its theme becomes more meaningful if viewed in relation
to the stages through which the poet had passed in attaining the
conception of his role here set forth. The opening four stanzas
rehearse the elements of the first part of the elegy when Tennyson
had devoted his art ritualistically to the private image of Hallam
enshrined in his heart. The summons from the sea, here as in
"Ulysses" and elsewhere a metaphor for the life of active commit-
ment in pursuit of transmundane goals, suggests through the device
of the river journey the severe struggle with doubt in the second
part of the poem, a struggle now looked back on as integral to the
attainment of artistic as well as spiritual maturity. The quest is con-
summated in the final stanzas where the poet is reunited with
Hallam—but a Hallam transubstantiated into the type of ideal
humanity to the service of which the writer will henceforth exert his
talents.

The third Christmas, observed in a new abode, ushers in the
great New Year's hymn (106) with its exultant proclamation of
progress toward the earthly paradise. His vision cleared and his pur-

pose steadied by the perception of a goal which will enlist the altruistic devotion enjoined on him by Hallam's example, Tennyson is now ready to don the bardic mantle: "Ring out, ring out my mournful rhymes, / But ring the fuller minstrel in." No longer will he embrace isolation out of a refusal to connect the life of the imagination with the general life:

> I will not shut me from my kind,
> And, lest I stiffen into stone,
> I will not eat my heart alone,
> Nor feed with sighs a passing wind . . .   (108)

No longer will he make the mistake of seeking the meaning of his experience in the cloudlands of subjective consciousness amidst the delusions of "vacant yearning": "What find I in the highest place, / But mine own phantom chanting hymns?" For in the wisdom sprung from associating his loss with the common lot, he can now perceive that all along "a *human* face" had shone on him from the "depths of death" within a landscape of sorrow overarched by "*human* skies" (italics added).

As the group of lyrics extending from one hundred and twenty to one hundred and twenty-five makes clear, the assumption of the Carlylean role of poetic sage paradoxically provided Tennyson with an argument in final vindication of the subjective mode of his elegy. Like the confessional writings of his great contemporaries, Carlyle's *Sartor Resartus*, Mill's *Autobiography*, and Newman's *Apologia*, the message of *In Memoriam* was addressed to the age; but the persuasiveness of the message in each of these works resided precisely in the essentially private nature of the experiential evidence which backed it up. The Victorian autobiographers thought of themselves as representative figures within the context of their times; and however intimate the circumstances from their lives selected for narration, they admitted nothing in which the particular could not be subsumed under the guise of the typical. Thus, when Tennyson declares, "I trust I have not wasted breath" (120), it is in the hope that the record of his own victory over doubt will guide others, similarly beset, along the road to faith.

The mood of affirmation which characterizes the concluding poems of *In Memoriam* is expressive not only of the poet's acceptance of love as the pervasive cosmological principle, but also of renewed delight in creative activity as an aspect of this faith. The boon conferred by willed belief has been

> To feel once more, in placid awe,
> The strong imagination roll
> A sphere of stars about my soul,
> In all her motion one with law.   (122)

And so Tennyson can invoke Hallam's genius to sustain poetic

utterance which, no longer shadowed by grief, will joyfully sing
once more its author's responsiveness to the beauty of the world:

> be with me now,
> And enter in at breast and brow,
> Till all my blood, a fuller wave,
>
> Be quicken'd with a livelier breath,
> And like an inconsiderate boy,
> As in the former flash of joy,
> I slip the thoughts of life and death;
>
> And all the breeze of Fancy blows,
> And every dew-drop paints a bow,
> The wizard lightnings deeply glow,
> And every thought breaks out a rose.

In the end, then, Tennyson turns back to the life of the imagina-
tion, rediscovering in its resources confirmation of the intuitions
which formed the basis of his religious faith: "But in my spirit will
I dwell, / And dream my dream, and hold it true" (123).[3] The
one hundred and twenty-fifth lyric develops in more straightforward
terms the quest motif embodied in the allegory of the one hundred
and third. In casting a backward glance over the stages of his spirit-
ual pilgrimage, the poet explicitly identifies with each a distinguish-
ing aesthetic manifestation:

> Whatever I have said or sung,
> Some bitter notes my harp would give,
> Yea, tho' there often seem'd to live
> A contradiction on the tongue,
>
> Yet Hope had never lost her youth,
> She did but look through dimmer eyes;
> Or Love but play'd with gracious lies,
> Because he felt so fix'd in truth;
>
> And if the song were full of care,
> He breathed the spirit of the song;
> And if the words were sweet and strong
> He set his royal signet there;
>
> Abiding with me till I sail
> To seek thee on the mystic deeps,
> And this electric force, that keeps
> A thousand pulses dancing, fail.

3. The one hundred and twenty-ninth lyric defines the substance of this dream, love being conceived as the harmonizing force which unites the poet's adulation of all that Hallam had stood for with his concern for human welfare in general: "Behold, I dream a dream of good, / And mingle all the world with thee."

And when, three poems later, he seeks a figure to encompass the organic totality of his experience, it is the process of artistic creation that comes to mind:

> I see in part
> That all, as in some piece of art,
> Is toil coöperant to an end.

Tennyson's emergence from his long night of sorrow over Hallam's death into the light of living faith is dramatized through the bold device of appending an epithalamion as epilogue to the elegy. He here takes final leave of the threnodic vein in which his suffering had found voice, "No longer coming to embalm / In dying songs a dead regret." The poetry born of subjective striving with private emotion no longer suffices the artist to whom the passing years have brought knowledge of the transcendant power of love:

> For I myself with these have grown
> To something greater than before;

> Which makes appear the songs I made
> As echoes out of weaker times,
> As half but idle brawling rhymes,
> The sport of random sun and shade.

The Prologue to *In Memoriam*, dated 1849, seven years later than the Epilogue, was clearly conceived as a set-piece to introduce the elegy; and this fact explains the deprecatory tone of its final stanza. The rather formal and perfunctory ring of these lines simply re-emphasizes the poet's intention, foreshadowed in the Epilogue, to devote himself henceforth to more public themes:

> Forgive these wild and wandering cries,
> Confusions of a wasted youth;
> Forgive them where they fail in truth,
> And in thy wisdom make me wise.

In the opening lyric of *In Memoriam* Tennyson had adumbrated the view of evolutionary progress which controls his method in the elegy and furnishes the key to the poem's structure: "men may rise on stepping-stones / Of their dead selves to higher things." These "stepping-stones," as psychologically distinguished by the author, ascend through three orders of consciousness: the emotional, identified with man's sensory being; the intellectual, identified with the human mind; and the intuitive, identified with the realm of spirit. Following Bradley's quadripartite arrangement, the consecutive stages of growth recorded in the poem may be roughly diagrammed as follows:

Part One: Despair (ungoverned sense)
Part Two: Doubt (mind governing sense, i.e. despair)
Part Three: Hope (spirit governing mind, i.e. doubt)
Part Four: Faith (spirit harmonizing sense and mind)

If now a corresponding diagram is constructed to illustrate the stages of aesthetic growth in the elegy, it will appear that the demands which Tennyson made on his art in each of the four parts were directly responsive to the psychological needs of the phase through which he was passing:

Part one: Poetry as release from emotion
Part Two: Poetry as escape from thought
Part Three: Poetry as self-realization
Part Four: Poetry as mission

In Memoriam, as a poem of spiritual quest, represents the Way of the Soul. It is not less surely a poem of aesthetic quest, which sets forth the Way of the Poet. Tennyson came to the writing of his elegy fresh from such compositions as "The Lady of Shalott," "Oenone," "The Palace of Art," and "The Lotos-Eaters." With its publication he was to attain the laureateship and to go on to the planning of *Maud* and the early *Idylls of the King*. Bridging, as it does, the earlier and later work, *In Memoriam* is quite as much testament to artistic as to philosophic growth.

JEROME BUCKLEY

In Memoriam: "The Way of the Soul," 1833–1850†

Diary-like, the virtually formless structure of *In Memoriam* gives it one particular advantage over other major elegies; the poet may explore at leisure the idea of death and all the contradictory emotions it engenders in him; he may contemplate his grief in time and make due allowance for his slow psychological recovery.

Since the way of the soul is neither direct nor entirely consistent but beset by waverings and alternatives, the unity of the poem as a whole derives less from its large loose argument than from the intensity and often the confusion of its single subject. Stylistic rather than architectonic, it depends above all on the recurrence of an imagery to which Tennyson's sensibility both consciously and unconsciously attaches particular meaning. Though admirable in itself, the "Dark house" lyric gains added strength from its context

† From *Tennyson: The The Growth of a Poet* (Cambridge, Harvard University   Press, 1960), 112–27.

in the sequence, for it brings together four basic images which have
already acquired a certain resonance: the dark (or night), the day
(or light), the rain (or water), and the hand. Throughout the
poem "dark" appears as the most frequent connotative epithet; and
the light-dark antithesis again and again provides a ready though
still compelling tension of opposites—which are the correlatives of
life and death, assent and denial—until at last, as in the climactic
ninety-fifth lyric, the polarities may be reconciled in a mystic half-
light, where

> . . . East and West, without a breath,
> Mixt their dim lights, like life and death,
> To broaden into boundless day.

Water—in the neo-Platonic tradition a common image of the
one and the many—is Tennyson's perpetual and ambiguous symbol
of changeless change. As ocean, sea, "dead lake," "Godless deep,"
"Lethean springs," river, brook, wave, flood, "greening gleam,"
cloud, frost, "spires of ice," possessive snow, killing or revitalizing
rain,[1] water is everywhere the token both of man's mutability and
of the infinite amorphous oneness of nature which mocks the tran-
sient human being. Eventually it is the water of life that must "rise
in the spiritual rock" bringing regeneration; but in much of the
poem it is the ominous "stillness of the central sea" or the tide that
wears away "the solid lands," and it holds for the individual the
terror of death by drowning and the menace of a "vast and wander-
ing grave." Thus the poet is fearful at the outset that the ship bear-
ing the dead man for burial in consecrated earth may founder and
the body be lost where

> . . . the roaring wells
> Should gulf him fathom-deep in brine,
> And hands so often clasp'd in mine,
> Should toss with tangle and with shells.

Here, as in "Dark house," the water is associated with the forces of
death and destruction, and the hands are a synecdoche for the
whole vanished life, for the physicality that once contained the
living object.

The image of the hand, found also in "Break, Break, Break," is
charged with unusual significance throughout *In Memoriam*.[2]
Having grasped the hand of the living Hallam, the poet now knows

1. In the imagery and descriptive pas-
sages of *In Memoriam* there are about
fifty distinct references to water in its
various forms. I here consider all as
"images" insofar as they illustrate the
developing emotion of the poem.
2. Some reference to the hand (or palm

or finger) or the act of touching will be
found in thirty of the lyrics that make
up the sequence. Cf. Professor C. R.
Sanders' comments on the image, "Ten-
nyson and the Human Hand," *Victorian
Newsletter*, No. 11 (1957), 5–14.

himself to have touched death, and in his own deathful bereavement he remains eager that the same hand should recall him to life. If Hallam could come back, he would, in proof of his essential vitality, "strike a sudden hand in mine." Since he cannot return in the flesh, his example may yet "Reach out dead hands to comfort me." At the climax of the poem, where the "I" briefly transcends time, Hallam reappears in an eternal present, and then "The dead man touch'd me from the past." Finally revisiting the dark house no longer dark, the poet can imagine the familiar gesture of friendship and sympathy:

> And in my thoughts with scarce a sigh
> I take the pressure of thine hand.

Elsewhere the hand is the symbol of aspiration—"I reach lame hands of faith"—or of agency—"the dark hand [death] struck down thro' time," or "Out of darkness came the hands / That reach thro' nature, moulding men," or again, in an image reversing Michelangelo's view of the Creation, "God's finger touch'd him, and he slept." Touch is the first and most basic sensation and soon the means by which the infant discovers his own identity:

> The baby new to earth and sky,
>   What time his tender palm is prest
>   Against the circle of the breast,
> Has never thought that "this is I:"
>
> But as he grows he gathers much,
>   And learns the use of "I," and "me,"
>   And finds "I am not what I see,
> And other than the things I touch."

The hand accordingly comes to represent the material body that defines and isolates the individual and pulses with the only sort of life he can immediately understand.

* * *

In Memoriam itself, as a finished "piece of art," is designed so that its many parts may subserve a single meaningful "end," a distinct if rather diffuse pattern of movement from death to life, from dark to light. The prologue, written last, when Tennyson had determined a suitable arrangement, suggests the course of the central argument and at the same time attempts to anticipate possible objection to what may seem "wild"—that is, morally and poetically undisciplined—in the separate lyrics. The three Christmas poems (sections **XXX**, **LXXVIII**, and **CV**) somewhat mechanically mark the passage of the years, and the parallel lines indicate by a shift of adverb the stages of the changing emotion:

And sadly fell our Christmas-eve. . . .
And calmly fell our Christmas-eve. . . .
And strangely falls our Christmas-eve. . . .

Numerous phrases from the earlier sections, carefully repeated in a new setting toward the conclusion, are likewise expected to rein-force the impression of unity.[3] And the epithalamium, which some critics have thought a most inappropriate epilogue, is consciously intended to dramatize in a joyful ritual the poet's final assent to life's purposes. Whatever the disorder of its original composition, *In Memoriam* is thus meant to escape the error of wildness, delirium, and mere subjective rhapsody; it is even, according to Tennyson's own rather ponderous description of its total design, to be read as "a kind of *Divina Commedia*, ending with happiness."[4]

But the happy ending is not, as in Dante, foreseen with certainty. The intellectual commitment of the early lyrics is to science rather than to theology. The poet assumes, perhaps too readily, that all real knowledge is scientific or at least empirical;[5] of the "larger hope" which seems essential to his will to live, he is quite persuaded that he "cannot know," since "knowledge is of things we see." He is driven, therefore, to ask whether the unseen God, to whom he lifts his lame hands of faith, can coexist with an amoral nature, the "scientific" view of which he endorses as proven and obviously accurate:

> Are God and Nature then at strife,
>   That Nature lends such evil dreams?
>   So careful of the type she seems,
> So careless of the single life?

The question, which could not have arisen in quite the same terms before Tennyson's time, foreshadows the precise problem that was to confront John Stuart Mill in "Nature," the first of his *Three Essays on Religion.* But Tennyson saw more clearly than Mill the ineffectuality of any attempt at a logical answer. The question merely prompts a more fearful one; if the testimony of "scarped cliff and quarried stone" proves Nature careless even of the type (she cries, "I care for nothing, all shall go"), must man, too, with all his bright illusions and high idealisms, perish as no more than another trial and error of the evolutionary process?

* * *

3. Cf. lines and phrases in sections VII and CXIX; LIV (stanza 5) and CXXIV (stanza 5); the "violet" of XVIII and CXV; references to the trance of XCV in CXXII and CXXIV (stanza 6). The deepest unity, of course, lies—as we have seen—in the more spontaneous re-currence of the images.

4. *Memoir,* I, 304.
5. Like Huxley and most of the Vic-torian scientists, Tennyson thinks of sci-ence as entirely inductive and empirical; he has no inkling of the extent to which later science will be deductive and con-ceptual.

It is irrelevant to object that *In Memoriam*, published nine years before *The Origin of Species* and more than twenty before *The Descent of Man*, is not proto-Darwinian insofar as it does not present the doctrine of natural selection and transmutation. For the elegist is concerned with the purpose and quality of human life rather than the means by which mankind reached its present state. His great question arises out of the precise intellectual atmosphere in which the Darwinian hypothesis was to be born, and it anticipates the serious debate that Darwinism in particular and Victorian science in general would provoke. Man, "who *seemed* so fair" under the older idealistic dispensation, now seems debased by a monistic naturalism which denies the soul and insists, with a dogged literalness, that "The spirit does but mean the breath." The fundamental conflict of the poem thus turns on an epistemological problem: the extent to which the old appearance did correspond with the reality, or to which the new "knowledge" (or "science") does give an adequate account of the human condition. The poet professes a deep devotion to knowledge and looks forward to its wide extension:

> Who Loves not Knowledge? Who shall rail
> Against her beauty? May she mix
> With men and prosper! Who shall fix
> Her pillars? Let her work prevail.

But he demands that knowledge "know her place," submit to the guidance of wisdom, learn that "reverence" must interpret and supplement the known and the knowable:

> Let knowledge grow from more to more,
> But more of reverence in us dwell;
> That mind and soul according well,
> May make one music as before.

When it lacks due reverence for the claims of the soul, knowledge forfeits its right to command the allegiance or respect of mankind; having regained his assent, the poet rather truculently declares suicide preferable to life in a world of "magnetic mockeries":

> Let Science prove we are, and then
> What matters Science unto men,
> At least to me? I would not stay.

He does not, of course, at the last believe knowledge capable of such proof; for he has once again warmed to the same "heat of inward evidence" that conquered the cold reason in "The Two Voices"; he has found life's necessary sanction quite beyond the things we see, altogether beyond knowing.

Concern with the mode of perception and the reality of the perceiving self turns the essential "action" of *In Memoriam* toward the inner experience. As in Tennyson's earliest verse, the dream and the

vision are called upon to explore and at last to validate the wavering
personality. In the night of despair, "Nature lends such evil
dreams" to the frail ego; and in hours of hope "So runs my dream,
but what am I?" Dreaming, the poet wanders across a wasteland
and through a dark city, where all men scoff at his sorrow, until "an
angel of the night" reaches out a reassuring hand. Half-waking, he
tries to recall the features of the dead Hallam, but these "mix with
hollow masks of night" and the nightmare images of Dante's hell:

> Cloud-towers by ghostly masons wrought,
> A gulf that ever shuts and gapes,
> A hand that points, and palled shapes
> In shadowy thoroughfares of thought;
>
> And crowds that stream from yawning doors,
> And shoals of pucker'd faces drive;
> Dark bulks that tumble half alive,
> And lazy lengths on boundless shores.

Only when "the nerve of sense is numb" and the self yields to the
calm of the hushed summer night does the moment of full appre-
hension come, the "epiphany" that reveals the continuous life for
which his whole heart hungers; as he reads Hallam's letters, the past
suddenly asserts its persistence and its infinite extension:

> And strangely on the silence broke
> The silent-speaking words, and strange
> Was love's dumb cry defying change
> To test his worth; and strangely spoke
>
> The faith, the vigour, bold to dwell
> On doubts that drive the coward back,
> And keen thro' wordy snares to track
> Suggestion to her inmost cell.
>
> So word by word, and line by line,
> The dead man touch'd me from the past,
> And all at once it seem'd at last
> His living soul was flash'd on mine,
>
> And mine in his was wound, and whirl'd
> About empyreal heights of thought,
> And came on that which is, and caught
> The deep pulsations of the world,
>
> Aeonian music measuring out
> The steps of Time—the shocks of Chance—
> The blows of Death. . . .[6]

6. Editions after 1880 were revised so that "His living soul" read "The living soul," and "mine in his" became "mine in this." The change was apparently in- tended to facilitate the transition from the awareness of the individual dead man to the perception of the One, the ultimate reality.

Eventually the trance is "stricken thro' with doubt"; the appearances of the world in all its "doubtful dusk" obscure the vision, and the poet returns to awareness of simple physical sensation. Yet he brings with him renewed purpose and composure; his experience has given him the certitude that "science" could not establish and therefore cannot destroy.

Though unable to sustain his vision, the "I" of the poem finds in his mystical insight the surest warrant for spiritual recovery. Tennyson, as we have seen, had been familiar with such "spots of time" from his childhood, and there was, of course, ample literary precedent for his use of "mystical" materials. In the Confessions of St. Augustine—to cite but one striking example—he might have found a remarkably similar passage recounting the ascent of the mind by degrees from the physical and transitory to the unchangeable until "with the flash of a trembling glance, it arrived at *that which is.*"[7] Yet he was perplexed as always by the difficulty of communicating what was essentially private and, in sensuous terms, incommunicable. The poet accordingly, having described his trance, at once recognizes an inadequacy in the description:

> Vague words! but ah, how hard to frame
> In matter-moulded forms of speech,
> Or ev'n for intellect to reach
> Thro' memory that which I became.

The mystical vision is assuredly the sanction of his faith, but he does not choose to seek fulfillment in a sustained and conscious pursuit of the mystic's isolation. Having found faith, he must assume his place in society and "rake what fruit may be / Of sorrow under human skies." And as poet, aware of his mission, he must work in his fallible yet inexhaustible medium, the "matter-moulded forms of speech."

But whether or not it defies translation into poetic language, the trance has for the poet a profound religious implication. Lifted through and beyond self-consciousness, his individual spirit attains a brief communion with universal Spirit; "what I am" for the moment beholds "What is." Yet Tennyson at no time insists that his private vision is representative or even that some way of "mysticism" is open to all others. He assumes only that each man will feel the necessity of believing where he cannot prove; and only insofar as he makes this assumption does he think of his voice in the poem

7. Confessions, Book VII, chap. xvii. sec. 23, *Confessions and Enchiridion,* trans. and ed. Albert C. Outler (Philadelphia, 1955), p. 151. Tennyson's trance is compared to St. Augustine's vision by Percy H. Osmond, *The Mystical Poets of the English Church* (London, 1919), pp. 309–310. The passage in the Confessions continues: "But I was not able to sustain my gaze. My weakness was dashed back, and I lapsed again into my accustomed ways." The ecstatic experience, in other words, took place some time before Augustine's conversion and had no direct relation to his decision to become a Christian.

as "the voice of the human race speaking through him." For his own part, he rejects the standard "proofs" of God's existence, especially Paley's argument from design, which the Cambridge Apostles had attacked and which a later evolutionary science seemed further to discredit:

> That which we dare invoke to bless;
> Our dearest faith; our ghastliest doubt;
> He, They, One, All; within, without;
> The Power in darkness whom we guess;
>
> I found him not in world or sun,
> Or eagle's wing, or insect's eye;
> Nor thro' the questions men may try,
> The petty cobwebs we have spun.

By intuition alone, the cry of his believing heart, can he answer the negations of an apparently "Godless" nature. His faith, which thus rests on the premise of feeling, resembles that of Pascal, who likewise trusted the reasons of the heart which reason could not know. Its source, like the ground of Newmans' assent, is psychological rather than logical, the will of the whole man rather a postulate of the rational faculty. And in its development, it is frequently not far removed from Kierkegaardian "existentialism," which similarly balances the demands of the inner life against the claims of nineteenth-century "knowledge."

In his *Concluding Unscientific Postscript*, which may serve as an unexpected yet oddly apposite gloss on the faith of *In Memoriam*, Kierkegaard describes his own inability to find God in the design of the objective world:

> I contemplate the order of nature in the hope of finding God, and I see omnipotence and wisdom; but I also see much else that disturbs my mind and excites anxiety. The sum of all this is an objective uncertainty. But it is for this very reason that the inwardness becomes as intense as it is, for it embraces this objective uncertainty with the entire passion of the infinite.

And to Kierkegaard *"an objective uncertainty held fast in an appropriation-process of the most passionate inwardness is the truth,* the highest truth attainable for an *existing* individual."[8] Such truth is apparently close to the faith that lives in "honest doubt," doubt that the physical order can in itself provide spiritual certainty. In a prose paraphrase of his poetic statement, Tennyson affirms the position even more emphatically than the philosopher:

8. Søren Kierkegaard, *Concluding Unscientific Postscript*, trans. David F. Swenson and Walter Lowrie (Princeton, 1944), p. 182; these passages are reprinted with an excellent brief introduction by Henry D. Aiken, *The Ages of Ideology* (New York, 1956), p. 239. I have quoted them from the 1944 edition with the kind permission of Princeton University Press.

God *is* love, transcendent, all-pervading! We do not get *this* faith from nature or the world. If we look at Nature alone, full of perfection and imperfection, she tells us that God is disease, murder and rapine. We get this faith from ourselves, from what is highest within us. . . .[9]

Believing that all "retreat to eternity *via* recollection is barred by the fact of sin,"[1] Kierkegaard questions the possibility of a complete mystical communion. Yet his faith requires "the moment of passion" comparable to the trance experience of *In Memoriam*, for "it is only momentarily that the particular individual is able to realize existentially a unity of the infinite and the finite which transcends existence."[2] Through passionate feeling, he maintains, and not by logical processes, the individual man may unify his life and achieve the dignity of selfhood. True self-awareness, as *The Sickness unto Death* tells us,[3] is born, paradoxically, of man's despair, the possibility of which is his "advantage over the beast," since in the deepest despair the soul faces its fear of imminent annihilation, "struggles with death" but comes to know the agonizing life-in-death, the torment of "not to be able to die" as prelude to acceptance of its indestructible obligation. Having also "fought with Death" and reached the level of total or metaphysical anxiety, the poet likewise finds his acute self-consciousness an essential element in his final self-realization. Such similarities are inevitable; for Tennyson, though he differs sharply from the philosopher in his estimate of the aesthetic and moral components of life, is ultimately, according to Kierkegaard's definition, "the subjective thinker": he is one who "seeks to understand the abstract determination of being human in terms of this particular existing human being."[4]

Fortified by his personal intuition, the elegist may at last give his sorrow positive resolution. He may assimilate the apparent confusions of history; he may trust that, though all political institutions are shaken in "the night of fear" and "the great Aeon sinks in blood," "social truth" nonetheless shall not be utterly destroyed; for

> The love that rose on stronger wings,
> Unpalsied when he met with Death,
> Is comrade of the lesser faith
> That sees the course of human things.

Subjectively reappraised, natural evolution itself may now be seen as the dimly understood analogue of a possible spiritual progress; and

9. *Memoir*, I, 314.
1. Kierkegaard, paraphrased by Howard Albert Johnson, "The Deity in Time," pamphlet published by the College of Preachers, Washington Cathedral, Washington, D.C., reprinted from *Theology Today*, January 1945. Cf. Tennyson's comment on the mists of sin and the far planet, quoted above, Chapter IV.
2. *Concluding Unscientific Postscript*, p. 176.
3. See *The Sickness unto Death*, trans. Walter Lowrie (New York, 1954), pp. 148–154.
4. *Concluding Unscientific Postscript*, p. 315.

God, whom faith has apprehended, may be construed as the origin and the end of all change, the "one far-off divine event, / To which the whole creation moves." Though the prologue addresses the Son of God as the principle of immortal Love, and thus as the warranty of the worth of human love, *In Memoriam* is seldom specifically Christian. Tennyson goes behind the dogmas of his own broad Anglicanism to discover the availability of any religious faith at all and finally to establish subjective experience as sufficient ground for a full assent to the reality of God and the value of the human enterprise. His poem accordingly is not a defense of any formal creed but an apology for a general "Faith beyond the forms of Faith." And as such it is at once universal in its implication and directly relevant to a Victorian England which was finding all dogmatic positions increasingly vulnerable.

CLYDE de L. RYALS

[Theme and Symbol in *In Memoriam*]†

***

It is because "In Memoriam" is such an all-encompassing work that it is so difficult to discuss in purely critical terms. One may object that the affirmation of Part IV is too easily achieved and, further, that it affirms too much. For in "In Memoriam" Tennyson seeks not only to assuage but also to remove the fear that is part of life. He did not share Wordsworth's realization that there must always be terror and fear, and he did not seek like Baudelaire to make a virtue of this realization. Tennyson's *paradis artificiel* is simply a realm beyond reality, which has none of the terrifying beauty of existence. It is, some critics feel, in this sense that "In Memoriam" is a poem of escape, a somewhat half-hearted answer to the problems proposed. Undoubtedly this is what T.S. Eliot means when he says that "In Memoriam" "is not religious because of the quality of its faith, but because of the quality of its doubt. Its faith is a poor thing, but its doubt is a very intense experience."

As far as its faith is concerned, "In Memoriam" is, I find, somewhat similar to Rossetti's "The Blessed Damozel." Ostensibly the elegy is concerned with a quest after belief in immortality. Yet at best the desire for everlasting life is subsumed by the poet's hope for a renewal of friendship with his dead friend. Tennyson may speak of Hallam as the ideal type of humanity, but still the Hallam

† From *Theme and Symbol in Tennyson's Poems to 1850* (Philadelphia: University of Pennsylvania Press, 1964), pp. 254–66. The author's footnotes have been omitted.

whom he wishes to find again is the Hallam as he knew him on earth. The Blessed Damozel wishes for this same continuance in heaven of her earthly love. To quote Eliot again, Tennyson's "desire for immortality never is quite the desire for Eternal Life: his concern is for the loss of man rather than for the gain of God."

Yet Tennyson works very hard at making his quest the search for the Incarnate God; he does this, as I have already suggested, by making Hallam a Christ-figure. In the New Year's hymn Hallam is, by implication at least, the prototype of the "larger heart, the kindlier hand," "the Christ that is to be" (CVI). Since the poem is a hymn in praise of a kind of Second Coming, the ringing of the bells which "ring out the old, ring in the new" reminds us of the New Covenant brought by Christ to supersede the Old Covenant made through Moses. This exultant proclamation of progress toward the earthly paradise results in the following lyrics of "In Memoriam" in a nearly complete fusion of Hallam with Christ, the new Hallam-Christ serving as the example which aspiring man is to follow and as the symbol by which and through which the poet asserts his confident faith.

The third group of Christmas poems brings us in our consideration of Hallam as Christ-figure to a speculation concerning the poet's insertion of these poems to indicate passage of time. One is tempted to associate this device with Tennyson's estimation of the superhuman qualities of Hallam. The traditional merriment of Christmas contrasts strongly with the grief that the Tennyson family experienced; but Tennyson's choice of this particular day of merriment to mark off prominently the divisions of the elegy seems to indicate something deeper than the contrast between extreme joy and sorrow. This supposition is further underlined by the fact that following the third Christmas poems comes a lyric (CVII), which celebrates the anniversary of the birth of Hallam, the first time that such has occurred in the elegy; and significantly it follows immediately upon the poet's representation of Hallam as Christ-figure.

If we examine the two celebrations, we shall see that there are distinct similarities between the two. Like Christmas, the anniversary occurs in the dead of winter, and this particular day, though cold, leaves "night forlorn." On Hallam's birthday, as in the second Christmas group, there is a burning log, there is wine drunk in remembrance, and there are songs—all of which, as at Christmastime, remind the family of the dead man. There is, however, a difference in the celebration of the third Christmas. Because the family has moved from the rectory at Somersby to High Beech and is thus in a strange place, Tennyson states that the old customs should not be observed, and consequently there is no burning log or drink or song. Yet, still in "the stranger's land" (CIV), they observe on Hallam's birthday the same customs as in the second Christmas poems, as though the anniversary of Hallam's birth has become more meaningful than Christ's, indeed has supplanted it.

It is not, however, *only* because the family has moved to a new home that the old Christmas customs are no longer observed. When the speaker asks, "For who would keep an ancient form / Thro' which the spirit breathes no more?" (CV), the query does not refer only to the removal from Somersby. The "ancient form" is almost certainly the observance of the Nativity, which is rejected in favor of a new nativity, Hallam's, in Section CVII. But the poet is careful to keep the implications muffled. And he ends the lyric with a passage suggesting that it is the spirit instead of the form which retains its vitality.

In Part IV we find again a number of retrospective lyrics, nearly all elucidating further Hallam's Christlike qualities. In CX we are told how Hallam, like Christ, delighted both young and old, how he caused the weak to forget their weakness, how near him the storm became mild, how he truly possessed "the Christian art," how the serpent (of Eden?) in his presence is made impotent. Even the imagery of Part IV suggests the likeness of Hallam to Christ, as in CXII where the images of tempest and calm recall Christ's calming the sea.

Section CXXVI affirms the reality of love and makes the identification of love with Christ almost explicit. But there is this ambiguity: Tennyson accepted the teaching of the Gospels that "God is Love," but he also made love, not faith, the means by which a knowledge of God is to be attained. God, then, is both Love as absolute and as means of reaching the absolute. Such a conclusion seems to have been entirely necessary for Tennyson's religious faith. Faced with the problem of the nineteenth-century Christian intellectual of preserving Christ as an emotionally significant image without going so far as to accept Santayana's later solution, Tennyson vaguely realized that his problem *vis-à-vis* the dead Hallam was essentially the same as the Christian's with regard to Christ. And realizing this, he sought in writing "In Memoriam" to identify his quest for the recapture of the spirit of a man with his desire for religious faith. Although he knew that he could not recapture the Spirit—that is, Christ as God—he felt that somehow he must receive Christ, an act of faith which could be effected by recreating Him as a person who was identifiable with His example. The poem, therefore, came to be not an elegy lamenting the death of a friend, but a religious quest concerned with the preservation of Hallam's personality through the preservation of the poet's personality. Thus Tennyson's faith in Christianity came through love—love of Hallam whom he made his Christ.

Tennyson explains his spiritual "way" perhaps best in lyric CXXIV. His faith in the "He, They, One, All; within, without; / The Power in darkness whom we guess" has come not through ratiocination ("I found Him not in world or sun"), but through the heart: "I have felt." The process can be explained as something like this: God is love; Christ is the embodiment of God's love for mankind; Hallam is identifiable with Christ and thus is himself an embodiment of ideal love which is immortal; I love Hallam; therefore I believe in Christ and in immortality. Having reached such a conclusion, Tennyson in the final lyrics goes still further in mingling the images of Christ and Hallam. In Poem CXXIX, for example, Hallam is addressed as "Known and unknown, human, divine," and as the "Dear heavenly friend that canst not die." In CXXX there is almost a note of jealousy when the poet, realizing that Hallam has become universal love and not merely personal love, says that the beloved friend is now a "diffusive power," but quickly adds, "I do not therefore love thee less." Hallam now belongs to every thing and to all; he is everywhere—in air, water, sun, star, and flower. And because the poet now is fully cognizant of his friend's union with the divine, he loses forever the sorrow born of grief and doubt. In its entirety Poem CXXX expresses Tennyson's completely unfolded love, which embraces more than the man he knew; his love now comprehends the man divine, the transcendental power, the God which gives him faith in both life and death.

* * *

One cannot leave "In Memoriam" without the impression that the elegy is really not a search for God. It is, the reader feels, one man's determination to hold on to God, a determination not to let Him go. The apotheosis of Hallam in the poem stems from the poet's desire to prove that God is, that Christianity, in spite of certain doubts which it must inevitably present to the mind of the thinking man, is the best faith to hold onto. "In Memoriam" is, thus, a refusal to say farewell to what one knows he has lost.

Tennyson enforces this impression in the last section. He invokes the "living will," which he explained as free-will (*Memoir*, I, 319), to rise in the "spiritual rock" and strengthen him in his faith. This is the will to believe in spite of all "proof" to the contrary, the will that brings the "faith that comes of self-control." As he explains in the Prologue, "Our wills are ours, we know not how; / Our wills are ours, to make them thine."

For Tennyson, God is absolutely necessary for man. If He does not exist, then man must create Him. Tennyson is what Professor Fairchild calls "an emotional pragmatist," and C. F. G. Masterman is quite right when he says that Tennyson posited God as "necessary for the satisfaction of the demands of the human race." Thus the poet in the Prologue affirms his faith in the "Strong Son of God" so that "Thou wilt not leave us in the dust." As he told his son, "I am ready to fight for *mein liebes Ich*, and hold that it will last for aeons of aeons" (*Memoir*, I, 320). This approach could be called a prudential proof of the existence of God for the purpose of being saved from extinction. His "living will" therefore is the resolve to "dream my dream, and hold it true" (CXXIII).

Part IV brings "In Memoriam" near to close with the roundest of declarations affirming the value of the life of the imagination. No longer is he distrustful that "so shall grief with symbols play / And pining life be fancy-fed" (LXXXV); rather, he discovers in the imagination a confirmation of his religious faith. Henceforward he will be a different kind of poet. In the New Year lyric he vows that he will undertake more general themes, will assume the role of bard: "Ring out, ring out my mournful rhymes, / But ring the fuller minstrel in." He will cease to be the "phantom chanting hymns" and will concern himself and his poetry with mankind:

* * *

His creative activity will become an aspect of his faith, and as the fuller minstrel he like the New Year's bell will sing of "the Christ that is to be."

Tennyson said of "In Memoriam": "It begins with a funeral and ends with a marriage—begins with death and ends in promise of new life—a sort of Divine Comedy, cheerful at the close." The value of the Epilogue has been questioned by critics who feel that this purpose was already achieved in Part IV. But I believe that the Conclusion has its purpose in that it serves to tie together the various themes of the elegy.

On the surface the Epilogue is merely another domestic idyll in which a girl marries the man she loves and presumably will live happily ever after. It is not at all strange, I think, that Tennyson, the laureate of domestic life, should begin his poem with his sister Emily's loss of her betrothed and close with his sister Cecilia's marriage to Edmund Lushington, another close friend of the poet; for marriage was very much on the poet's mind, since he was himself to be wedded to Emily Sellwood in the same year that his elegy was published. Furthermore, the frequent allusions to marriage in such metaphors as "widow'd race" constitute a kind of countertheme to the theme of loneliness, and the marriage in the Epilogue seems to serve as a symbol that the old Tennysonian hero, the Byronic outcast, would forever be banished from the poet's verse as a pole of sympathy.

In part the epithalamium is composed in Tennyson's most mannered, picturesque style. A line like "the foaming grape of eastern France" is the kind of elegant locution that the modern reader cannot abide: it sounds just as artificial as Pope's "finny denizens of the deep," it is as though Wordsworth had never lived. But these faults must not be allowed to obfuscate the good things in the poem. The picture of the bride standing on the tombstones, "pensive tablets round her head, / And the most living words of life / Breathed in her ear"—this is a fine symbolic situation. It is the Hesper-Phosphor image carried out of art into actuality; for this is a concrete, human image of Life-in-death, a kind of objective correlative uniting all the themes of the elegy.

Gone is the grief and despair; the world has become alive and shows its beauty everywhere. The bells have no sorrow touched with joy; they tell only "joy to every wandering breeze." Furthermore, "The dead leaf trembles to the bells," for they herald a new life. The flower image is likewise pushed to its utmost value: today's flowers are only seeds of what will be:

> For all we thought and loved and did,
> And hoped, and suffer'd, is but seed
> Of what in them is flower and fruit.

The marriage of the couple is symbolic of a new and better life, for in the child resulting from their union there shall be "a closer link / Betwixt us and the crowning race."

The moral exhortation at the end of CXVIII is here developed into a prophecy of a higher plane of human existence in which the individual intelligence participates as a creative energy:

> A soul shall draw from out the vast
> And strike his being into bounds,
>
> And, moved thro' life of lower phase,
> Result in man, be born and think,
> And act and love, a closer link
> Betwixt us and the crowning race
>
> Of those that, eye to eye, shall look
> On knowledge; under whose command
> Is Earth and Earth's, and in their hand
> Is Nature like an open book;
>
> No longer half-akin to brute. . . .

The prophecy is that through emotional purgation and intellectual aspiration man will be freed from the animal chain to which he is now bound.

The Epilogue makes it clear that there are two kingdoms with which "In Memoriam" is concerned—an Earthly Paradise, which will result from evolutionary development, and a Heavenly Paradise, which is to be attained through Christian faith. And just as clearly the Epilogue shows that it is Hallam, the Christlike superhuman, who serves as an example and a link by which the two kingdoms are to be gained. The poet greets the putative child of his sister Cecilia and Edmund Lushington as a still further link between man at present and the future "crowning race," of whom, it is clearly implied, Hallam was one. Hallam, however, came too early, "Appearing ere the times were ripe." This statement of course suggests Christ's being rejected by those whom He came to help: the world is, the poet says, not ready to receive its saints. But for Tennyson the time for reception of the Christ-figure will come, for eventually the earth shall hold those in whose hand—and here the poet employs one more time the image of the hand—"Is Nature like an open book." And having approached perfection on earth, they shall be part of the Divine, like "That friend of mine who lives in God."

Masterman remarks that Tennyson "looked for the ideal man in man and never found the Christ." The poet's acceptance of Christianity, however, could for him come only through the finding of the ideal in man. Although he had Scriptural authority for his apotheosis of love (First Epistle of St. John, IV: 7, 16), he was, ironically, led most probably to his religious point of view by Hallam himself. In the " Theodicaea Novissima," an essay read to the Apostles at Cambridge, Hallam, basing his argument on the Biblical statement "God is Love," wrote that that which prompted God to temporal creation was love of Christ. Christ is the Son of God, but "the Godhead of the Son has not been a fixed, invariable thing from the beginning: he is more God now than he was once; and will be perfectly united to God hereafter, when he has put all enemies under his feet." Hallam thus allows for the evolutionary growth of "Godliness" in Christ; and since this is true, it is likewise possible that man through love of Christ may progress toward divinity; for "love of the Eternal Being will require similarity in the object that excites it." To know God, then, one must experience love, and this love of man, God's image, can lead to love and knowledge of God:

> But God, we have seen is love; love for all spirits in His image, but above all, far above all, for His son. In order to love God perfectly we must love what He loves; but Christ is the grand object of His love; therefore we must love Christ before we can attain that love of the Father, which alone is life everlasting. Before the Gospel was preached to man, how could a human soul have this love, and this consequent life? I see no way; but now that Christ has excited our love for him by shewing unutterable love for us; now that we know him as an Elder Brother, a being of like

thoughts, feelings, sensations, sufferings with ourselves, it has become possible to love as God loves, that is, to love the express image of God's person: in loving him we are sure we are in a state of readiness to love the Father, whom we see, he tells us, when we see him. Nor is this all: the tendency of love is towards a union so intimate, as virtually to amount to identification; when then by affection towards Christ we have become blended with his being, the beams of Eternal Love falling, as ever, on the one beloved object will include us in him, and their returning flashes of love out of his personality will carry along with them some from our own, since ours has become confused with his, and so shall we be one with Christ and through Christ with God.

There is, of course, an important difference between the love that proceeds from God to man and the love between men or from man toward God. On this point Hallam, in the foregoing quotation, is relatively clear; Tennyson is not. For Hallam, Christ is the expression of God's love toward man; man's love toward God through Christ is the response to that love. Hallam is, I believe, still orthodox enough to mean Christ objectively. Tennyson, on the other hand, means "Christ" subjectively—as a term for the love between human beings, which in its "highest" manifestation is "divine," that is, of transcendent but perhaps not of transcendental value.

The knowledge of God through love of the ideal in man is a sentiment which Tennyson was to repeat time and again. "I believe in God, not from what I see in Nature, but from what I see in man," he once said. And it is the idea of love of God through love of man that informs the religious ideal of the Round Table in the "Idylls of the King." * * *

By means of seeking for the Christ in man, Tennyson was able to maintain his faith in Christianity. But his Christianity was, he was aware but never admitted, a deception, not formulated as such because of his willing suspension of disbelief. Tennyson, whatever his limitations as a philosopher, knew he could never take its symbolic rightness for scientific truth; indeed, approaching religion in the spirit of poetry, transcending its dependence on "science" or "knowledge," is, as I see it, the main business of the poet in "In Memoriam." The lesson which the speaker learns is that religion is an imaginative achievement, a symbolic representation of moral reality having as its most important function the stimulation and vitalization of the mind.

In the beginning of the elegy the "I" finds, to his dismay, that religion is not a literal representation of truth and life, yet he also learns that his knowledge is not comprehensive enough to cover all existence. What within the course of the poem he does learn is that religion is a symbolic representation of human experience and, further, that there can be no moral allegiance except to the ideal. It is for this reason, then, that Hallam as the manifestation of the ideal becomes the "Christ," the "divine" man of the "crowning race," who replaces or is to replace the New Testament Christ. It was through this substitution that the speaker could cling to his belief, as expressed in the concluding lines of the Epilogue, in "That God, which ever lives and loves." This was a kind of "new Mythus" for which Carlyle had asked in *Sartor Resartus,* a mythus embodying "the divine Spirit" of Christianity "in a new vehicle and vesture."

ALAN SINFIELD

In Memoriam and the Language of Modern Poetry†

> What hope is here for modern rhyme
> To him, who turns a musing eye
> On songs, and deeds, and lives, that lie
> Foreshorten'd in the tract of time?   (lxxvii)

The reader who has followed with sympathy my explorations into the structure of the language of *In Memoriam* may admire, as I do, the subtlety and complexity of the interactions which Tennyson creates. Yet, as I have indicated at various points, critical opinion has not always been approving. This is doubtless due in part to the fact that not all Tennyson's poetry is as good as *In Memoriam*; but then, such inconsistencies are to be found in the work of all poets. At the risk of seeming impertinent, I would like to suggest that critical attitudes to Tennyson have been formed almost entirely by people whose parents were Victorians. Sir Harold Nicolson claimed, at the start of his highly influential study published in 1923, that it was becoming possible to see the Victorians in perspective, that the details which had obscured the general outline had faded and the principal landmarks become evident. But notice the kinds of reaction to this state of affairs which he envisaged:

> The individual emotions aroused by this change of aspect will vary according to temperament. For some the immensities of the Victorian background will but emphasize what they regard as the complacent futilities of the foreground; others, again, will feel a stirring of indignation at the thought of so vast an opportunity having fallen to a generation seemingly so ignorant, so optimistic and so insincere. And there will be some who, from the troubled waters of our insecure age, will look back wistfully at what may

† From *The Language of Tennyson's "In Memoriam"* (Oxford: Basil Black-   well, 1971), pp. 196–210.

appear to them as the simple serenities, the sun-lit confidence, the firm dry land which formed the heritage of that abundant epoch.[1]

One could hardly call these responses detached—complacent futilities, sun-lit confidence, wistfulness, stirrings of indignation; it is *Look Back in Anger* thirty years before!

To a younger commentator, who may be aroused and yet irritated by the apparently uncomplicated heroics of the Spanish Civil War —or even of the Campaign for Nuclear Disarmament—Tennyson's period is no more, and no less, personally significant than Chaucer's. There will still be prejudices, but they will be of a different character, and it should be possible to take some tentative steps towards a new perspective. Some such reaction against the art of the previous age as Nicolson describes seems to be an indispensible condition for the achievement of an individual voice in the new generation. Nevertheless, it also appears to be the case that a movement is rarely as different from its predecessors as its theorists may like to claim. In Chapter II I suggested some relationships between *In Memoriam* and Enlightenment and Romantic thought; by way of conclusion I wish to point out that there are elements of continuity as well as contrasts in the language of nineteenth- and twentieth-century English poetry (to include American works would be hopelessly ambitious), and that the seeds at least of later developments can be found in *In Memoriam*. Such a purpose must inevitably produce partial and over-generalized results, but they may nevertheless prove suggestive.

Of course, the differences between Tennyson's use of language and, say, Eliot's are very marked. An attempt to place in context Nicolson's comments on his contemporaries does not make the feelings he describes any less influential, and in such a climate of opinion we would not expect poetry to remain the same. The changes for the most part involve the qualities which in Chapter II I called 'classical'—the claim to speak for the whole of mankind, the cultivation of unobtrusive nuances rather than broad or startling effects, and the persistent stylization of language which makes us always aware of the artificiality of *In Memoriam*. The twentieth-century poet is always conscious that any opinion may be his alone; he may well use abrupt contrasts to express his alarm, his frustration, or his sense of the fragmentation in society; and he is liable to reject self-conscious artifice as insincere and 'rhetorical'—metre, syntactical inversions[2] and poetic diction are all questioned or completely abandoned.

1. Nicolson, *Tennyson*, pp. 1–2.
2. For a general discussion of factors influencing the syntax of modern poetry, see William E. Baker, *Syntax in English Poetry, 1870–1930* (Berkeley and Los Angeles, 1967), chapter five.

> Why should not old men be mad?
> Some have known a likely lad
> That had a sound fly-fisher's wrist
> Turn to a drunken journalist;
> A girl that knew all Dante once
> Live to bear children to a dunce;
> A Helen of social welfare dream,
> Climb on a wagonette to scream.

Yeats' poem rhymes, though not always fully, and has vestiges of a metre, but its diction is completely colloquial and its syntax largely straightforward. Unusual and unexpected juxtapositions (Helen of Troy and old age pensions) convey the strength of the poet's disappointment at the failing of the old aristocratic ideals. Though the first line may give the impression that a general statement is intended, the poem immediately becomes highly personal in its allusions; despite some more inclusive remarks in the second sentence, Yeats can really be sure of only his own feelings, and in the last line he relinquishes the claim to speak for others: 'Know why *an* old man should be mad.'

Tennyson believed that progress was possible if man could 'Move upward, working out the beast, / And let the ape and tiger die' (cxviii); but in *The Waste Land* we find 'hooded hordes swarming/ Over endless plains', in his last poem Wilfred Owen prophesies that 'None will break ranks, though nations trek from progress', and Yeats' rough beast slouches towards Bethlehem for the horrific Second Coming. In such circumstances we should hardly expect poets to be able to identify hopes and ideals held in common by our civilization or delicately to balance their phrases and rhythms as Pope and Tennyson had done. These manifestations would suggest at least some confidence in the sanity of the ultimate order of things. Tennyson's *Maud* closes with the hero's regeneration through war:

> And hail once more to the banner of battle unroll'd!
> Tho' many a light shall darken, and many shall weep
> For those that are crush'd in the clash of jarring claims,
> Yet God's just wrath shall be wreak'd on a giant liar.

The exclamation and repetition in the syntax, the heavy alliteration, the archaisms and the gradiloquent tones which allow the speaker to wave aside individual suffering all proclaim Tennyson's conviction that such simple solutions are viable. In the First World War Owen saw and heard

> the blood
> Come gargling from the froth-corrupted lungs,

248 · *Alan Sinfield*

> Obscene as cancer, bitter as the cud
> Of vile, incurable sores on innocent tongues.

When our forebears all believed that 'Dulce et decorum est pro patria mori' they dignified the notion by retaining the ancient expression of it. Tennyson, in that tradition, employed elevated language as his hero went off to fight in the Crimea, but Owen, conscious of his alienation from the aspirations of many of his countrymen, draws his diction and syntax from ordinary language and communicates his horror through the violence of his imagery. The old certainties become, as Owen says, the old lies, and the classical tones characteristic of *In Memoriam* lose their point. It is no longer feasible that one man should speak for a nation so divided, let alone the race; delicate nuances seem insufficiently dramatic to express the deep perplexities of modern life; and rhetoric of all kinds—with its traditional assumptions about what is valuable and what worthless, its assurance, which seems to imply that all shall eventually be well and, above all,, its tone of confidence in the worth of human endeavour—seems meretricious. It is dismissed in this period by Pound as 'perdamnable' and by T. E. Hulme as 'divorced from any real vision', and Yeats declares that 'We make out of the quarrel with others, rhetoric, but of the quarrel with ourselves, poetry'.[3]

Irony becomes the dominant mode in twentieth-century poetry —not the Popean variety, which makes its affirmation by striking off against unacceptable values and so achieves unison with prevailing cultural norms, but an irony which is simply destructive, or in which the assertion is either minor or personal and idiosyncratic. Yeats, the earliest major poet whom we call modern, resisted the negative impulse of his age, not because he did not feel it, but because he thought that 'if I affirm that such and such is so, the more complete the affirmation, the more complete the proof, and even when incomplete, it remains valid within some limit. I must kill scepticism in myself . . .'[4] Inconsistencies did not matter to Yeats; the point was that one should always be reaching towards some kind of positive statement, however uncertain, for human nature demands that we strive to transcend incompleteness. This position is nevertheless far from Tennyson's devotion to his belief which, though no more than a hope, was most fervently held.

The irony of Eliot's early poetry seems to me almost entirely pessimistic and destructive (and I must insist that I do not regard these terms as constituting adverse criticism).

3. Ezra Pound, in *Poets on Poetry*, ed. Charles Norman (New York, 1962), p. 329; T. E. Hulme, 'Notes on Language and Style', *The Criterion*, III (1925), 487; Yeats, *Selected Criticism*, ed. Norman Jeffares (London, 1964), p. 170.
4. Quoted by Richard Ellmann, *The Identity of Yeats* (paperback, London, 1964), p. 239.

The host with someone indistinct
Converses at the door apart,
The nightingales are singing near
The Convent of the Sacred Heart,

And sang within the bloody wood
When Agamemnon cried aloud,
And let their liquid siftings fall
To stain the stiff dishonoured shroud.

'Sweeney Among the Nightingales' juxtaposes the brothel-keeper with the Christian shrine, the murder of the victor of Troy by his adulterous relatives, and the droppings of the bird which, in *In Memoriam*, 'Rings Eden thro' the budded quicks' (lxxxviii). One might maintain that the ironic treatment of the traditionally lofty images serves to place the squalor of modern life, but the disillusionment and the distaste for sex—and indeed, for humanity—are so violent as to leave us with no positive values at all. I find the same features in *The Waste Land*. It is not very helpful just to be told that one is lacking in spiritual values, and the aversion to sex unbalances the presentation to the extent that, although we know of Eliot's respect for 'objectivity', it becomes hard to see the poem as any more impersonal than *In Memoriam*. We may also notice that the irony is by no means always gentle or subtle—outside the typist's window are 'perilously spread / Her drying combinations touched by the sun's last rays'. Eliot evidently does not intend to permit any reader to continue in the 'complacent futilities' attributed by Nicolson's contemporaries to the Victorians.

Other poets retain in their language the restraint and unobtrusiveness of *In Memoriam*, but not the stylization or the confidence.

About suffering they were never wrong,
The Old Masters: how well they understood
Its human position; how it takes place
While someone else is eating or opening a window or just walking
   dully along.

In Auden's '*Musée des Beaux Arts*' the irony is in the theme itself, and the whole subject is presented in just that casual manner in which suffering is said to occur. The diction and syntax are yet again those of ordinary language—almost to the point of bravado. But this is not the gentle tone of Tennyson when he writes, for instance,

> But in my spirit will I dwell,
>   And dream my dream, and hold it true;
>   For tho' my lips may breathe adieu,
> I cannot think the thing farewell.   (cxxiii)

The poet is here undertaking a major statement of the principle upon which he bases his whole existence, and the quiet intonation, though tinged with a note of defiance in the face of scepticism, embodies his inner assurance. The unassuming language of Auden's poem is right because the subject makes no pretensions to grandeur or even to originality—the Old Masters have already expressed it very well. The tone is almost apologetic; it seems to be saying, This is just an odd idea I thought I would mention, nothing special—I am not Prince Hamlet ... A lot of modern poetry is like this. A small incident gives rise to a small moral and it seems that to venture further is too risky—hence, perhaps, the death of the long poem.

Twentieth-century English poetry, then, tends towards the negative, or towards the small or personal affirmation; the more common mode is a tentative irony which eschews large statements. It does not seem extravagant to relate the developments in sensibility I have described to the disappearance of the classical qualities Tennyson cultivated in *In Memoriam*. The claim to speak for all men becomes invalid, the sensitive restraint becomes inadequate or the vehicle for relatively unambitious reflections, and the stylization becomes irrelevant. But these features represent only one side of the linnet and artifact dichotomy which I have distinguished in Tennyson's creative impulse. The other is the Romantic, with its opposition to rationalism and science, its dependence upon subjective and even mystical experience, and its desire to employ only such forms as are dictated by the subject matter. These aspects of Tennyson's approach are not rejected, but are taken up with even greater enthusiasm by the Symbolist and Imagist movements of the later nineteenth and early twentieth centuries. Frank Kermode and Marshall McLuhan have already argued impressively for this continuity,[5] but it is worth examining again in the specific context of the language of *In Memoriam*.

For Arthur Symons, the publicizer of Symbolism in England, the writings of Gérard de Nerval, Villiers de L'Isle-Adam, Rimbaud, Verlaine, Laforgue, Mallarmé and Huysmans were essentially a reaction against materialism, 'an attempt to spiritualize literature'. He declared that Symbolism consisted in

> this revolt against exteriority, against rhetoric, against a materialistic tradition; in this endeavour to disengage the ultimate essence, the soul, of whatever exists and can be realised by the consciousness; in this dutiful waiting upon every symbol by which the soul of things can be made visible. . . .[6]

5. Frank Kermode, *Romantic Image* (London, 1957); and McLuhan's two articles in Killham, *Critical Essays*.
6. Arthur Symons, *The Symbolist Movement in Literature*, 2nd edn. (London, 1911), pp. 8–9. For further discussion see Wilson, *Axel's Castle*, and C. M. Bowra, *The Heritage of Symbolism* (London, 1943).

Tennyson too hated materialism; Symbolism is a more extreme statement of his position. The Symbolist locates reality exclusively in his own mind, thus carrying much further the concentration on individual experience which I have pointed out in *In Memoriam* and earlier Romantic poetry. The elements in Tennyson's approach which are discarded are those we should expect—rhetoric, the concern with social issues and mankind in general, the long poem. Symons observes that Verlaine admired *In Memoriam*—'Only, with Verlaine, the thing itself, the affection or regret, is everything; there is no room for meditation over destiny, or search for a problematical consolation'.[7] To seize the essence of a mood is the Symbolist's one endeavour; he is not interested in circumstances, opinions, analysis of motive or consequence, but in evoking the quality of an immediate experience. A long poem is therefore a contradiction in terms. On the last point, Symons conveniently phrases his belief so that it fits in neatly with my argument on *In Memoriam*: 'no long poem was ever written; the finest long poem in the world being but a series of short poems linked together with prose'.[8] Tennyson can be seen as approaching an awareness of this doctrine in the way he explicitly builds *In Memoriam* out of a series of short poems, for he establishes a distinct split between the sections at the highest tension, each embodying one moment when the poet's immediate and unalloyed emotions break through, and the others leading up to and away from them.

Tennyson's dependence upon mystical experience also relates him to the Symbolists—who revered Blake above all other poets. But, again, the Symbolists went further. For them all experience was ultimately supernatural in character—there was no disjunction between the world of the senses and the world of ideal beauty which they wished to capture in their verse. Many Symbolists, including Yeats, involved themselves in spiritualism or magic, thus setting themselves at the furthest remove from the methods of scientific enquiry. They placed at the centre of their ontology a mode of experience which had been for Tennyson only intermittent. Hence the title of the movement: 'they attempted', says Bowra, 'to convey a supernatural experience in the language of visible things, and therefore almost every word is a symbol and is used not for its common purpose but for the associations which it evokes of a reality beyond the senses'.[9] The danger in this approach is of poetry becoming so inward-looking as to be inaccessible to most or all readers. For many people, obscurity is the most obvious feature of modern poetry and its language. The neo-classical aspirations in Tennyson's writing preserve him from this fate; indeed, he seems at times to be making a last desperate attempt to write for the whole

7. *The Symbolist Movement in Literature*, p. 93.
8. *The Symbolist Movement in Litera-*
ture, p. 134.
9. *The Heritage of Symbolism*, p. 5.

culture, and there is no doubt that this impulsion sometimes leads him into vulgarity. Yet he did succeed, and he was the last to do so, for later English authors seem suddenly to abandon as hopeless any such pretensions. Then, in revulsion against the apparent compromises of their predecessors, they swing completely to the opposite extreme, and poetry becomes the preserve of a very select few.

The most significant result for poetic language of the Symbolist determination to view every object as an emblem of a transcendent beauty is the extensive use of the symbol, as I defined it in Chapter VIII. The image represents ideas and feelings which cannot be neatly rendered in other terms and whose literal referent is left unstated. Now this procedure is decked out in the fully self-conscious theories of Mallarmé, for whom literal and figurative are simply not distinct. He rejects as 'brutal' any ordering of images by direct thought—Symons translates:

> To be instituted, a relation between images, exact; and that therefrom should detach itself a third aspect, fusible and clear, offered to the divination. Abolished, the pretension, aesthetically an error, despite its dominion over almost all the masterpieces, to enclose within the subtle paper other than, for example, the horror of the forest, or the silent thunder afloat in the leaves; not the intrinsic, dense wood of the trees.[1]

I have shown how Tennyson feels his way towards this position through the blurring of the literal and figurative, leading to the disappearance of the literal element. He is nearest to the Symbolists in a section like cxxi, 'Sad Hesper', which I discussed at the end of Chapter VIII. The poet describes the boat drawn upon the shore, the wakeful bird and the movements of the sun, and we understand that the reality of love and eternal life is his ultimate theme. In the last stanza he resorts to the literal and states explicitly a part of his thought, and we can see that he is still held by rationalist assumptions. But the impulse towards the Symbolist aesthetic is there too.

In England, the Pre-Raphaelites were writing poetry which in many ways approximates to Symbolist theories—Rossetti's 'The Woodspurge' describes a walk in the countryside in a time of grief, and concludes with a defence of the moment in and for itself:

> My eyes, wide open, had the run
> Of some ten weeds to fix upon;
> Among those few, out of the sun,
> The woodspurge flowered, three cups in one.
>
> From perfect grief there need not be
> Wisdom or even memory:
> One thing then learnt remains to me,—
> The woodspurge has a cup of three.

1. *The Symbolist Movement in Literature*, p. 131.

But the major exponent of Symbolism in English is the early Yeats, to whom Symons dedicated his book.

> I went out to the hazel wood,
> Because a fire was in my head,
> And cut and peeled a hazel wand,
> And hooked a berry to a thread;
> And when white moths were on the wing,
> And moth-like stars were flickering out,
> I dropped the berry in a stream
> And caught a little silver trout.

The fish turns into a 'glimmering girl':

> Though I am old with wandering
> Through hollow lands and hilly lands,
> I will find out where she has gone,
> And kiss her lips and take her hands;
> And walk among long dappled grass,
> And pluck till time and times are done
> The silver apples of the moon,
> The golden apples of the sun.

'The Song of the Wandering Aengus' is more ethereal and enigmatic than anything in *In Memoriam*, and the symbolic trout and apples are made more prominently the focus than is usual with Tennyson. What we do find here, and in just the same kind of way as in *In Memoriam*, are two linguistic features which I have already associated with Tennyson's development of the symbol: the use of incidental landscape to evoke mood, and a preference for analogical syntax which is at times almost no syntax at all. The mind of the speaker is the principal concern for both Tennyson and Yeats, and external 'background' objects—here, the moths, stars and long dappled grass—are significant because of their contribution to the atmosphere, and so to our impression of the speaker's emotions. The syntax is also very close to Tennyson's practice. Yeats repeats the same kind of clause, and avoids clauses of condition, cause and result, which would characterize an analytical approach. The syntax is self-effacing, so that we are left to pass through a series of images; we feel that we are experiencing the poet's immediate mental sensations, with the minimum of intervention from any conscious organizing faculty. In these respects Symbolist language is in a direct line from the mode of writing which Tennyson employs in *In Memoriam*. In theory and in practice there is full continuity.

English Symbolism, because of its late appearance, blurs into Imagism—Eliot's *Prufrock* volume shows signs of Laforgue whereas *The Waste Land* was influenced by Pound. The principal differences seem to be that the transcendental justifications are replaced by a concentration on aesthetic effectiveness and psychologically based conceptions of the nature of the mind, and that vague evocation gives way to irony (which we already find in Laforgue) and to a preference for hard, precise diction and images.

The theorist of this development is T. E. Hulme, and the correspondences between his thought and Tennyson's practice as I have described it are very revealing. Hulme, who leans heavily towards a Roman Catholic position, denies completely that man is capable of progress, and here at once we seek the break with Tennyson: the faith in mankind is absent. Hulme insists upon the absolute disjunction between three facets of our experience—the inorganic world of the physical sciences, the organic world of biology and related approaches, and the world of religious and ethical values.[2] He represents these three fields as contained within concentric circles, thereby using the very same image as Tennyson in *In Memoriam*. The great achievement for the poet there is to gain the belief that all the circles are one, that all differences of time, space and matter can be transcended in the moment of mystical awareness; but for Hulme, right thinking depends upon keeping the circles separate.

Yet Hulme is really tackling the same problem—the status of the creative imagination in a scientific age. He and Tennyson are both in the same Romantic tradition. To the early nineteenth century it seemed that science had spoilt the rainbow, but there was plenty of scope left for the individual, and rationalist methods could be disregarded. For Tennyson the position was far more serious; he could not avoid the 'brooding over scientific opinion' which Yeats considered so deleterious.[3] Science was as meaningful to him as the gyres were to Yeats (and a good deal more meaningful to his readers). Tennyson was just able to absorb the discoveries of the geologists, but by the time of Yeats and Hulme such inclusiveness had become impossible. The only answer was to deny completely the validity of science and to live entirely within the self—'Only in the fact of consciousness', says Hulme, 'is there a unity in the world'.[4]

But this was basically Tennyson's position too, and when Hulme asserts the value of intuitive as well as analytical thinking,[5] he is only endorsing Tennyson's faith in the heart standing up and answering 'I have felt', and advocating the kind of thought process which Tennyson exemplifies through his analogical syntax. Hulme draws upon Bergson's view of existence as a formless flux upon which, because of the structure of our minds, we impose an artificial order; Tennyson evidently sensed that a form founded on analytical

2. T. E. Hulme, *Speculations* (paperback, London, 1960), pp. 3–11.
3. 'The Symbolism of Poetry' (1900), William Butler Yeats, *Essays and Introductions* (London, 1961), p. 163.
4. Hulme, *Speculations*, p. 222.
5. This is the main argument of 'Notes on Language and Style'. Cf. Baker, *Syntax in English Poetry*, chapter five.

processes could falsify, for *In Memoriam* is built upon the principle of following the poet's consciousness. The issue is imperfectly revealed—imperfectly grasped, no doubt—by Tennyson, but the seeds are there. It is by no means true that Imagist theory and Tennyson's practice in *In Memoriam* are irreconcilably at odds. In his general outlook, his attitude to form, and his syntax Tennyson either anticipates or is recognizably a predecessor of Hulme.

There is no definite evidence of a connection between Hulme's thinking and Eliot's poetry, but the two are certainly not inconsistent. The very striking technique, specially prominent in *The Waste Land*, of baldly juxtaposing images so that the whole poem is pieced together like a mosaic can be related to Hulme's insistence that reality is distorted by the logical connecting processes we have learnt to apply. As I have suggested, Tennyson shows an awareness of this issue in *In Memoriam*. His repetitions of the same syntactic structures verge at times upon the simple effect of a sequence of images ungoverned by any rational procedures. There is little of the violence of Eliot, and the verse form, the inversions and the punctuation distract our attention from the implications of the technique; but consider these lines from section xcv, which I have altered only by moving one or two phrases:

> The brook alone was heard far-off
> And the fluttering urn on the board
> And bats in fragrant skies
> Went round.
>
> And the filmy shapes
> Wheeled or lit, that haunt the dusk with ermine capes
> And woolly breasts and beaded eyes,

Now here is part of 'What the Thunder said':

> A woman drew her long black hair out tight
> And fiddled whisper music on those strings
> And bats with baby faces in the violet light
> Whistled, and beat their wings
> And crawled head downward down a blackened wall
> And upside down in air were towers
> Tolling reminiscent bells, that kept the hours
> And voices singing out of empty cisterns and exhausted wells.

The sequences of relationships between the clauses in the two passages are really very similar. Tennyson's repetitions of structure, which I have called analogical syntax, make the connections between clauses as simple and undemanding as possible, so that we are left to move through a series of images. Eliot makes this the primary rationale of his verse; often the juxtapositions are more jerky

than in the lines I have quoted, but fundamentally the method is
the same.

The tendency to invest external objects with qualities indicative
of the mental state of the speaker is also shared by Tennyson and
Eliot. This too can be explained in terms of Hulme's Bergsonian
account of the relationship between consciousness and the material
world. Imagist theory tends to claim that the natural object should
be presented just for itself, but in fact it usually seems the bearer of
emotive connotations which we are expected, in Tennysonian fash-
ion, to relate to the theme or the speaker. This is always true in
Eliot—what could be more evocative, and in just the same way as
sections x and xi of *In Memoriam*, than part IV of *The Waste
Land?*—

> Phlebas the Phoenician, a fortnight dead,
> Forgot the cry of gulls, and the deep sea swell
> And the profit and loss.
>   A current under sea
> Picked his bones in whispers. As he rose and fell
> He passed the stages of his age and youth
> Entering the whirlpool.

As in *In Memoriam*, the detail indicates the exact significance: the
second line seems to contain both the pathos and the grandeur of
life; the whispers of the current suggest the reverence with which
we are to regard the event; and the whirlpool may be either that
where Phlebas' remains finally disintegrate or the vicissitudes of life.
The example may not seem altogether typical of Eliot because the
image is natural rather than urban, but exactly the same process is
at work when he speaks of 'the dull canal / On a winter evening
round behind the gashouse'.

I have written of the absence of an established and agreed system
of images whose connotations would be relied upon; this lack has
clearly become much greater since 1850. One answer which Eliot
finds is literary allusion, which enables him to draw upon systems
which other men have created. Tennyson does this too, though to a
much lesser extent. Like Eliot, he employs Dante as a source of
spiritual imagery; the pastoral convention serves a similar function
in *In Memoriam*, but the myth is doubtless too simple to act as a
credible antithesis to twentieth-century conditions. However, the
most fundamental and important link between the practice of Ten-
nyson and his successors is the use of recurring images which
achieve the status of symbols. This becomes the usual method of
creating a coherent and yet evocative system of value-bearing images
to which the reader can be referred for an indication of the poet's
intellectual and emotional attitude. Yeats (like Blake) evolved an

entire mythology which exists, as a rule, in an abstract and private world of its own somewhere above the poem; we must make ourselves sufficiently informed to be able to pluck it down and apply it at the poet's whim. Eliot, with brilliant inspiration, uses in *The Waste Land* the vegetation myths of *The Golden Bough*. Thus he draws upon the symbolic system which *other* societies found significant—societies, that is, which had not suffered the fragmentation of modern western Europe. The very mention of the Hanged God is ironical because it reminds us of the absence of such deep-rooted and generally accepted symbols in our own culture.

In *The Waste Land*, as in *In Memoriam*, the major point to notice is that these symbols are not static: they change their connotations with the development of the experience of the poet. 'I sat upon the shore / Fishing, with the arid plain behind me', which occurs a few lines from the end, is filled with echoes from the rest of the poem—indeed, without them it would be practically meaningless. Both Tennyson and Eliot build up round certain images a strong group of associations which fertilize, and are fertilized by, each successive appearance, so that by the end of the poem a brief mention can recall the whole of the poet's experience. We again find the Romantic elements in Tennyson's use of language persisting into the twentieth century.

The connections I have been making may seem surprising, for it is well-known that Eliot wrote slightingly of Tennyson in this period. He thought him a 'reflective poet. Tennyson and Browning are poets, and they think; but they do not feel their thought as immediately as the odour of a rose.'[6] Yet Arthur Hallam, in his review of Tennyson's 1830 volume, contrasted him with Milton and Wordsworth and linked him with Shelley and Keats, whom he called 'poets of sensation rather than reflection'. He makes his point in terms very like Eliot's:

> So vivid was the delight attending the simple exertions of eye and ear, that it became mingled more and more with their trains of active thought, and tended to absorb their whole being into the energy of sense. Other poets *seek* for images to illustrate their conceptions; these men had no need to seek; they lived in a world of images.[7]

There is a clear similarity in ideas here. I believe that Eliot is the successor to a line of thinking about poetry and language which is gradually clarified and emphasized by the Symbolists and others during the nineteenth century—McLuhan points out that Yeats found Hallam's essay an invaluable key to Symbolism.[8] The quali-

6. *Selected Prose*, p. 110.
7. Motter (ed.), *The Writings of Arthur*

Hallam, p. 186.
8. Killham, *Critical Essays*, p. 67.

ties in the language of *In Memoriam* which might commend them-
selves to our insecure century are completely interwoven with forms
which we have felt obliged to discard, but in general terms I see a
continuity. The anxieties which Tennyson faced have intensified so
that his form of resolution is no longer acceptable, and correspond-
ingly certain features of his use of language have been accentuated
and others largely abandoned. This makes him a very difficult poet
for us, since it is hard to disconnect him completely from our
modern sensibility, but impossible to see him as a satisfactory
expression of it.

Selected Bibliography

I. BIBLIOGRAPHY AND BIOGRAPHY

The newest and fullest Tennyson bibliography is Sir Charles Tennyson and Christine Falls's *Alfred Tennyson: An Annotated Bibliography* (Athens, Ga., 1967). A well-annotated critical bibliography, it includes works about, as well as by, Tennyson. E. D. H. Johnson's "Tennyson," in *The Victorian Poets: A Guide to Research*, second edition (Cambridge, Mass., 1968), contains bibliographical information but also affords an excellent selective survey of modern Tennyson scholarship. *A Tennyson Handbook*, by George O. Marshall, Jr., is useful for summary information and quick reference.

Sir Charles Tennyson's study, *Alfred Tennyson* (New York, 1949), is the most authoritative and comprehensive biography. The biographically oriented works listed below also contain much useful information about such matters as the genesis, composition, publication, and reception of *In Memoriam*.

Fausset, Hugh I'A. *Tennyson: A Modern Portrait*. New York, 1923.

Knowles, James. "Aspects of Tennyson: A Personal Reminiscence." *Nineteenth Century, 33* (1893), 164–88.

Nicolson, Sir Harold. *Tennyson: Aspects of His Life, Character and Poetry*. London, 1923.

Rader, Ralph W. "Tennyson in the Year of Hallam's Death." *PMLA, 77* (1962), 419–24.

Richardson, Joanna. *The Pre-Eminent Victorian*. London, 1962.

Sanders, Charles R. "Carlyle and Tennyson." *PMLA, 76* (1961), 82–97.

Tennyson, Sir Charles. "The Somersby Tennysons." *Victorian Studies*, Christmas Supplement, 1963.

Tennyson, Hallam, Lord. *Alfred, Lord Tennyson: A Memoir by His Son*. 2 vols. New York, 1897.

II. EDITIONS

The standard text of *In Memoriam* is found in the Eversley Edition of Tennyson's *Works* edited by Hallam Tennyson (1907–8). Other, more modern editions are useful, however, especially for the notes and critical introductions written by their editors. The newest, best, and most authoritative edition of Tennyson's verse is Christopher Ricks's *The Poems of Tennyson* (Longmans Annotated English Poets; London, 1969).

Auden, W. H., ed. *A Selection from the Poems of Alfred, Lord Tennyson*. Garden City, N.Y., 1944.

Buckley, Jerome H., ed. *Poems of Tennyson*. Boston, 1958.

Bush, Douglas, ed. *Tennyson: Selected Poetry*. New York, 1951.

De Vane, William C., and Mabel P. De Vane, eds. *Selections from Tennyson*. New York, 1940.

Hill, Robert W., Jr., ed. *Tennyson's Poetry*. New York, 1971.

Rolfe, W. J., ed. *The Poetic and Dramatic Works of Alfred, Lord Tennyson*. Boston, 1898.

Tennyson, Sir Charles, ed. *Poems of Alfred, Lord Tennyson*. London, 1954.

III. GENERAL STUDIES

The works below, mostly modern, are concerned with those aspects of the intellectual, literary, social, or scientific temper of the Victorian age which are relevant to an informed reading of *In Memoriam*. The list is selective, the primary criterion for inclusion of a work being its direct relevance to *In Memoriam*. Most of the studies, indeed, contain significant, extended analyses of the poem.

Beach, Joseph Warren. *The Concept of Nature in Nineteenth-Century English Poetry*. New York, 1936.

Buckley, Jerome. *The Victorian Temper: A Study in Literary Culture.* Cambridge, Mass., 1951.
Bush, Douglas. *Mythology and the Romantic Tradition in English Poetry.* Cambridge, Mass., 1937.
———. *Science and English Poetry.* New York, 1950.
Evans, Sir B. Ifor. *Literature and Science.* London, 1954.
Fairchild, Hoxie Neale. *Religious Trends in English Poetry,* vol. 4, 1830–80. New York, 1957.
Houghton, Walter E. *The Victorian Frame of Mind, 1830–1870.* New Haven, 1957.
Johnson, E. D. H. *The Alien Vision of Victorian Poetry,* Princeton, 1952.
Langbaum, Robert. *The Poetry of Experience.* New York, 1957.
Miller, J. Hillis. *The Disappearance of God: Five Nineteenth-Century Writers.* Cambridge, Mass., 1968.
Millhauser, Milton. *Just Before Darwin.* Middletown, Conn., 1958.
Miyoshi, Masao. *The Divided Self: A Perspective on the Literature of the Victorians.* New York, 1969.
Roppen, Georg. *Evolution and Poetic Belief: A Study in Some Victorian and Modern Writers.* No. 5 in *Norwegian Studies in English.* Oslo, 1965.
Stevenson, Lionel. *Darwin Among the Poets.* Chicago, 1952.
Willey, Basil. *More Nineteenth-Century Studies: A Group of Honest Doubters.* New York, 1955.

IV. CRITICISM

The following works have been selected from among the large numbers of studies which comprise the critical literature on *In Memoriam.* Each work either takes *In Memoriam* for its sole subject or contains an analysis of Tennyson's verse in which *In Memoriam* is of central concern. The emphasis is on modern criticism. Studies from which selections have been reprinted in this volume have been omitted.

August, Eugene R. "Tennyson and Teilhard: The Faith of *In Memoriam.*" *PMLA, 84* (1969), 217–26.
Bishop, Jonathan. "The Unity of 'In Memoriam.' " *Victorian Newsletter,* No. 21 (1962), pp. 9–14.
Bradley, A. C. *A Commentary on Tennyson's "In Memoriam."* London, 1930.
Brashear, William B. *The Living Well: A Study of Tennyson and Nineteenth-Century Subjectivism.* The Hague, 1969.
Carr, Arthur J. "Tennyson as a Modern Poet." *University of Toronto Quarterly, 19* (1950), 361–82.
Danzig, Allan. "The Contraries: A Central Concept in Tennyson's Poetry." *PMLA, 77* (1962), 577–85.
Forsythe, R. A. "The Myth of Nature and the Victorian Compromise of the Imagination." *English Literary History, 31* (1964), 213–40.
Fulweiler, Howard W. "Tennyson and the 'Summons from the Sea.' " *Victorian Poetry, 3* (1965), 25–44.
Gatty, Alfred. *A Key to Tennyson's In Memoriam.* London, 1881.
Genung, John W. *Tennyson's "In Memoriam": Its Purpose and Its Structure.* Boston, 1884.
Gibson, Walker. "Behind the Veil: A Distinction between Poetic and Scientific Language in Tennyson, Lyell, and Darwin." *Victorian Studies, 2* (1958), 60–68.
Grandsen, K. W. *Tennyson: In Memoriam.* No. 22 in *Studies in English Literature.* London, 1964.
Grant, Stephen A. "The Mystical Implications of *In Memoriam.*" *Studies in English Literature, 2* (1962), 481–95.
Hirsch, Gordon D. "Tennyson's *Commedia.*" *Victorian Poetry, 8* (1970), 93–106.
Hough, Graham. "The Natural Theology of *In Memoriam.*" *Review of English Studies, 23* (1947), 244–56.
Hunt, John D. "The Symbolist Vision of *In Memoriam.*" *Victorian Poetry, 8* (1970), 187–98.
James, D. G. "Wordsworth and Tennyson." *Proceedings of the British Academy, 1950, 36* (1956), 113–29.
Joseph, Gerhard. *Tennysonian Love: The Strange Diagonal.* Minneapolis, 1969.
Jump, John D., ed. *Tennyson: The Critical Heritage.* New York, 1967.
Killham, John, ed. *Critical Essays on the Poetry of Tennyson.* London, 1960.
Kissane, James. "Tennyson: The Passion of the Past and the Curse of Time." *English Literary History, 32* (1965), 85–109.

Marshall, George O., Jr. "Tennyson's 'O! That 'twere Possible': A Link between *In Memoriam* and *Maud*." *PMLA, 78* (1963), 225–29.
Masterman, C. F. G. *Tennyson as a Religious Thinker.* London, 1900.
Mays, J. C. C. "*In Memoriam:* An Aspect of Form." *University of Toronto Quarterly, 35* (1965), 22–46.
Millhauser, Milton. " 'Magnetic Mockeries': The Background of a Phrase." *English Language Notes, 5* (1967), 108–13.
———. "Tennyson. *Vestiges,* and the Dark Side of Science." *Victorian Newsletter,* No. 35 (1969), pp. 22–25.
Morton, Edward P. "The Stanza of *In Memoriam*." *Modern Lauguage Notes, 21* (1906), 229–31.
Ostricker, Alicia. "The Three Modes in Tennyson's Prosody." *PMLA, 82* (1967), 373–84.
Paden, W. D. "A Note on the Variants of *In Memoriam* and *Lucretius*." *The Library,* 5th ser., *8* (1953), 259–73.
———. *Tennyson in Egypt: A Study of the Imagery in his Earlier Work.* Lawrence, Kan., 1942.
Pitt, Valerie. *Tennyson Laureate.* London, 1962.
Potter, George R. "Tennyson and the Biological Theory of the Mutability of Species." *Philological Quarterly, 16* (1937), 321–43.
Preyer, Robert. "Alfred Tennyson: The Poetry and Politics of Conservative Vision." *Victorian Studies, 9* (1966), 325–52.
———. "Tennyson as an Oracular Poet." *Modern Philology, 55* (1958), 239–51.
Rutland, William R. "Tennyson and the Theory of Evolution." *Essays and Studies by Members of the English Association, 26* (1940), 7–29.
Ryals, Clyde de L. "The Heavenly Friend: The 'New Mythus' of *In Memoriam*.". *The Personalist, 43* (1962), 383–402.
Sanders, Charles R. "Tennyson and the Human Hand." *Victorian Newsletter,* No. 11 (1957), pp. 5–14.
Sendry, Joseph. "*In Memoriam* and *Lycidas*." *PMLA, 82* (1967), 437–43.
Shannon, Edgar F., Jr. *Tennyson and the Reviewers: A Study of His Literary Reputation and the Influence of the Critics upon His Poetry, 1827–1850.* Cambridge, Mass., 1952.
Shaw, W. David. "The Transcendentalist Problem in Tennyson's Poetry of Debate." *Philological Quarterly, 46* (1967), 79–94.
Sinfield, Alan. "Matter-Moulded Forms of Speech: Tennyson's Use of Language in *In Memoriam*." In *The Major Victorian Poets: Reconsiderations,* ed. Isobel Armstrong. London, 1969.
Schmiefsky, Marvel. " 'In Memoriam': Its Seasonal Imagery Reconsidered." *Studies in English Literature, 7* (1967), 721–39.
Smith, Elton E. *The Two Voices: A Tennyson Study.* Lincoln, Neb., 1964.
Sonn, Carl R. "Poetic Vision and Religious Certainty in Tennyson's Early Poetry." *Modern Philology, 57* (1959), 83–93.
Svaglic, Martin J. "A Framework for Tennyson's *In Memoriam*." *Journal of English and Germanic Philology, 61* (1962), 810–25.
Taafe, James G. "Circle Imagery in Tennyson's *In Memoriam*." *Victorian Poetry, 1* (1963), 123–31.
Tennyson, Sir Charles. *Six Tennyson Essays.* London, 1954.
Wain, John. " 'Stranger and Afraid': Notes on Four Victorian Poets." *Preliminary Essays,* pp. 93–120. London, 1957.